FUNCTIONAL
KOREAN

A Communicative Approach Textbook

FUNCTIONAL KOREAN

by Namgui Chang
Yong-chol Kim

HOLLYM

First published in 1989
Fourth printing, 1993
by Hollym International Corp.
18 Donald Place, Elizabeth, New Jersey 07208 U.S.A.
Phone: (908)353-1655 Fax: (908)353-0255

Published simultaneously in Korea
by Hollym Corporation; Publishers
14-5 Kwanchol-dong, Chongno-gu, Seoul 110-111, Korea
Phone: (02)735-7551~4 Fax: (02)730-5149

ISBN: 0-930878-65-5
Library of Congress Catalog Card Number: 89-83648

Printed in Korea

Preface

This book is designed for those who wish to acquire basic survival skills in Korean. At the end of this language course, we hope that the learner will have attained the minimal functional proficiency in Korean, dealing with common situations such as meeting people, obtaining accommodations and services, getting around, doing shopping, dining out, and the like.

Unlike many other existing Korean-language textbooks, *Functional Korean* is concerned with communicative aspects of language. Most textbooks of Korean have taken in the past a structural view of language, concentrating on the grammatical system. It is certainly true that some of these grammar-oriented methods cannot be dispensed with. Nevertheless, we strongly feel that the structural approach to language needs to be supplemented with some other approach, if language is to be taught as a means of communication.

Functional Korean embodies the results of many years of our research and labor, infused with our belief in communicability. The book pays systematic attention to functional as well as structural aspects of the Korean language. We hope that combining the two approaches will help make this book a more fully communicative teaching material.

The word "functional" implies an emphasis on communicative functions rather than language functions in the narrow sense of the terms. While the latter is primarily concerned with the structure of a sentence (which is stable and straightforward), the former is more concerned with the situational and social aspects of language (which are variable and sometimes ambiguous). We want to point out again that our book puts stress on communicative functions, but not necessarily ignoring the importance of structures. Hence, the user of *Functional Korean* will acquire not only a rare knowledge of the communicative functions in Korean, but also a basic ability to understand the linguistic structures and vocabulary of the language.

This knowledge of communicative functions includes the learner's ability to relate the linguistic forms to appropriate non-linguistic knowledge, such as situational knowledge and social knowledge. Our book abounds with sections designed for this type of knowledge.

Functional Korean consists of 18 lesson units, each of which dealing with one set of related topics and situations. Each lesson has the following parts.

∗ Lesson Objectives

The format of this unit derives from an educational theory emphasizing the importance of learning objectives to the learner. According to this theory, the more specific the learning objectives are, the more effective the learning becomes. We believe that it is highly desirable for the learner to have his/her learning objectives set at the beginning of a lesson. In every lesson, the learning objectives are described in terms of the requirements of functional as well as linguistic proficiency.

∗ Cultural Notes

This unit has been provided roughly in line with the topics and situations of the lesson. There is no doubt that the Korean language is an integral part of Korean culture. One can easily infer from this that the more one knows about the Korean people and their culture, the more enriching will be the language learning experience.

∗ Communicative Exchanges

This core unit contains several sub-units, and each of them is called Frame 1, Frame 2, Frame 3 and so on. The unit is designed to meet the learner's need to acquire a wide range of variables in situational and social knowledge. In each frame, there is a column called "substitution" at the bottom of the page. This column is designed to bring the learner's attention to a broad range of vocabulary usable within that particular topic or situation.

∗ Grammar and Usage

For most English-speaking learners, Korean grammar can be a very difficult task to deal with. This holds true particularly because Korean and English have little in common with each other. In this unit, however, the learner's attention has been brought to many of the contrastive aspects of both languages. For example, many of grammatical features in Korean are explained in such a way that a learner having a basic knowledge of English grammar will understand Korean grammar in proper perspective.

Even if the learner feels that he/she does not make as much progress in Korean grammar as desired, that should not be the source of his/her disappointment. We feel that grammar is something that a learner gradually forms, consciously or unconsciously, out of many sentences, not something that the learner must have mastered before using sentences. In fact, grammar may often hinder one's speech if one gets overly conscious of rules of grammar.

This grammar unit is also devoted to "usage," the way in which Korean words and phrases are actually used in particular contexts. The learner will find that many of the items discussed under "usage" have something to do with unique Korean ways of thinking and living.

✴ Exercises

In the early phase of this course, emphasis is placed on exercises in listening and speaking, and this particular emphasis is sustained throughout the textbook. The exercises become more varied in kind and more complex in quality as the lessons reach the middle and later phases, where the learner's ability to relate linguistic forms to appropriate communicative functions command increasing attention.

✴ Reading and Writing

This unit, provided in the middle and later phases of the course, is designed to help the learner to comprehend reading material effectively and communicate his/her messages and ideas in written Korean. Although listening and speaking skills are given greater emphasis throughout the textbook, it is important to note that a learner's ability to read and write in the target language enhances his/her overall communicative ability.

✴ Words and Phrases

This unit is for the learner's review of the lexical items and useful expressions already introduced in the lesson. It is always to the learner's benefit to pause and go over these items before moving into the next lesson.

This book has a special reference section in its final part. This particular section consists of:

Han-gŭl : The Letters and Sounds

Numbers in Korean

Time : Hours, Days, Months and Years

It is a good idea for the learner to start with the section on Han-gŭl, so that he/she may be able to get a fairly good idea about the Korean script before moving into the lessons.

The learner will find that the first five lessons have used a romanization system (the McCune-Reischauer system in this case) together with the Han-gŭl material. This was to facilitate the understanding of the beginning student of Korean. Once the learner becomes used to the sound values of Korean through Roman letters—though we are aware of a theory that the use of Roman letters only delays the learning—we hope that he/she will soon be able to pronounce Korean sounds accurately with the aid of the instructor or that of any educated Korean speaker.

Namgui Chang

Yong-chol Kim

Contents

Greetings

Lesson Objectives

1. Greet a friend or an acquaintance whom you see for the first time in a day, using an appropriate gesture (a bow or a nod). Specifically you will:
   (a) Address your friend, using his/her name and title.
   (b) Use one of the common greeting phrases.

2. Say that you haven't seen him/her for a long time.

3. Greet a fellow worker whom you have already seen more than once in a day. Specifically you will:
   (a) Ask if your fellow worker is busy.
   (b) Answer that you are busy or not busy.
   (c) Ask how things are going with your fellow worker.
   (d) Answer that things are going fairly well with you.

4. Know some general facts about Korean sentences and Korean names, specifically:
   (a) How Korean sentence-endings vary depending upon the speaker's attitude toward the hearer.
   (b) How the first and last names of a Korean man or woman are arranged, and how some of the titles are used.

Cultural Notes
Korean Expressions of Good Will

An important part of Korean greetings is the formal bow or the more casual nod. The age and status of the person being greeted are major factors that determine how deeply you should bow. If the person you greet is your senior in age or status, you are expected to bow more deeply or nod more emphatically than he does. But don't overdo it. Nowadays, a bow does not exceed 30 degrees, and you don't have to repeat it more than once. If you are unsure as to the appropriateness of a gesture, just imitate what the other person does.

A greeting between men often includes a handshake, and to the handshake a bow may be added depending upon the social relationship of the two persons.

A nod may or may not be accompanied by words of greeting. Koreans are not very talkative when greeting acquaintances. This does not mean that they are unfriendly, but simply that they are reserved with people they do not know well.

As a rule, strangers do not greet each other on their own in Korea. A friendly American, who often greets a stranger on the street in America, may do the same in Korea. But, if you greet a stranger and he looks perplexed, it simply means that he is not used to being greeted by a person he does not know.

Communicative Exchanges

FRAME 1

Greeting a Friend or an Acquaintance

When you meet a friend or acquaintance for the first time in a day, at any time of day, most commonly greetings such as these occur.

박 : 안녕하세요?	How are you? (Literally, "Are you in
Park : Annyŏnghaseyo?	good health?")
김 : 네. 안녕하세요?	Yes. (I'm well.) How are you?
Kim : Ne. Annyŏnghaseyo?	

NOTE : 안녕하세요? in this context is not so much a question as a form of greeting. A typical response to this greeting form is to acknowledge it with 네 and then repeat 안녕하세요? The acknowledging word 네 can make sense to you if you perceive the greeting quite literally, that is, "Are you in good health?"

FRAME 2

Greeting a Friend after not Seeing Him for a While

Two friends see each other after a time of separation. Obviously, the exchange can get more lively and spirited.

윤 : 미스터 김, 안녕하세요 ?
Yun : Mist'ŏ Kim, annyŏnghaseyo ?

Mr. Kim, how are you ?

김 : 아, 미스터 윤, 안녕하세요 ?
Kim : A, mist'ŏ Yun, annyŏnghaseyo ?

Oh, Mr. Yun, how are you ?

윤 : 오래간만입니다. [1]
Yun : Oraeganmanimnida.

It's been a long time.

김 : 네. 오래간만입니다.
Kim : Ne. Oraeganmanimnida.

Yes. It's been a long time.

윤 : 반갑습니다.
Yun : Pangapsŭmnida.

I'm glad (to see you again).

SUBSTITUTION

1. 오랜만입니다.   It's been a long time.
   Oraenmanimnida.

FRAME 3

Formal Greetings to an Acquaintance
or a Person Older than You

Mr. Kim and Mr. Nam are relatively new acquaintances. In such cases, the greetings become more formal than those used in previous frames.

김 : 남 선생님, 안녕하십니까?   Mr. Nam, how are you?

Kim: Nam sŏnsaengnim, annyŏnghashim-
      nikka?

남 : 네. 김 선생님, 안녕하십니까?   Yes. (I'm fine.) How are you,

Nam: Ne. Kim sŏnsaengnim, annyŏngha-   Mr. Kim?
      shimnikka?

김 : 잘 지냅니다. 요즘 바쁘십니까?   I'm getting on well. Are you

Kim: Chal chinaemnida. Yojŭm pappŭ-   busy lately?
      shimnikka?

남 : 네. 요즘 꽤 바쁩니다.   Yes, I'm quite busy these days.

Nam : Ne. Yojŭm kkwae pappŭmnida.

NOTE : 안녕하세요? and 안녕하십니까? mean the same, the latter being more formal. Note that the courtesy title-word 선생님 is used here. See pages 23-24 for the usage of 미스터 and 선생님.

FRAME 4

Informal Greetings in the Hallway

Two acquaintances exchange greetings in the hallway of the office area. It is not the first time they have seen each other that day.

송 : 바쁘세요?   Are you busy?
Song: Pappŭseyo?

한 : 별로 안 바빠요.   I'm not too busy.
Han : Pyŏllo an pappayo.

　　　선생님은 어떠세요?   How is everything with you?
　　　Sŏnsaengnimŭn ŏttŏseyo?

송 : 많이 바빠요.[1]   (I'm) very busy.
Song: Mani pappayo.

SUBSTITUTION
1. 그저 그래요.   So-so.
　 Kŭjŏ kŭraeyo.

Grammar and Usage

1. Idiomatic Expressions

You have learned four idiomatic expressions, for which rough English equivalents are given below. You do not have to know yet exactly how such meanings have developed from the components of the sentences.

안녕하세요?　　　　How are you?

안녕하십니까?　　　(A more formal expression than 안녕하세요?)

오래간만입니다.　　It's been a long time (since I saw you last).

어떠세요?　　　　　How is everything (with you)?

Another utterance, 바쁘세요? is not idiomatic, but it is often used as a greeting.

2. Sentence-Endings

Korean sentence-endings are determined by how polite or formal the speaker becomes in addressing the hearer. The ending -요 represents an attitude polite enough, but not as formal as the ending 습니다. While the ending 습니다 is commonly used for a statement, 습니까 is used for a question.

3. Addressing Korean Adults

In general, Korean adults do not use their first names when they address their friends or acquaintances. Instead, they may use a title, such as 선생님, preceded by a surname. You should never address a Korean with his/her last name alone. But a title is rarely used when you introduce yourself.

For a male who is your senior in age or status, use SURNAME+선생님, as in 김 선생님. For a male who is your equal or junior in age or status, use SURNAME+선생, as in 김 선생. A career woman may be addressed, as 김 선생님 or 김 선생, depending upon her age or status. For a male who is your equal or junior in age or status, also use 미스터+SURNAME, as in 미스터 남.

Another title 씨, loosely translated as "Mr." is used in many different ways. You may use SURNAME or GIVEN NAME or FULL NAME+씨, as in 김 씨 or 종일 씨 or 김 종일 씨. Sometimes, regardless of her marital status, a woman may be addressed with 씨, as in 유 경자 씨. (In this case, it is not customary to use 씨 together with her surname only.) It is true that nowadays the use of 씨 preceded by a last name or a full name is appropriate only for one who is your equal or junior. But you should know that in a public announcement, for example, it is quite appropriate to call someone with 씨. You must also know that the use of 씨 together with someone's given name suggests an intimate relationship, as in 종일 씨.

If a woman is married (or apparently married) or older than you, use MAIDEN NAME+여사님, as in 박 여사님 (A Korean woman does not adopt her husband's name when she marries.). For a woman of similar standing, you may also use 미시즈+HUSBAND'S NAME, as in 미시즈 김. If a woman is the wife of a prominent man or of your senior, use simply 사모님 with no last name attached to it. For a young, unmarried female, 미스+SURNAME is most often used, as in 미스 남. You may also use SURNAME+양, as in 남 양.

4. How the Korean Full Name Is Arranged

A person's full name is always arranged in the order of LAST NAME+FIRST NAME, as in 박 인구. When a Korean full name is put into English, it is often arranged in the English way; hence, In-ku Park. Nowadays, however, more and more Koreans go the Korean way when they put their names into English, as in Park In-ku.

5. Typical Korean Last Names

Last names in Korea are relatively limited in number. With the exception of a few, typical last names have only one syllable. (Most given names are typically of two syllables.) Listed below are some of the most common last names and their common English spellings.

김 Kim	정 Chŏng	권 Kwon
이 Lee/Yi/Rhee	조 Cho	서 Sŏ/Suh
박 Pak/Park	한 Han/Hahn	유 Yoo/Yu/Ryu
최 Choi/Ch'oe	장 Chang	강 Kang

Exercises

A. What Do You Hear?

Cover the Han-gŭl text below and say aloud the English equivalent for each utterance that your instructor makes.

1. 미스터 김, 안녕하세요?
2. 오래간만입니다.
3. 한 선생님, 안녕하십니까?
4. 바쁘세요?
5. 박 선생님, 오래간만입니다.
6. 어떠세요?
7. 그저 그래요.
8. 별로 안 바빠요.

B. What Do You Say?

Work with your instructor or classmate in the following series of role-playing.

1. You see a friend in the street and you want to greet him. What do you say?
2. Walking down the street, you meet a friend whom you have not seen for some time. You say, "How are you?" and now you want to add that it has been a long time since you saw him last. What do you say?
3. You want to greet an older person on a formal occasion. You bow, and now you want to say, "How are you, sir?" using a formal expression. What do you say?
4. You run into a friend from another office in the hallway. It is not the first time you have seen him today. You want to exchange casual greetings. What do you say?
5. You see Mr. Lee, a good friend of yours, working next door. He greets you first, saying, "Are you busy?" Respond to his greeting.
6. On the way home you meet Miss Han, whom you have not seen for a month or so. She greets you, saying, "It's been a long time." Respond appropriately to her greeting.

Words and Phrases

그저 그래요.	So-so.
네	yes
많이	very; a great deal, much
미스	Miss
미스터	Mr.
미시즈	Mrs.
바빠요.	(One) is busy.
바쁘세요?	Are you busy?
바쁘십니까?	Are you busy? (formal)
바쁩니다.	(One) is busy. (formal)
반갑습니다.	I'm glad.
별로	(not) particularly; (not) too
사모님	Mrs. (one's senior's wife)
선생님	Mr.; teacher
씨	Mr.
아	oh
안	not
안녕하세요?	How are you?
안녕하십니까?	How are you? (formal)
양	Miss
어떠세요?	How is everything with you?
오래간만입니다.	It's been a long time.
오랜만입니다.	It's been a long time.
요즘	lately
잘 지냅니다.	(One) is getting on well.

Meeting People

Lesson Objectives

1. Introduce your friend or colleague to someone in the office or at a social gathering. Specifically you will:
   (a) Say that you want to introduce your friend to him/her.
   (b) Ask both parties to greet each other.
   (c) State the name and title of the person being introduced.

2. Exchange appropriate greetings when you meet someone for the first time or when someone introduces you to another. Specifically you will:
   (a) Introduce yourself by name.
   (b) Say that you are glad to meet the person.

3. Bid farewell to a departing visitor or a host.

4. Know some general facts about Korean grammar, specifically:
   (a) The omission of the subject of a sentence.
   (b) The normal position of the verb in a sentence.
   (c) Verb endings determining types of expression.
   (d) The verb of "equation" or "identification."

Cultural Notes
Korean Introduction Customs

As far as the introduction customs are concerned, there is no great difference between the Korean way and the Western way, except for the custom of bowing (already noted in Lesson 1).

One's status or age is an important factor to consider. For if you are to introduce an old man and a young man to each other, you should address the older man first and introduce the younger man to the older, not vice versa.

Among men, name (or business) cards are frequently used for introduction purposes. The business card enables you to know instantly the other person's status or profession and to choose proper levels of language or proper gestures.

As a rule, you are not supposed to tap someone on the shoulder or any other part of his body during introductions, unless he is a very close friend of yours. Especially, touching someone on the head is considered extremely rude even among close friends.

Communicative Exchanges

FRAME 1

Introducing a Friend

Mr. Kim introduces Mr. Chang to Mr. Han in his office.

김 : 제 친구 소개하겠습니다.
Kim : Che ch'in-gu sogaehagessŭmnida.

I'd like to introduce my friend to you.

이분은 장 홍수 씨입니다.
I punŭn Chang Hong-su ssiimnida.

This gentleman is Mr. Hong-su Chang.

장 : 처음 뵙겠습니다.[1]
Chang: Ch'ŏŭm poepkessŭmnida.

I am glad to meet you.
(Literally: I think I meet you for the first time.)

한 : 처음 뵙겠습니다.
Han : Ch'ŏŭm poepkessŭmnida.

I am glad to meet you.

저는 한 기수입니다.
Chŏnŭn Han Ki-suimnida.

I am Ki-su Han.

SUBSTITUTION

1. 처음 뵙습니다.   I am glad to meet you.
   Ch'ŏŭm poepsŭmnida.

NOTE : This is slightly more casual in tone.

FRAME 2

Meeting People at a Party

Mr. Kim brings a young lady (Miss Myŏng-sun Yun) to a social gathering and introduces her to Mr. Han.

김 : 한 선생님, <u>인사하십시오.</u> [1]
Kim : Han sŏnsaengnim, insahashipshio.

     이 분은 윤 명순 씨입니다.
     I punŭn Yun Myŏng-sun ssiimnida.

윤 : 처음 뵙겠습니다.
Yun : Ch'ŏŭm poepkessŭmnida.

한 : 네, 처음 뵙겠습니다.
Han : Ne, ch'ŏŭm poepkessŭmnida.

     한 기수입니다.
     Han Ki-suimnida.

Mr. Han, I want you to meet each other.

This is Miss Myŏng-sun Yun.

I am glad to meet you.

I am glad to meet you.

I'm Ki-su Han.

SUBSTITUTION

1. 인사하세요.   I want you to meet each other.
   Insahaseyo.

NOTE : This form is more casual or familiar in tone.

FRAME 3

Saying Good-bye

Miss Yun has been visiting Mr. Han and is now taking her leave.

윤 : 그럼 또 뵙겠습니다.
Yun: Kŭrŏm tto poepkessŭmnida.

Well, then, I'll see you again.

한 : 또 뵙겠습니다. <u>안녕히 가십시오.</u> [1]
Han: Tto poepkessŭmnida. Annyŏnghi kaship-
shio.

I'll see you again. Good-bye.
(Literally, "Go in peace.")

윤 : 네, <u>안녕히 계십시오.</u> [2]
Yun: Ne, annyŏnghi kyeshipshio.

Yes, good-bye. (Literally,
"Stay in peace.")

SUBSTITUTION

1. 안녕히 가세요.   Good-bye.
   Annyŏnghi gaseyo.
   조심하세요.   Take care.
   Choshimhaseyo.
2. 안녕히 계세요.   Good-bye.
   Annyŏnghi kyeseyo.

NOTE : These are more casual or familiar in tone.

Grammar and Usage

1. Omission of the Subject

Koreans often drop the subject of a sentence when they think the intended meaning gets across without the subject-word, especially the word referring to the speaker ("I") and the hearer ("you"). Koreans prefer, that is, not to use personal pronouns in their verbal communication. You will soon learn that the Korean speaker, being self-conscious in this matter, keeps on using people's names or titles instead of personal pronouns.

2. Normal Position of the Verb

One of the basic features of Korean grammar is that the verb is almost always placed at the end of a sentence. Compare the positions of the verbs (underlined) as they are found in different types of verbal expression in Korean and English.

(Statement)	이 사람은 제 친구입니다.	This is my friend.
(Question)	이분은 친구입니까?	Is this your friend?
(Request)	이리 오세요.	Come this way.

3. Verb-endings Determining Types of Expression

We find that a verb-ending in Korean is an important factor determining the type of a verbal expression, whereas the position of a verb plays a similar role in English. To cite more examples,

(Statement)	오래간만입니다.	It has been a long time.
(Question)	안녕하십니까?	How are you?
(Request)	인사하십시오.	Greet each other, please.

We can now identify some of the verb-endings which are commonly used:

―입니다, ―입니까, ―십니까, ―십시오 (or ―세요).

4. The "Identification" Verb

One of your basic needs in Korean is an ability to identify persons and objects or to equate one thing to another. Obviously you need to become familiar with a type of sentence designed for such use. For convenience's sake, we will call this type of sentence an "identification sentence" or an "equation sentence."

이분이　　장 홍수 씨<u>입니다.</u>

$\left(\begin{smallmatrix}\text{subject}\\\text{omitted}\end{smallmatrix}\right)$ 한 기수<u>입니다.</u>

In the sentences cited above, 입니다 serves as an "identification" or "equation" verb. In many European languages the form of this verb alters (or inflects) to indicate different grammatical relations. In English, the form of the verb <u>be</u> changes according to the person and the number, as in I <u>am</u>, you <u>are</u>, he <u>is.</u> There is no such verb inflection in Korean.

The vowel 이 in —입니다 may be dropped when the preceding noun ends with a vowel. For instance, you can say 정 영잡니다 instead of 정 영자입니다 because the final sound in the syllable 자 is a vowel.

Exercises

A. What Do You Hear ?

Cover the Han-gŭl text below and say aloud the English equivalent for each utterance that your instructor makes.

1. 처음 뵙겠습니다.
2. 안녕히 계십시오.
3. 또 뵙겠습니다.

4. 안녕히 가십시오.
5. 제 친구 소개하겠습니다.
6. 인사하십시오.

B. What Do You Say ?

Work with your instructor or classmate in the following series of role-playing.

1. Say to your old acquaintance that you would like to introduce a friend of yours to him.
2. Say that the person being introduced is Mr. Hong-su Chang.
3. Mr. Kim is introducing his friend to you. Tell that person that you are glad to meet him, and introduce yourself by stating your name.
4. Two of your friends are with you. You want to get them to meet each other. What do you say ?
5. Introduce your female friend Myŏng-sun Yun to Ki-su Han, another friend of yours, by using the former's name and title.
6. Take the role of Myŏng-sun Yun, and tell Ki-su Han that you are glad to meet him.
7. Now take the role of Ki-su Han and tell Myŏng-sun Yun that you are glad to meet her, and introduce yourself by stating your name.
8. After a visit with someone, you are about to take your leave. What do you say ?
9. Your visitor has said a farewell greeting. How do you respond to that ?
10. How do you respond to the farewell greeting of your host, the one you have been visiting ?

Words and Phrases

그럼	then
또 뵙겠습니다.	I'll see you again.
소개하겠습니다.	Let me introduce….
안녕히 가세요.	Good-bye. (to a departing person)
안녕히 가십시오.	Good-bye. (to a departing person) (formal)
안녕히 계세요.	Good-bye. (to the host)
안녕히 계십시오.	Good-bye. (to the host) (formal)
—은	subject-marking suffix
—이	subject-marking suffix
이분	this person
인사하세요.	Please meet….
인사하십시오.	Please meet…. (formal)
저	I
제	my
조심하세요.	Take care.
처음 뵙겠습니다.	Glad to meet you. (formal)
처음 뵙습니다.	Glad to meet you.
친구	friend

Office Visits

Lesson Objectives

1. Carry on a conversation with the receptionist when visiting a friend in his office. Specifically you will:
   (a) Greet the receptionist.
   (b) Ask the receptionist if your friend is in the office.
   (c) Understand the receptionist's instructions (e.g., wait, sit down, go in).

2. Carry on a conversation, as receptionist, with a visitor. Specifically you will:
   (a) Ask the visitor who he/she is.
   (b) Give him/her necessary instructions (e.g., wait, sit down, go in).

3. Carry on a conversation with your friend in his office. Specifically you will:
   (a) Greet your friend appropriately.
   (b) Understand his/her offer of refreshments, such as tea, coffee, or a cold drink.
   (c) Decline or thank your friend for his/her offer of refreshments.

4. Understand fully some general rules about sentence-endings (either the long or short form), so that you may easily recognize:
   (a) "Polite request" sentences.
   (b) Question sentences.
   (c) Statement sentences.

Cultural Notes
Korean Modesty

When someone makes a visit with you, you may want to offer that person some refreshment. It is socially correct for a Korean visitor to accept such hospitality. However, sometimes a Korean visitor might hesitate to accept, or even decline the host's offer. This initial refusal can often be a mere sign of modesty on the visitor's part. Therefore, you should make sure of your visitor's true intention by repeating your offer two or three times. In urban areas, however, you will find more Koreans who are open and direct in their behavior.

Communicative Exchanges

FRAME 1

Arriving at an Office

테일러 Taylor	: 수고하십니다.¹ : Sugohashimnida.	Hello. (Literally, "With due re- spect to your hard work.")
	김 선생님 계세요? Kim sŏnsaengnim kyeseyo?	Is Mr. Kim in?
접수안내원 Receptionist	: 네, 계십니다. : Ne, Kyeshimnida.	Yes, he is.
	누구시지요?² Nugushijiyo?	May I ask who you are?
테일러 Taylor	: 존 테일러입니다. : Chon T'eillŏimnida.	I'm John Taylor.
접수안내원 Receptionist	: 네. 잠깐 기다리세요. : Ne. Chamkkan kidariseyo.	I see. Wait a moment, please.

SUBSTITUTION

1. 안녕하세요? How are you?
   Annyŏnghaseyo?
   NOTE: Used to greet a person or draw his/her attention.
2. 성함이 어떻게 되시지요? What is your name, please?
   Sŏnghami ŏttŏk'e toeshijiyo?

FRAME 2

Being Received in the Office

The receptionist asks Mr. Taylor to wait for a moment and shows him in a while later.

접수안내원 :	잠깐 기다리세요.	Please wait a moment.
Receptionist :	Chamkkan kidariseyo.	
	이리 앉으세요.	Have a seat here, please.
	Iri anjŭseyo.	
테일러 :	네	Yes.
Taylor :	Ne.	

(A while later)

접수안내원 :	이리 오십시오.	Come this way, please.
Receptionist :	Iri oshipshio.	
	자, 들어가세요.	Now, you may go in.
	Cha, tŭrŏgaseyo.	

FRAME 3

Social Greetings in Your Friend's Office

Mr. Taylor is now in Mr. Kim's office. The two friends exchange social greetings.

테일러: 김 선생님, 안녕하세요?　　　　　Mr. Kim, how are you?
Taylor : Kim sŏnsaengnim, annyŏnghaseyo?

오래간만입니다.　　　　　　　　It's been a long time.
Oraeganmanimnida.

김　　: 아, 참 오래간만입니다.　　　　Yes, it's been a long time
Kim　　: A, ch'am oraeganmanimnida.　　indeed.

이리 앉으세요.　　　　　　　　Please sit down here.
Iri anjŭseyo.

테일러: 네.　　　　　　　　　　　　Yes.
Taylor : Ne.

김　　: 커피[1] 한잔 하시겠어요?　　　Would you like to have a
Kim　　: K'ŏp'i hanjan hashigessŏyo?　　cup of coffee?

테일러: 네, 감사합니다.[2]　　　　　Yes, thank you.
Taylor : Ne, kamsahamnida.

SUBSTITUTION
1. 차　any hot drink (generic term)　　　인삼차　ginseng tea
　ch'a　　　　　　　　　　　　　　insamch'a.

　홍차　Lipton tea　　　　　　　　　콜라　　Coca or Pepsi Cola
　hongch'a　　　　　　　　　　　　k'olla

2. 아니오, 괜찮습니다.　　　　　　　No, never mind.
　Anio, kwaench'anssŭmnida.

Grammar and Usage

1. How to Make a Polite Request

The following sentences are used to politely urge someone to do something. This kind of expression will be called, for convenience's sake, a "polite request sentence."

인사하세요.	Please greet each other.
안녕히 가십시오.	Good-bye. (to a person leaving)
안녕히 계십시오.	Good-bye. (to a person staying)
잠깐 기다리세요.	Please wait for a moment.
이리 앉으세요.	Please sit down here.
들어가세요.	Please go in.

You may notice in the polite request sentences above two different endings:

—세요.	(SHORT FORM)
—십시오.	(LONG FORM)

They are almost always interchangeable and have practically no difference in meaning. The long form, however, is more formal and is used exclusively for request sentences.

The short form is more informal; it is used more commonly by women, and may be used in other types of expressions as well. Read aloud each of the following sentences until you become fully acquainted with the two different endings involved:

인사하세요.	인사하십시오.
안녕히 가세요.	안녕히 가십시오.
안녕히 계세요.	안녕히 계십시오.
잠깐 기다리세요.	잠깐 기다리십시오.
이리 앉으세요.	이리 앉으십시오.
들어가세요.	들어가십시오.

2. How to Ask a Question

Let us review some sentences that are used to ask questions:

안녕하세요?	How are you ?
안녕하십니까?	How are you ?
어떠세요?	How is everything ?
이분 아세요?	Do you know this lady/gentleman ?
김 선생님 계세요?	Is Mr. Kim in ?

As in polite request sentences, two different endings are used in the question sentences. Similarly, the long form is used strictly in question sentences, but the short form may be used for other types of expressions as well.

—세요?	(SHORT FORM)
—십니까?	(LONG FORM)

Read aloud each of the following sentences until you become fully acquainted with the two different endings involved.

안녕하세요?	안녕하십니까?
어떠세요?	어떠십니까?
이분 아세요?	이분 아십니까?
김 선생님 계세요?	김 선생님 계십니까?

3. How to Make a Statement

Let us now review some sentences that are used to make statements :

오래간만입니다.	It's been a long time.
안 바빠요.	I am not busy.
또 뵙겠어요.	I'll see you again.
감사합니다.	(I) thank you.

In the statement sentences given above, you may again notice two different endings :

—요.	(SHORT FORM)
—ㅂ니다.	(LONG FORM)

The long form is used exclusively to make statements, while the short form may be used to form other types of expression as well, which will be introduced later.

Read aloud each of the following sentences until you become fully acquainted with the two different endings involved.

오래간만이에요.   오래간만입니다.
안 바빠요.   안 바쁩니다.
또 뵙겠어요.   또 뵙겠습니다.
괜찮아요.   괜찮습니다.

Exercises

A. What Do You Hear?

Cover the Han-gŭl text below and say aloud the English equivalent of each utterance that your instructor makes.

1. 이 선생님 계십니다.
2. 수고하십니다.
3. 감사합니다.
4. 커피 한잔 하시겠어요?
5. 잠깐 기다리세요.

6. 이리 앉으세요.
7. 조 선생님 계세요?
8. 들어가십시오.
9. 이리 오십시오.
10. 누구시지요?

B. What Do You Say?

Work with your instructor or classmate in the following series of role-playing.

1. You are entering an office as a visitor. How would you greet the receptionist?
2. Inquire of him/her if Mr. Cho, the one you are visiting, is in.
3. Take the role of a receptionist and ask your visitor what his/her name is.
4. Ask your visitor to please wait for a moment.
5. Pointing to a seat nearby, tell your visitor to please sit down.
6. Ask your visitor to go right into another office.
7. You are now walking into the main office as a visitor. As you find Mr. Cho there, draw his attention by calling his name and greeting him.
8. Take the role of Mr. Cho and greet your visitor whom you have not seen for a long time.
9. Ask your visitor to please sit down and offer him/her something to drink.
10. As a visitor, either accept with thanks or decline Mr. Cho's offer of refreshments.

C. Grammar Exercise

1. For each utterance with a long ending that your instructor makes, say aloud its counterpart with a short ending. For example, if you hear 안녕

하십니까? and say 안녕하세요?

    (a) 김 선생님 계십니까?   (d) 들어가십시오.
    (b) 잠깐 기다리십시오.   (e) 이리 오십시오.
    (c) 이리 앉으십시오.

2. For each utterance with a short ending that your instructor makes, say aloud its counterpart with a long ending. For example, if you hear 안녕하세요? say 안녕하십니까?

    (a) 이리 앉으세요.   (d) 김 선생님 계세요?
    (b) 들어가세요.   (e) 이리 앉으세요.
    (c) 잠깐 기다리세요.

Words and Phrases

감사합니다.	Thank you.
괜찮습니다.	Never mind. (formal)
괜찮아요.	Never mind.
계세요?	Is (one) in?
계십니까?	Is (one) in? (formal)
계십니다.	(One) is in.
기다리세요.	Please wait.
누구시지요?	May I ask who you are?
들어가세요.	Please go in.
성함이 어떻게 되시지요?	What is your name, please?
수고하십니다.	Hello. (used as a greeting)
아니오.	No.
접수안내원	receptionist
앉으세요.	Please sit down.
오십시오.	Please come.
이리	this way
인삼차	ginseng tea
자	now, well
잠깐	a moment
차	hot drink (a generic term)
참	very; indeed
커피	coffee
콜라	cola
한잔 하시겠어요?	Would you like to have a drink?
홍차	black tea

Going Places

Lesson Objectives

1. Carry on a conversation with your friend or acquaintance about going to different places. Specifically you will:
   (a) Ask your friend where he/she is going.
   (b) State where you are going, naming your destination.
   (c) Explain why you are taking a particular trip.

2. Indicate for your friend the location of a city on the map.

3. Use correctly the following grammatical forms:
   (a) The sentence-ending indicating the speaker's politeness (known as the "honorific marker").
   (b) The word "who" or "anyone" in a question sentence.

4. Understand fully some general rules about the subject-marking suffixes —이 and —가, so that you may easily recognize them by listening.

Cultural Notes
Korea's Land and Cities

Did you ever wonder what's the language you are now learning called ? It's 한국말 (han-gukmal). What about the country where that language has been spoken over many centuries? It's 한국 (Han-guk). At present, unfortunately, we have two Koreas: South Korea and North Korea.

South Korea, officially named 대한민국 (Taehanmin-guk, meaning "the Republic of Korea"), has diplomatic ties with all nations of the Free World. (The culture and language being introduced in this book are, of course, those prevailing in South Korea today.) 한국 is a term in common use, meaning "Korea." There is a geo-politically slanted term 남한 (Namhan), meaning "South Korea" as against 북한 (Puk' an), meaning "North Korea." However, North Koreans themselves call their own territory 북조선 (Puk-chosŏn), 조선 (Chosŏn) being one of the old names of Korea. For political reasons, South Koreans do not refer to North Korea as 북조선; they prefer the name 북한.

Following are some of the important cities in South Korea. (For city locations see the map on next page.)

1. 서울 (Sŏul) : The name, meaning "capital," is spelled "Seoul" in English. Seoul has about 10 million people, one fourth of the nation's population.
2. 인천 (Inch'ŏn) : A principal port lying to the west of the capital, Inch'ŏn is well known for General Douglas MacArthur's Inch'ŏn landing operations during the Korean War.
3. 수원 (Suwon) : Suwon, capital of Kyŏnggi-do Province situated to the south of Seoul, is noted for the ancient gates and walls dating from the 18th century.
4. 대전 (Taejŏn) : The capital of Ch'ungch'ŏngnam-do Province, Taejŏn is about two hours south of Seoul.
5. 대구 (Taegu) : Korea's third largest city, Taegu is famed as an important

college town and as the center of Korea's apple and textile industry.

6. 경주 (Kyŏngju) : Often called the "museum without walls" because of its numerous historical buildings and treasures, Kyŏngju is one of the most important historical centers of Korea.

7. 부산 (Pusan) : Pusan is Korea's second largest city and principal port lying at the southeastern tip of the peninsula.

8. 광주 (Kwangju) : Kwangju is a major city in the entire west coast area.

9. 제주 (Cheju) : Cheju-do Island is one hour's flight from Seoul off the southwestern coast of the peninsula. The city of Cheju is both the location of an international airport and the center for various activities on the island.

1. 서울
   Sŏul

2. 인천
   Inch'ŏn

3. 수원
   Suwon

4. 대전
   Taejŏn

5. 대구
   Taegu

6. 경주
   Kyŏngju

7. 부산
   Pusan

8. 광주
   Kwangju

9. 제주
   Cheju

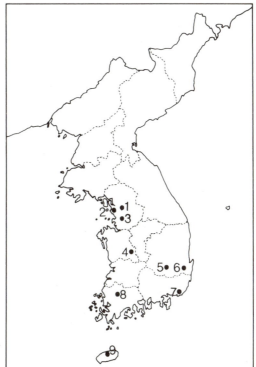

Communicative Exchanges

FRAME 1

Going to Korea

Kim and Taylor talk about the former's trip to Korea.

테일러: 미스터 김, 어디 가세요 ?　　　　Where are you going, Mr. Kim ?
Taylor : Mistŏ Kim, ŏdi kaseyo ?

김　　: 아, 한국에 갑니다.　　　　　　Oh, I'm going to Korea.
Kim　　: A, Han-guge kamnida.

테일러: 한국에요 ?　　　　　　　　　　To Korea ?
Taylor : Han-gugeyo ?

　　　　가족이 계세요 ?　　　　　　　Do you have your folks in Korea ?
　　　　Han-guge kajogi kyeseyo ?

김　　: 네, 우리 어머니하고 아버지　　　Yes. My mother and father are in
　　　　가 부산에 계십니다.　　　　　　Pusan.
Kim　　: Ne, uri ŏmŏnihago abŏjiga Pu-
　　　　sane kyeshimnida.

테일러: 네 ! 그러세요 ?　　　　　　　　Oh ! Is that so ?
Taylor : Ne ! Kŭrŏseyo ?

FRAME 2

Going into the Countryside

Kim and Chŏng talk about the former's trip to his native town.

정   : 김 선생님, 어디 가십니까?
Chŏng : Kim sŏnsaengnim, ŏdi kashimnikka ?

Mr..Kim, where are you going ?

김   : 아, 시골에 갑니다.
Kim   : A, shigore kamnida.

Oh, I'm going into the countryside.

정   : 시골 어디에 가십니까?
Chŏng : Shigol ŏdie kashimnikka ?

Where in the countryside are you going ?

김   : 홍성에 갑니다.
Kim   : Hongsŏng-e Kamnida.

Going to Hongsŏng.

정   : 홍성에요? 좋겠군요!
Chŏng : Hongsŏng-eyo? Chok'etkunyo!

To Hongsŏng ? That's good ! (Literally, "It must be good.")

잘 다녀오세요.
Chal tanyŏoseyo !

Have a good trip ! (Literally, "Have a good trip and come back safely.")

FRAME 3

Going to the Korean Folk Village

Kim and Taylor talk about a trip to the Korean Folk Village near Suwon.

테일러: 김 선생, 주말에 어디 가세요 ?　　　Where are you going during
Taylor : Kim sŏnsaeng, chumare ŏdi kaseyo ?　the weekend, Mr. Kim ?

김　　: 민속촌에 갑니다.　　　　　　　　　I'm going to the Folk Village.
Kim　　: Minsokch'one kamnida.

테일러: 그것이 어디 있습니까 ?　　　　　　Where is it located ?
Taylor : Kŭgŏshi ŏdi issŭmnikka ?

김　　: 수원 가까이에 있습니다.　　　　　It's near Suwon.
Kim　　: Suwon kakkaie issŭmnida.

(Kim points to Suwon on the map.)

김　　: 여기가 수원입니다.　　　　　　　This is Suwon.
Kim　　: Yŏgiga Suwonimnida.

　　　　그리고 민속촌은 여기입니다.　　　And the Folk Village is here.
　　　　Kŭrigo minsokch'onŭn yŏgiimnida.

FRAME 4

Coming and Going

People always come and go as in the following scene.

김 : 고 선생, 어디 가세요?
Kim : Ko sŏnsaeng, ŏdi kaseyo?

Where're you going, Mr. Koh?

고 : 서울역에 갑니다.
Koh : Sŏullyŏge kamnida.

Going to Seoul Station.

김 : 그러세요? 저도 서울역에 갑니다.
Kim : Kŭrŏseyo? Chŏdo Sŏullyŏge kamnida.

Really? I'm going to Seoul Station, too.

고 : 여행 가십니까?
Koh : Yŏhaeng kashimnikka?

Are you going on a trip?

김 : 네, 경주에 갑니다.
Kim : Ne, Kyŏngjue kamnida.

Yes, I'm going to Kyŏngju.

선생님도 여행 가십니까?
Sŏnsaengnimdo yŏhaeng kashimnikka?

Are you going on a trip, too?

고 : 아니오. 친구가 대구에서 옵니다.
Koh : Anio. Ch'in-guga Taeguesŏ omnida.

No, I'm not. A friend of mine is coming from Taegu.

Grammar and Usage

1. Sentences Expressing Coming and Going

You have learned the following Korean sentences that express the idea of coming or going.

안녕히 $\left\{ \begin{array}{l} 가세요. \\ 가십시오. \end{array} \right.$ Good-bye. (Literally, "Please go in peace.")

미국에 갑니다.   I am going to America.

수원에 가요.   I am going to Suwon.

한국에 가세요?   Are you going to Korea?

이리 오십시오.   Come this way, please.

누가 옵니까?   Who is coming?

Let us sum up some general facts about these sentences.

1. The verb is always placed at the end of a sentence.
2. The stem of the verb "to go" is 가— and it is always followed by an ending; 오— is the stem of the verb "to come."
3. The phrase expressing the destination of coming or going has the suffix —에, which is equivalent to "to" in English, but this suffix is often omitted in short sentences.
4. A question word such as 어디 ("where") is not necessarily placed at the beginning of a sentence, which is not the case in English. In Korean it is placed where the answering word such as 한국에 ("to Korea") would be found. For example,

주말에 <u>수원에</u> 갑니다.   I am going to Suwon during the weekend.
       ↓
(ANSWERING WORD)
       ↑
주말에 <u>어디(에)</u> 가세요?   Where are you going during the week-end?

2. More on the Sentence-Endings

In sentences, such as 이리 앉으세요. ("Please sit down.") and 한잔

하시겠어요？ ("Would you like to have a cup ?"), the endings begin with —시 or—세. These elements are indicators of the speaker's respect for the subject of a sentence. We shall call these indicators "honorific markers" for convenience's sake. They may be used in any kind of expression—a statement, a question, or a request.

An honorific marker refers only to the listener or a third party as subject. Using an honorific marker it would not be appropriate when the speaker himself is the subject, since he would be paying respect to himself. This explains the two different verb endings in the following conversation.

Kim　：어디(에) 가세요？　　Where are you going ?
Taylor：한국(에) 갑니다.　　I am going to Korea.

The question contains —세요, but the answer, in which Taylor himself is the subject, contains no honorific marker (—시 or —세).

The complex use of the honorific marker cannot be mastered in a short period of time. You need to be exposed to more examples and more detailed explanations.

There is another instance when the honorific marker is not used. When you are speaking to a close friend or to someone with whom you needn't be very polite or formal, you may omit the honorific marker in a question or a request, as in the following example:

Kim　：한국(에) 갑니까？　　Are you going to Korea ?
Taylor：네, 한국(에) 갑니다.　　Yes, I am going to Korea.

3. Identifying Places

In Lesson 2, you learned how to identify persons or objects. In this lesson, you are learning how to identify places, following essentially the same pattern. The following formula shows the general form of sentences that is used for identifying people or things.

Subject	Suffix	Predicate
{NOUN ENDING IN A CONSONANT	+이}	NOUN+입니다
{NOUN ENDING IN A VOWEL	+가}	

"Subject" and "predicate" are the labels we shall use to identify the major parts of such sentences. If you need more information on them, consult a dictionary or any grammar reference book at hand. Note that the subject suffix takes two forms, —이 and —가, the former when the preceding noun ends with a consonant, and the latter when the noun ends with a vowel. For example,

서울이 어디 있습니까?	Where is Seoul?
경주가 어디 있습니까?	Where is Kyŏngju?
서울이/경주가 여기(에) 있습니다.	Seoul/Kyŏngju is here.
여기가 경주입니다.	This (place) is Kyŏngju.

Again, the question word 어디 is in the predicate (second word) because that is where the answering noun will appear. The question word in Korean, is not necessarily at the beginning of a sentence, as we noted earlier.

Note in the fourth example above that the place noun 여기 is to be translated "this" or "this place" when it is the subject of a sentence. In the third example, however, 여기(에) is to be translated "here" because it is used adverbially.

4. Are the Noun Suffixes Absolutely Necessary?

In this lesson you have seen nouns accompanied by short suffixes such as —에, —이 and —가.

수원에 가요.	I am going to Suwon.
수원이 어디(에) 있습니까?	Where is Suwon located?
여기가 수원입니다.	This (place) is Suwon.

Such a noun suffix usually indicates the role of the noun in a given sentence and is often called a "postposition" or a "particle." Generally speaking, these noun suffixes are like English prepositions, and would therefore be expected to play important roles. The suffixes introduced so far, however, are exceptions to the above rule in that they are commonly absent in short sentences (unless the noun is emphasized). In short, you are not always required to use the subject-marking —이, —가 and the destination-marking 에 suffixes in your speech; you only have to know what they are when you hear them. In other words, the following are acceptable as spoken forms:

수원 가요.	I am going to Suwon.
수원 어디 있습니까?	Where is Suwon located?

여기 수원입니다.   This is Suwon.

CAUTION: Other suffixes that will be introduced later may not always be omitted in the same way. For example, if you say, "I come America" for "I come from America" (omitting "from"), you will not be understood. The same is true in Korean.

---

5. The Question Word "Who"

The question word 누구 ("who"), when used as the subject of a sentence, is 누가 rather than 누구가. For example,

누가 옵니까?   Who is coming?
누가 계세요?   Who is there?

CAUTION: In sentences such as "Who is he?", 누구 is found in the predicate and therefore should remain 누구 (not 누가). For example,

그는 누구입니까?   "Who is he?"

Exercises

A. What Do You Hear?

Cover the Han-gŭl text below and say aloud the English equivalent of each utterance your instructor makes.

1. 미스터 신, 어디 가세요?
2. 한국에 가족이 계세요?
3. 시골에 갑니다.
4. 여기가 경주입니다.
5. 친구가 부산에서 옵니다.

B. What Do You Say?

Work with your instructor or classmate in the following series of role-playing.

1. Someone asks you where you are going. Tell him/her, one at a time, that you are going to (a) Korea, (b) America, (c) Taejŏn, (d) the countryside, and (e) the Folk Village.
2. Your friend says he is going on a trip. You want to wish him/her a nice trip. How would you say?
3. You want to ask your friend where he/she is going during the weekend. How would you say?
4. Your friend is going to (a) Suwon, (b) Taejŏn, (c) Kwangju, or (d) Pusan. Ask him/her where each of these places is located.
5. Tell your friend that the Folk Village is near Suwon.

C. Grammar Exercise

1. For each utterance that your instructor makes, say aloud its counterpart with the honorific marker —시 or —세.

   (a) 어디 가요?
   (b) 한국에 갑니까?
   (c) 수원에 가요?
   (d) 주말에 어디 갑니까?
   (e) 누가 옵니까?

2. Complete the following utterance by filling in the blank with each of the five place names below, followed by the proper subject suffix —이 or

一가.

_____이/가 어디 있습니까?

(a) 수원   (b) 경주   (c) 서울   (d) 광주   (e) 부산

3. Respond to the question 어디 갑니까? by using each of the cues given below.

> *Example* : Question : 어디 갑니까?
> Cue : 한국
> Response : 한국(에) 갑니다.

Cues : (a) 미국   (b) 일본   (c) 서울   (d) 수원   (e) 광주

4. Respond to the question 어디 가세요? by using each of the cues given below. Note in the example that, although the questions are in honorific form, your responses should still be in plain form.

> *Example* : Question : 어디 가세요?
> Cue : 한국
> Response : 한국(에) 갑니다. (not 한국(에) 가십니다.)

Cues : (a) 서울   (b) 경주   (c) 수원   (d) 대구   (e) 부산

5. Respond to the question 어디 있습니까? by using each of the cues given below.

> *Example* : Question : 어디 있습니까?
> Cue : 대구
> Response : 대구에 있습니다.

Cues : (a) 수원   (b) 경주   (c) 대전   (d) 인천   (e) 제주

6. Using a map of Korea, point to the correct location of each of the following cities. As you do that, say the Korean expression for "This (place) is...."

> *Example* : 여기가 서울입니다.

Cues : (a) 부산   (b) 광주   (c) 인천   (d) 대전   (e) 경주

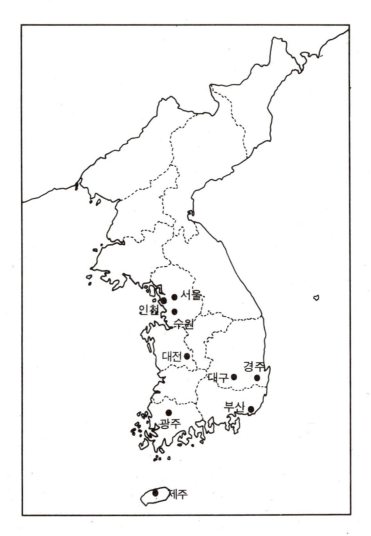

Words and Phrases

—가	subject-marking suffix
가족	family
가까이에	near
가세요?	Are you going?
가십니까?	Are you going? (honorific)
그것	it, that
그러세요?	Is that so?
그리고	and
누가	who
—도	too (subject-marking suffix)
시골	countryside
아버지	father
어디	where
어머니	mother
—에 갑니다.	(One) is going to….
—에서 옵니다.	(One) is coming from….
여기	this place; here
여행 가십니까?	Are you going on a trip?
우리	my; our
있습니다.	(One) is (or exists); (something) is (or exists).
잘 다녀오세요.	Have a good trip (or outing).
주말	during the weekend
—하고	(NOUN) and

Asking Directions

Lesson Objectives

1. Obtain information from a stranger on how to get to your destination. Specifically you will:
   (a) Politely attract the attention of a passerby.
   (b) Ask the person about the location of a place of interest you have in mind.
   (c) Ask the person how to get to the place of interest being discussed.

2. Understand the typical directions that a passerby gives you.

3. Thank the passerby for his/her help.

4. Use correctly the following grammatical forms:
   (a) Two sets of words indicating a direction or location relative to where you and the hearer are situated.
   (b) Two negative forms, according to the type of sentence involved.

Cultural Notes
Where to Go in Seoul

Seoul, capital of the Republic of Korea, is the political, financial, diplomatic, commercial, educational and cultural center of Korea. The city abounds with numerous public office buildings and places of interest, old and new. The following is the list of important public offices and well-known places of interest.

1. Government Offices / Foreign Embassies
   The Blue House (청와대) (The President's official home)
   Unified Government Building (정부 종합 청사)
   National Assembly Building (국회 의사당)
   Seoul City Hall (서울 시청)
   Seoul Metropolitan Police Dept. (서울시 경찰국)
   Seoul Central Post Office (서울 중앙 우체국)
   U.S. Embassy (미국 대사관)
   British Embassy (영국 대사관)
   Japanese Embassy (일본 대사관)

2. Royal Palaces / Ancient Gates
   Ch'angdŏkkung Palace (창덕궁)
   Kyŏngbokkung Palace (경복궁)
   Tŏksugung Palace (덕수궁)
   Namdaemun Gate (남대문)
   Tongdaemun Gate (동대문)

3. Museums / Performing Arts Facilities
   National Central Museum (국립 중앙 박물관)
   Drama Center (드라마 센터)
   The National Museum of Contemporary Art (국립 현대 미술관)
   Seoul Arts Center (예술의 전당)
   Hoam Art Hall (호암 아트 홀)
   National Theater (국립 극장)

Sejong Cultural Center (세종 문화 회관)

4. Parks / Sports Facilities
   Olympic Park (올림픽 공원)
   Pagoda Park (파고다 공원)
   Seoul Grand Park (서울 대공원)
   Changch'ung Gymnasium (장충 체육관)
   Seoul Sports Complex (서울 종합 운동장)

5. Shopping and Amusement Districts
   Myŏng-dong (명동)
   Insa-dong (인사동)
   Itaewon (이태원)
   Yŏngdong (영동)
   Lotte Department Store (롯데 백화점)
   Shinsegye Department Store (신세계 백화점)
   Midopa Department Store (미도파 백화점)
   Hyundai Department Store (현대 백화점)

6. Hotels
   Hotel Lotte (롯데 호텔)
   Seoul Plaza Hotel (서울 프라자 호텔)
   Westin Chosun (조선 호텔)
   Hotel Shilla (신라 호텔)
   Sheraton Walker Hill (세라톤 워커힐 호텔)
   Seoul Hilton International (서울 힐튼 호텔)
   Hyatt Regency Hotel (하이야트 호텔)
   Ramada Olympia Hotel (라마다 올림피아 호텔)

Communicative Exchanges

FRAME 1

Asking the Way to a Hotel

Mr. Jones, on a street in Seoul, asks a passerby the way to the Westin Chosun Hotel.

존스 Jones	: 실례합니다. : Shillyehamnida.	Excuse me, sir.
행인 Passerby	: 네. : Ne.	Sure.
존스 Jones	: 조선 호텔이 어딥니까?[1] : Chosŏn hot'eri ŏdimnikka?	Where is the Chosun Hotel?
행인 Passerby	: 바로 저기입니다. : Paro chŏgiimnida.	It's right over there.
존스 Jones	: 감사합니다.[2] : Kamsahamnida.	Thank you.
행인 Passerby	: 천만에요. : Ch'ŏnmaneyo.	You're welcome.

SUBSTITUTION

1. 조선 호텔에 어떻게 갑니까?   How do I get to the Chosun Hotel?
   Chosŏn hot'ere ŏttŏk'e kamnikka?

2. 고맙습니다.   Thank you.
   Komapsŭmnida.

FRAME 2

Finding Your Way to a Public Office Building

Mr. Jones now asks of a passerby the directions to the American Embassy in Seoul.

존스	: 실례합니다.	Excuse me, sir.
Jones	: Shillyehamnida.	
	말씀 좀 묻겠습니다.	May I ask you a question?
	Malssŭm chom mutkessŭmnida.	
행인	: 네.	Sure.
Passerby	: Ne.	
존스	: 미국 대사관에 어떻게 갑니까?[1]	How do I get to the American
Jones	: Miguk taesakwane ŏttŏk'e kamnikka?	Embassy?
행인	: 이리 곧장 가십시오.[2]	Go straight down this way.
Passerby	: Iri kotchang kashipshio.	
	저기 크고 하얀 건물입니다.	It's that big white building.
	Chŏgi k'ŭgo hayan kŏnmurimnida.	
존스	: 네, 알겠습니다. 고맙습니다.	Oh, I see. Thank you.
Jones	: Ne, algessŭmnida. Komapsŭmnida.	

SUBSTITUTION

1. 미국 대사관은 어느 길로 갑니까?   Which way do I go for the
   Miguk taesagwanŭn ŏnŭ killo kamnikka?   American Embassy?

2. 이 길로 가세요.   Go this way.
   I killo kaseyo.

FRAME 3

Finding the Right Way to Your Destination

Mr. Jones wants to find out the right way to the Tŏksugung Palace.

존스 : 실례합니다.
Jones : Shillyehamnida.

Excuse me. Do I go this way to the Tŏksugung Palace ?

덕수궁은 이 길로 갑니까?
Tŏksugungŭn i killo kamnikka ?

행인 : 그 길이 아닙니다.
Passerby : Kŭ kiri animnida.

No, it's not that way.

덕수궁은 이 길로 가세요
Tŏksugungŭn i killo kaseyo.

For the Tŏksugung Palace, go this way.

존스 : 롯데 호텔은 어느 길로 갑니까?
Jones : Lotte hot'erŭn ŏnŭ killo kamnikka ?

Which way do I go to get to Hotel Lotte ?

행인 : 롯데 호텔은 저 길로 갑니다.
Passerby : Lotte hot'erŭn chŏ killo kamnida.

To Hotel Lotte, you can go that way.

존스 : 대단히 감사합니다.
Jones : Taedanhi kamsahamnida.

Thank you very much.

행인 : 천만에요.
Passerby : Ch'ŏnmaneyo.

Not at all.

Grammar and Usage

1. Pointer Words

You have learned two sets of pointer words, one indicating the location and the other the direction, relative to where you (the speaker) and the hearer are situated. In English, there are two basic words or phrases for each set: "here" and "there"; "this way" and "that way." In Korean, there are three:

(a) Referring to the location

여기	here	a place near the speaker
거기	there	a place near the hearer
저기	{there ; over there}	a place away from both the speaker and hearer

(b) Referring to the direction

이리	this way	a direction toward, or close by, the speaker
그리	that way	a direction in which the hearer is headed
저리	that way	a direction away from both the speaker and hearer

2. Negation

You have learned two negative forms, one for negating identification sentences and the other for negating all other types of verbs.

(a) Negating identification sentences

Affirmative ("A is B.")	Negative ("A is not B.")
A $\left\{ \begin{array}{l} \text{이/가} \\ \text{은/는} \end{array} \right\}$ +B입니다.	A $\left\{ \begin{array}{l} \text{이/가} \\ \text{은/는} \end{array} \right\}$ B $\left\{ \begin{array}{l} \text{이} \\ \text{가} \end{array} \right\}$ + 아닙니다.

Example :
여기가 조선 호텔입니다.   This is the Chosun Hotel.
여기는 우체국이 아닙니다.   This is not the post office.

CAUTION: The two negative forms are used in statements and questions, but <u>not</u> in request sentences. The negative request form (for example, "Don't...") will be introduced later.

(b) Negating all other types of verbs

Affirmative ("A does ...")	Negative ("A does not ...")
A $\begin{Bmatrix} 이/가 \\ 은/는 \end{Bmatrix}$ + VERB	A $\begin{Bmatrix} 이/가 \\ 은/는 \end{Bmatrix}$ + 안 + VERB

Example :

제가 거기 <u>갑니다.</u>   I go there.

저는 거기 <u>안 갑니다.</u>   I don't go there.

Exercises

A. What Do You Hear?

Cover the Han-gŭl text below and say aloud the English equivalent of each utterance that your instructor makes.

1. 아니오, 미국 대사관이 아닙니다. 4. 덕수궁은 이 길로 가세요.
2. 이리 곧장 가십시오.   5. 롯데 호텔은 저 길로 갑니다.
3. 저기 큰 건물입니다.

B. What Do You Say?

Work with your instructor or classmate in the following series of role-playing.

1. What do you say to get the attention of a passerby on the street?
2. You want to ask the passerby where each of the following is located: (a) the Namdaemun Gate, (b) the Seoul Sports Complex, (c) the Westin Chosun Hotel, (d) the Itaewon shopping district, and (e) the American Embassy. Say one at a time.
3. You want to ask him how to get to each of the following: (a) the National Assembly Building, (b) the Japanese Embassy, (c) the National Central Museum, (d) the Sejong Cultural Center, and (e) the Lotte Department Store. Say one at a time.
4. You want to find out from a passerby the right way to each of the following destinations: (a) the Kyŏngbokkung Palace, (b) the Myŏng-dong shopping district, (c) the Sheraton Walker Hill, (d) the Seoul Central Post Office, and (e) the Hyundai Department Store.
5. How do you thank someone who has given you directions.

C. Grammar Exercise

1. Say aloud the negative counterpart for each of the utterances that your instructor makes.

   (a) 여기가 정부 종합 청사입니다.
   (b) 저기가 명동입니다.

(c) 미국 대사관에 갑니다.

(d) 김 선생님은 계십니다.

(e) 우리 어머니는 서울에 계십니다.

2. Answer the following questions, using one of the three pointer words, according to the following cues.

> Cues :   "Speaker"—Use the word referring to a place near you (the speaker).
> "Hearer"—Use the word referring to a place near the hearer.
> "Away"—Use the word referring to a place away from you and the hearer.
>
> ———— • ————
>
> *Example* :   Question: 서울 시청이 어딥니까?
> Cue: "Away"
> Response: 저기가 서울 시청입니다.

(a) Question: 미국 대사관이 어딥니까?
   Cue: "Away"

(b) Question: 조선 호텔이 어딥니까?
   Cue: "Speaker"

(c) Question: 중앙 우체국이 어딥니까?
   Cue: "Hearer"

3. Respond negatively to each of the following questions.

> *Example* :   Question: 여기가 경복궁입니까?
> Response: 아니오, 여기는 경복궁이 아닙니다.

Questions:

(a) 여기가 세종 문화 회관입니까?

(b) 저기가 신라 호텔입니까?

(c) 여기가 미국 대사관입니까?

Words and Phrases

가십시오.	Please go.
거기	there (a place near the hearer)
건물	building
고맙습니다.	Thank you.
곧장	straight
그 길	that way
그리	that way (in the direction the hearer is headed)
대단히	a great deal, very
말씀 좀 묻겠습니다.	May I ask you a question?
바로	right
실례합니다.	Excuse me.
아닙니다.	(It) is not.
알겠습니다.	I see/ understand
어느 길로	in which way
어떻게	how
여기	here
우체국	post office
이 길로	this way
저기입니다.	It's over there.
천만에요.	You are welcome.; Not at all.
크고	big
하얀	white

Looking for Things

6

Lesson Objectives

1. Carry on a conversation with your friend or acquaintance about the identity, presence or whereabouts of something. Specifically you will:
   (a) Ask your friend if a certain thing you name is at hand; if not, ask him/her where it is.
   (b) Ask your friend what a particular thing you are pointing to is.
   (c) Ask your friend what he/she is looking for.
   (d) Answer the above-listed questions, as needed.

2. Use correctly the following grammatical forms:
   (a) Verbs denoting existence or location.
   (b) Pointer words ("this," "that," etc.) in reference to where you and the hearer are located.

3. Recognize correctly the subject of a sentence when different suffixes (은, 는, 이, 가) are attached to it.

4. Read and write in Han-gŭl:
   (a) Selected words from lesson material.
   (b) Selected phrases and sentences from lesson material.

Cultural Notes

Obtaining Newspapers and Maps in Korea

It is true that local newspapers and maps can be important source of information for anyone traveling in a foreign country. But an English-speaking traveler would find it rather difficult to obtain first-hand information from a Korean newspaper because some pages of the newspaper use both Chinese characters and Han-gŭl. Luckily, there are two English-language daily newspapers, the *Korea Herald* and the *Korea Times.* Both English- and Korean-language newspapers are available at hotels and many offices. In case you need local papers for yourself, you may get them from newspaper vendors on city streets. In Seoul, you will find newspaper vendors at subway stations or in subway trains.

All different kinds of maps are available at hotels or bookstores, but only a limited number of them can be used by English-speaking travelers. Korean gasoline stations ordinarily do not provide their customers with road maps, as some American gasoline stations do.

Communicative Exchanges

FRAME 1

Looking for Today's Newspaper

Mr. Jones is looking for today's newspaper and asks Mr. Lee if he has one.

존스 : <u>오늘 신문</u>¹ 어디 있어요?	Where is today's newspaper?
이 : 오늘 신문이요? 여기 없습니다. 이것은 오늘 신문이 아닙니다. 어제 신문입니다.	Today's paper? It's not here. This isn't today's newspaper; it's yesterday's paper.

(While Mr. Lee looks for today's paper, Mr. Jones points to another paper.)

존스 : 이것은 무엇입니까?	What's this?
이 : 아, 그것이 오늘 신문입니다.	Oh, that's today's paper!

SUBSTITUTION

1. 한국 지도   map of Korea
   서울 지도   map of Seoul
   미국 지도   map of U.S.A.

FRAME 2

Asking for Stationery Items

Mr. Jones needs stationery for writing letters and asks Mr. Park to bring him some.

존스 : 봉투¹ 있어요 ?	Are there (any) envelopes ?
박　 : 여기 없습니다.	There are none here.
존스 : 어디 있어요 ?	Where are they ?
박　 : 옆방에² 있습니다.	They are in the next room.
존스 : 제 방에 좀 갖다 주십시오.	Please bring some to my room.
박　 : 네, 알겠습니다.	O.K.

SUBSTITUTION	
1. 연필	pencil
볼펜	ball-point pen
종이	paper
2. 사무실에	in the office
책상 위에	on the desk

FRAME 3

Helping Someone to Find Things

Mr. Jones helps Mr. Han to find his passport that has been misplaced.

존스 : 무엇 찾으세요?	What are you looking for?
한　 : 제 <u>여권</u>¹ 찾아요.	I'm looking for my passport.
존스 : <u>까만 것</u>²입니까?	Is it a black one?
한　 : 아니오, 누런 것입니다.	No, it's a brown one.
존스 : 아, 여기 있습니다.	Oh, it's here!

SUBSTITUTION

1. 지갑	purse
안경	eyeglasses
2. 하얀 것	a white one
파란 것	a blue one

Grammar and Usage

1. Verbs Expressing Existence

In English, the same verb ("to be") is used to express both identity and existence. Compare the following:

Identity   : This gentleman <u>is</u> Mr. Jones.
                (This gentleman <u>is identified as</u> Mr. Jones.)
Existence : Mr. Jones <u>is</u> here.
                (Mr. Jones <u>exists</u> or <u>is present</u> here.)

In Korean, a different verb is used for each type of expression.

Identity	: A이/가	B입니다.	A is B.
		B이/가 아닙니다.	A is not B.
Existence	: A이/가	있습니다.	A is (present).
		없습니다.	A is not (present).

The verb 있습니다 (with the stem 있—) is translated either by a form of the verb "to be," as above, or by the phrase "there is/are," or by a form of the verb "to have." For example,

호텔이 있습니다.   { There is a hotel.
                        { We have a hotel.

봉투가 있습니까?   { Are there (any) envelopes?
                        { Do you have (any) envelopes?

The negative form of 있— is obtained by replacing it with 없—.

봉투가 없습니다.   { There are no envelopes.
                        { We have no envelopes.

You will find at least three negative forms in use, depending on the type of verb involved.

A는 B가 아닙니다.   (Non-identification)

A가 없습니다.   (Non-existence)

A가 안 갑니다.   (All other types of verb in negation.
                               Add 안 before the verb.)

2. Phrases Specifying Location

A verb denoting existence often goes with a phrase specifying location, which we will call a "location phrase." Such a phrase ends with the suffix —에. For example,

의자가 옆방에 있습니다.   The chairs are in the next room.

CAUTION : Unlike the destination suffix —에, the location suffix is not normally dropped, except after 어디, "where."

서울에 가요.
서울 가요.   I am going to Seoul. (Destination Suffix)

서울에 있어요.   It is in Seoul.   (Location suffix)

서울   있어요.   (This sentence is not acceptable because the location phrase lacks a suffix.)

3. More Pointer Words

In Lesson 5 you learned two sets of pointer words: 이리, 그리, and 저리 on one hand and 여기, 거기, and 저기 on the other.

In this lesson you have learned: 이것, "this (thing)," something near the speaker; 그것, "that (thing)," something near the hearer; and 저것, "that (thing)," something away from both the speaker and hearer. They are combinations of the adjectives 이—, 그—, and 저—, and the noun 것, "thing," as shown below.

이것 : 이 "this" + 것 "thing"	an object near the speaker
그것 : 그 "that" + 것 "thing"	an object near the hearer; or an object mutually understood (equivalent to "the")
저것 : 저 "that" + 것 "thing"	an object away from both the speaker and hearer

이—, 그—, and 저— may also be combined with other nouns, such as 분, "person," as in the following examples.

이분 아세요?	Do you know this lady/gentleman?
그분 계세요?	Is the lady/gentleman in?
저분이 누구입니까?	Who is that lady/gentleman?
이분이 윤 명순 씨입니다.	This (lady) is Miss Myŏng-sun Yun.

4. Suffixes Added to the Subject

In Lesson 4 you learned that the subject of a sentence is generally marked by the suffix —이 when the subject ends with a consonant, and by —가 when it ends with a vowel. This is, however, a slight oversimplification. Often, particularly when the subject is not emphasized, it has no subject-marking suffix at all. For example,

김 선생님 계세요?	Is Mr. Kim in?
(No suffix)	

When the subject is introduced as a new topic in contrast with something previously talked about, it may take a different suffix: —은 after a consonant and —는 after a vowel. We will call this the "topic-marking" suffix for convenience's sake. For example,

이것은 무엇입니까?	What is this (as opposed to something mentioned before)?
그것은 오늘 신문입니다.	That's today's newspaper (as opposed to another newspaper just mentioned).

But this is not the whole story on the use of subject-marking suffixes. All you need to know at this stage is the fact that a subject may have —이/—가 or —은/—는 or neither. In the first phase of your experience with Korean conversation, you need not worry about the subject-marking suffix since you can often get your message across without it.

5. Words Ending in ㅅ

The consonant ㅅ at the end of a word is pronounced like [t] unless it is followed by a suffix beginning with a vowel. When you pronounce the following words in isolation, you must pronounce them as though they would

end in [t]

이것	igŏt	저것	chŏgŏt
그것	kŭgŏt	무엇	muŏt

The same principle applies when each of these words come without a suffix in a sentence. For example,

이것 무엇입니까 ?   Igŏt muŏshimnikka ?
                            (What is this ?)

그것 서울 지도입니다.   Kŭgŏt Sŏul chidoimnida.
                            (That's a map of Seoul.)

In conversation, the final consonant of these words is further weakened and often totally dropped, as follows:

저거 무엽니까 ?   Chŏgŏ muŏmnikka ?
저거 오늘 신문입니다.   Chŏgŏ onŭl shinmunimnida.

When the final ㅅ is followed by a suffix vowel, such as the subject-marker —이, it is pronounced like [s] (or [ʃ] when followed by [i]). Say aloud the following words :

이것이 this (thing)   (an object near the speaker)

그것이 that (thing)   (an object near the hearer)

저것이 that (thing)   (an object away from the speaker and the hearer)

Exercises

A. What Do You Hear?

Cover the Han-gǔl text below. The model voice will say the two sets of verbal exchange in Korean, each set voiced twice. As you listen, put the Korean exchanges into English.

Exchange I	Exchange II
A: 타자기 있어요?	A: 무엇 찾으세요?
B: 여기 없어요.	B: 제 지갑 찾아요.
A: 어디 있어요?	A: 까만 것입니까?
B: 사무실에 있어요.	B: 아니오. 누런 것입니다.

B. What Do You Say?

Work with your instructor or classmate in the following series of role-playing.

1. You wish to read today's newspaper. How would you ask someone if today's newspaper is at hand?
2. Point to something which is away from both you and the hearer and ask what it is.
3. The hearer has a newspaper in front of him/her. Ask that person if it is today's paper.
4. Ask your colleague if there are (a) any envelope, (b) any pencil, or (c) any ball-point pen that you can use.
5. Someone is asking for one of the three items stated above. Respond to that person that it is not available here, but that it is (a) in the next room, (b) in the office, or (c) over there. Say one at a time.
6. Ask politely someone to bring some item: (a) a map of Korea, (b) a ball-point pen, or (c) a pair of eyeglasses.
7. Someone seems to be looking for something anxiously. Ask that person what he/she is looking for.
8. To such a question as one given above, you want to tell your friend that

you are looking for (a) your pencil, (b) your purse, or (c) your passport.
How would you say ?

9. Tell your friend that (a) your pencil is a blue one, (b) your purse is a black
one, or (c) your passport is a brown one.

C. Vocabulary Exercise

Each of the following model sentences is accompanied by a list of cues.
After reading to each sentence, say a new one by replacing the appropriate
word with the Korean equivalent of each cue.

> *Example* :   You read : 신문 있어요 ?
> Cue : chair
> You say : 의자 있어요 ?

1. 의자 있어요 ?
Cues : (a) envelope   (b) map   (c) today's newspaper

2. 의자 있습니까 ?
Cues : (a) paper   (b) Miss Park   (c) yesterday's newspaper

3. 그것 좀 갖다 주십시오.
Cues : (a) passport   (b) chair   (c) purse

4. 저기 있습니다.
Cues : (a) next door   (b) here   (c) over there

D. Grammar Exercise

1. When you hear "A, B, or C" in random order, say aloud "이것," "그것," or
"저것," by using the following diagram which assumes that you are at the
speaker's position.

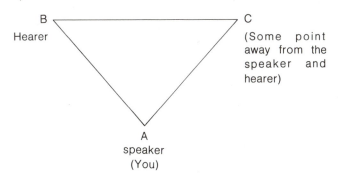

B
Hearer

C
(Some point away from the speaker and hearer)

A
speaker
(You)

2. You are going to be asked : 이것이/그것이/저것이 무엇입니까?
   Answer the question by using each of the cues below and an appropriate
   pointer word.

Example :   Question : 이것이/그것이/저것이 무엇입니까?
               Cue   : a map
               Answer   : 그것은/이것은/저것은 지도입니다.

(a) 이것이 무엇입니까?
    Cues : a chair
(b) 그것이 무엇입니까?
    Cues : an envelope
(c) 저것이 무엇입니까?
    Cues : a newspaper

(d) 그것이 무엇입니까?
    Cues : coffee
(e) 저것이 무엇입니까?
    Cues : a passport

Reading and Writing

     From this lesson on, a section will be devoted to the practice of reading and writing Han-gŭl. Since you have learned some of the basic facts about Han-gŭl, this section will focus on irregularities in, and discrepancies between, spelling and pronunciation, using some of the words and phrases already introduced in the lesson.

1. Read each of the following words and phrases aloud, and then say its English equivalent.

    (a) 어제 신문   (e) 오늘 신문

    (b) 누런 것   (f) 갖다 주십시오.

    (c) 옆방에   (g) 찾으세요?

    (d) 없습니다.   (h) 까만 것

2. Write the following words four times each, saying them aloud as you write them. Note that ㅅ is pronounced [t] when it is not followed by a vowel.

무엇   _____ _____ _____ _____

이것   _____ _____ _____ _____

그것   _____ _____ _____ _____

저것   _____ _____ _____ _____

3. Write the following words three times each, saying them aloud as you write them. Note that ㅅ in these words is pronounced [s].

무엇이   _____ _____ _____

이것이   _____ _____ _____

그것이   _____ _____ _____

저것이   _____ _____ _____

Summary of Verb Forms

이다 ("to be")

STATEMENT	LONG	SHORT
HON	—이십니다	—이세요
PLN	—입니다	—이에요*

QUESTION	LONG	SHORT
HON	—이십니까?	—이세요?
PLN	—입니까?	—이에요?*

Note : Request forms are not introduced for this verb.

없다 ("not to exist")

STATEMENT	LONG	SHORT
HON	안 계십니다	안 계세요
PLN	없습니다	없어요

QUESTION	LONG	SHORT
HON	안 계십니까?	안 계세요?
PLN	없습니까?	없어요?

REQUEST	LONG	SHORT
HON	계십시오	계세요
PLN	(not introduced)	

갖다 주다 ("to bring")

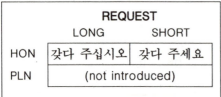

REQUEST	LONG	SHORT
HON	갖다 주십시오	갖다 주세요
PLN	(not introduced)	

Note : This verb is introduced only in request forms.

*This is a variant of —이어요 and is more commonly used.

Words and Phrases

까만	black
누런	brown
무엇을 찾으세요?	What are you looking for?
방	my room
볼펜	ball-point pen
봉투	envelope
사무실	office
신문	newspaper
안경	eyeglasses
어디 있어요?	Where is...?
어제	yesterday
없습니다.	(Something) is not available.
여권	passport
연필	pencil
옆방	next room
오늘	today
위	on; upon
의자	chair
이것	this thing, this one
저것	that one (over there)
저분이 누구입니까?	Who is that person?
좀 갖다 주십시오.	Please bring (me)....
종이	paper
지갑	purse
지도	map
책상	desk
파란	blue

Looking for People

Lesson Objectives

1. Carry on a conversation with a new acquaintance (such as a receptionist/ typist in the office you are visiting) about the presence, whereabouts, or absence of someone. Specifically, using appropriate honorific or plain forms, you will:
   (a) Ask your listener if a certain person (your senior or junior friend) is in.
   (b) Ask him/her where the person you are looking for is.
   (c) Take the role of a receptionist or typist in the office and answer some of the above-listed questions, as needed.

2. Use correctly the following grammatical forms:
   (a) The honorific forms of nouns and verbs.
   (b) The plain forms of nouns and verbs.

3. Read and write in Han-gŭl:
   (a) Selected words from lesson material.
   (b) Selected phrases and sentences from lesson material.

Cultural Notes

Interpersonal Relationships in Korea

One of the most conspicuous differences between the Korean and American cultures is the greater importance Koreans attach to "vertical" relationships of people. They tend to look upon another person either as senior or junior—in age, position, or status—and feel awkward when their interpersonal relationships are not clearly defined in terms of seniority. In a family, age establishes seniority. In society there are more factors, such as position, rank, sex, or status. When the relative status of two strangers or new acquaintances is not clear, both parties can be polite and formal in an attempt to yield senior status to each other.

The Korean language reflects this traditional aspect of Korean culture in its speech levels and styles. You have already learned the "polite" level of speech in two slightly different styles, the long and short forms. This level is almost always used when one speaks to his senior.

Another factor reflected in Korean speech is the status of the person spoken about, that is, the subject or topic of a sentence. When the subject of a sentence is your senior, you use "honorific" forms.

Communicative Exchanges

FRAME 1

Asking for Your Senior Friend

Mr. Parker enters an office and asks the receptionist for the company president.

파커	: 손 사장님¹ 계십니까?	Is president Sohn in?
접수안내원	: 지금 안 계십니다.	He is not in now.
파커	: 어디 계십니까?	Where is he, please?
접수안내원	: 휴게실²에 계십니다.	He is at the lounge.
	휴게실은 아래층입니다.	The lounge is downstairs.

SUBSTITUTION	
1. 임 선생님	Mr. Im
고 시장님	Mayor Koh
2. 옆방	next room
식당	restaurant

FRAME 2

Asking for Your Junior Friend

Mr. Parker enters an office and asks a middle-aged receptionist in the office for Mr. Kwon, a young friend of Mr. Parker's.

파커	: 미스터 권 있습니까?	Is Mr. Kwon in, please ?
접수안내원	: 지금 없습니다.	He is not in now.
파커	: 어디 갔습니까?	Where is he, please ?
접수안내원	: 화장실[1]에 갔습니다.	He went to the rest room.
	좀 기다리십시오.	Why don't you wait a while ?
파커	: 저 지금 바쁩니다.	I'm busy now.

SUBSTITUTION

1. 회의실	conference room
휴게실	lounge
시청	City Hall

FRAME 3

Asking for Your Younger Acquaintance

Mr. Jones enters an office and asks the typist if Mr. Han, a young acquaintance, is there. (Note that Mr. Jones uses the plain verb form and the typist uses the honorific form.)

존스	: 여기 미스터 한 있습니까?	Is Mr. Han here?
타자수	: 지금 여기 안 계십니다.	He is not here now.
존스	: 어디 있습니까?	Where is he, please?
타자수	: 식당¹에 계십니다.	He is at the restaurant.
존스	: 식당이 어디에 있습니까?	Where is the dining hall?
타자수	: 이층²에 있습니다.	It's on the second floor.
존스	: 감사합니다.	Thank you.

SUBSTITUTION

1.	다방	tearoom; teahouse
	사장실	company president's office
	커피숍	coffee shop
2.	아래층	downstairs
	15층	the 15th floor

Grammar and Usage

1. Honorific Verb Forms

In Lesson 4, you learned this exchange:

어디 가세요?   Where are you going ?

서울(에) 갑니다.   I am going to Seoul.

You were told at that time not to use the form 가세요 in the answer. The element 세 (or 시 at other times) denotes the speaker's respect toward the subject of a sentence. It would naturally be out of place to show respect to yourself, "I" (the speaker), in the answer.

The element 세 or 시 in a verb form is called an "honorific marker," and a verb form containing such an element is called an "honorific form."

Generally speaking, honorific forms are identifiable by 세 in the short verb form (STEM+세요), as in 가세요, and by 시 in the long verb form (STEM+십니다), as in 가십니다. Some verbs, however, are irregular and require changes in the stem. You are learning one such verb, 있습니다. "to exist, to be," whose honorific form is 계십니다 rather than 있으십니다.

	Plain form	Honorific form
Short form	있어요	계세요
Long form	있습니다	계십니다

The conversational frames in this lesson show three different situations. In Frame 1, the two persons are talking about a third person who is senior to both of them. Therefore, honorific forms are used in both the question and the answer. In Frame 2, the speakers are talking about a third person who is equal to or junior to both of them, and so neither of them uses an honorific form. In Frame 3, the person spoken about is junior to the first speaker, who doesn't use an honorific form, but senior to the second speaker, who does.

2. Agreement between Nouns and Verbs

When an honorific verb form is used in a sentence, a noun or pronoun referring to the subject or topic should agree by also expressing respect. You have already learned the suffix —님, which is added to a noun to express one's respect, as in 김 선생님, "Mr. Kim" (rather than 김 선생).

김 선생 있습니까?	Is Mr. Kim in ? (plain)
김 선생님 안 계십니다.	Mr. Kim is not in. (honorific)

3. Request Forms with the Honorific Marker

Requests are almost always made with honorific forms since the speaker tends to be respectful when asking someone to do something.

기다리십시오.	Please wait.
들어가세요.	Please go right in.
잠깐 여기 계십시오.	Please stay here for a moment.

Exercises

A. What Do You Hear?

Cover the Han-gŭl text below. The model voice will say the two sets of verbal exchange in Korean, each set voiced twice. As you listen, put the Korean, exchange into English.

Exchange I	Exchange II
A : 한 선생님 계십니까?	A : 미스터 신 어디 있습니까?
B : 지금 안 계십니다.	B : 휴게실에 계십니다.
A : 어디 계십니까?	A : 휴게실이 어디 있습니까?
B : 커피숍에 계십니다.	B : 이층에 있습니다.

B. What Do You Say?

Work with your instructor or classmate in the following series of role-playing.

1. In the company president's office, you (as an employee) are about to ask his/her secretary if he is in. How would you say?
2. You are visiting Mayor Kwon. Ask his secretary if he is in.
3. You are stepping into the office of Mr. Han, a junior friend of yours. How would you ask his office mate where he is?
4. Someone steps into your office and asks where Mr. Im, your supervisor, is. Tell the visitor that Mr. Im is at the lounge.
5. Someone asks where Mr. Han, your colleague, is at the moment. Tell the visitor that Mr. Han has gone to the City Hall.
6. You are told that the man you want to see is not in. Ask the speaker where he is.
7. A visitor asks you if your company president is in. Tell the visitor that your company president is not in now.

C. Vocabulary Exercise

Each of the following model sentences is accompanied by a list of cues.

After reading to each sentence, say a new one by replacing the appropriate word with the Korean equivalent of each cue.

> *Example* : You read : 의자 있어요 ?
>
>   Cue : envelope
>
>   You say : 봉투 있어요 ?

1. 정 선생님 계십니까 ?
   Cues : (a) Mr. Kim (b) Miss Kwon   (c) (company) president Sohn

2. 식당에 계십니다.
   Cues : (a) lounge   (b) next room   (c) teahouse

3. 미스터 박 있습니까 ?
   Cues : (a) Mr. Koh (b) Mrs. Yun   (c) Miss Han

4. 식당에 갔습니다.
   Cues : (a) lounge   (b) U.S. Embassy (c) City Hall

5. 여기 안 계십니다.
   Cues : (a) there   (b) next room   (c) coffee shop

D. Grammar Exercise

1. Using each of the cues below, ask your listener if he has that particular item.

> *Example* : Cue : 신문
>
>   Response : 신문 있습니까 ?

   Cues :   (a) 봉투   (b) 지도   (c) 의자   (d) 볼펜   (e) 연필

2. Using each of the cues below, ask your listener if that particular person is in. Assuming you do not have to be deferential to that person, use the plain verb form.

> *Example* : Cue : 미스 한
>
>   Response : 미스 한 있습니까 ?

   Cues :   (a) 한 선생   (b) 미스터 장   (c) 미스 송   (d) 김 씨

3. Using each of the cues below, ask your listener that particular person is in. This time you may use an honorific form.

> *Examle* : Cue : 남 선생님
> Response : 남 선생님 계십니까?

Cues :   (a) 박 선생님   (b) 민 선생님   (c) 정 사장님

4. Answer the following questions negatively, using the honorific form.

> *Example* : Question : 이 선생님 계세요?
> Answer : 아니오, 이 선생님 안 계세요.

Questions : (a) 한 선생님 계세요?   (c) 김 사장님 계세요?
           (b) 박 선생님 계십니까?   (d) 미스터 김 계세요?

5. Answer the following questions negatively, using the plain form.

> *Example* : Question : 미스터 홍 있어요?
> Answer : 아니오, 미스터 홍 없어요.

Questions : (a) 미스 박 있습니까?   (c) 미스 한 있어요?
           (b) 미스터 권 있어요?   (d) 미스 양 있습니까?

6. Answer the following questions, using the cues given.

> *Example* : Question : 미스터 한 어디 있어요?
> Cue : 옆방
> Answer : 옆방에 있어요.

Question : (a) 미스터 박 어디 있어요?
         Cue : 저기
      (b) 미스 고 어디 있습니까?
         Cue : 식당
      (c) 미스터 김 어디 있습니까?
         Cue : 회의실
      (d) 미스터 남 어디 있어요?
         Cue : 다방

Reading and Writing

1. Read each of the following words and phrases aloud, and then say its English equivalent.

   (a) 휴게실에   (e) 아래층에
   (b) 옆방에   (f) 회의실에
   (c) 김 사장님   (g) 사장실
   (d) 커피숍   (h) 고 시장님

2. Write the following verbs six times each, saying them aloud as you write them. Note that the verb stem ending with a consonant is spelled separately from the ending and that ㅂ in 습니다 is pronounced [m] not [p].

   있습니다   _____ _____ _____

              _____ _____ _____

   없습니다   _____ _____ _____

              _____ _____ _____

3. Write the following honorific verb forms six times, saying them aloud as you write them.

   계십니다   _____ _____ _____

              _____ _____ _____

   계십니까?   _____ _____ _____

              _____ _____ _____

Words and Phrases

갔습니다.	(One) went; (One) has gone.
갔어요.	(One) went; (One) has gone.
다방	tearoom; teahouse
사장	company president
사장실	company president's office
시장	mayor
아래층	downstairs; bottom floor
없어요.	(One) is not available.
지금	now
층	floor
커피숍	coffee shop
화장실	rest room; bath room
회의실	conference room
휴게실	lounge

Conversing at the Lounge

8

Lesson Objectives

1. Carry on a conversation on personal matters with a co-worker whom you've just met. (You are at the lounge to take a break.) Specifically you will:
    (a) Ask your listener if he/she works for this organization here.
    (b) Ask that person what his/her name, nationality, or office is.
    (c) State your name, your nationality, or the office you belong to.
    (d) Ask that person if he/she speaks English.
    (e) Compliment that person on his/her ability to speak English.
    (f) State that you can speak Korean a little.

2. Use correctly the following grammatical forms:
    (a) The long and short forms of verb endings for statements, questions, and requests
    (b) The suffix indicating the place of events
    (c) The irregular honorific forms, 계세요 and 계십니다

3. Read and write in Han-gŭl:
    (a) Selected words from lesson material.
    (b) Selected phrases and sentences from lesson material.

Cultural Notes

Korean Behavior in Social Relationships

Koreans do not make acquaintances in exactly the same way as Americans do. For one thing, they are not eager to know a person's full name, especially his/her first name, when they first meet. Rather, Koreans prefer to know the full name indirectly, if possible, before meeting, or as they cultivate each other's acquaintance further. This is partly because they are used to employing one's last name with a title.

Nevertheless, since life in Korean cities is becoming increasingly westernized, it is not out of place for you to introduce yourself and ask politely your new acquaintance's full name.

Despite this trend, you may find that Koreans, especially women, will not readily tell you their full names. Do not press them. You will get to know their names as you cultivate each other's acquaintance further.

Remember also that Koreans almost always go by their last names. Avoid calling them by their first names.

Americans directly express gratitude when complimented by others. They say "Thank you" when someone compliments them on, say, their ability to speak a foreign language. In Korean culture, a flattered person usually reserves, out of modesty, his gratitude and even mildly declines the compliment.

Communicative Exchanges

FRAME 1

Striking up a Friendship with Your Co-worker

Mr. Jones encounters one of his co-workers at the lounge in his office building and starts a friendly talk.

존스 : 여기서 근무하세요?	Do you work here?
한　 : 네. <u>총무과</u>[1]에서 일합니다.	Yes. I work in the Business Office.
선생님도 여기서 일하세요?	Do you work here, too?
존스 : 네. 저는 홍보과에 있습니다.	Yes, I'm with the Public Relations Office.
한　 : 선생님은 어느 나라 분이세요?	What country are you from?
존스 : <u>미국 사람</u>[2] 입니다.	I'm an American.
한　 : 아, 그러세요?	Oh, really?

SUBSTITUTION
1. 인사과　　　　　　　Personnel Office
　　비서실　　　　　　　Secretariat
　　통신과　　　　　　　Communications Office
　　회계과　　　　　　　Accounting Office
2. 영국 사람　　　　　　Englishman
　　독일 사람　　　　　　German
　　프랑스 사람　　　　　Frenchman

FRAME 2

Asking a Person's Name

Mr. Jones introduces himself and asks his co-worker's name.

존스 : 제 이름은 존스입니다.   My name is Jones.
      성함이 어떻게 되십니까?   What is your name?

한   : 한 기태입니다.   I am Ki-t'ae Han.

존스 : 우리 홍보과에도 <u>한 씨</u>[1]가 한   We have a Mr. Han in our Public
      분 있습니다.   Relations Office, too.

한   : 아, 그러세요? 미국에 <u>존스</u>   Oh, is that so? Are there many
      <u>씨</u>[2]가 많아요?   Joneses in America?

존스 : <u>그렇게 안 많아요.</u>[3]   There aren't so many.

SUBSTITUTION

1. 이 씨	Mr. Lee
정 씨	Mr. Chŏng
2. 앤더슨 씨	Mr. Anderson
스미스 씨	Mr. Smith
3. 좀 있어요.	There are some.
아주 많아요.	There are very many.

FRAME 3

Talking about Someone's Foreign Language Facility

Mr. Han compliments Mr. Jones on his Korean while Mr. Jones is curious to know about Mr. Han's knowledge of English.

한	: 한국말¹ 잘 하십니다.	You speak Korean well.
존스	: 아니오, 잘 못합니다.	No, I speak it poorly.
한	: 한국말 어렵습니까?	Is Korean difficult for you?
존스	: 네, 어려워요. 미스터 한은 영어 하세요?	Yes, it is. Do you speak English, Mr. Han?
한	: 네, 조금 합니다.²	Yes. I speak it a little.

SUBSTITUTION	
1. 영어	English
프랑스어	French
독어	German
2. 전혀 못합니다.	I cannot speak it at all.

Grammar and Usage

1. Verb Forms and Their Uses—with More Verbs

In Lesson 3, you already learned the basic features of short and long forms of Korean verbs. In this lesson this important aspect of the Korean verb will be seen more broadly and methodically.

Short form (Used, with the appropriate intonation, in any of the three types of expression : statement, question, and request.)

	Honorific	Plain
Statement :		
Question :	가세요	가요
Request :		

Long form (Each form is specialized for a statement, a question, or a request)

	Honorific	Plain
Statement :	가십니다	갑니다
Question :	가십니까	갑니까
Request :	가십시오	(not used)

When they are used : Short and long forms are intermixed in conversation. The short forms are more often used in casual conversation; the long forms are more common in conversation where formalities are required.

In your speech, you may either mix long and short forms or, if you prefer, use only one form exclusively. However, you need to understand both forms as you hear them.

How verbs are formed : All verbs are made up of at least one stem and one ending. The general rules for making up the verb forms are as follows:

		Honorific	Plain
SHORT FORM	Statement Question Request	STEM + (으)세요	STEM + 어요
LONG FORM	Statement Question Request	STEM + (으)십니다 STEM + (으)십니까 STEM + (으)십시오	STEM + (습)니다 STEM + (습)니까

What "STEM + 어요" means : Although the short plain form is obtained simply by adding the ending —어요 to the stem, the combination often results in additional changes which are not altogether regular. At this stage, it is best for you to simply memorize each verb in its short plain form. Later on, you will learn additional rules for making up this form. Following is a list of the verbs you have learned so far in the short plain form:

Stem		Stem + 어요
NOUN + 이—	to be + NOUN	NOUN + 이에요
NOUN + 아니—	not to be + NOUN	NOUN + 아니에요 (Negative of 이에요)
하—	to do	해요
있—	to exist	있어요
없—	not to exist	없어요
가—	to go	가요
오—	to come	와요
앉—	to sit	앉아요
기다리—	to wait for	기다려요

What "STEM + (으)" means : The rest of the forms (i.e., the short honorific, the long honorific, the long plain) are obtained in two ways, depending on whether the stem ends in a vowel or a consonant. If the stem ends in a vowel, simply add it to the appropriate ending.

Stem		Ending			
가	+	세요	→	가세요	(short honorific)
하	+	십니다	→	하십니다	(long honorific)
오	+	ㅂ니다	→	옵니다	(long plain)

If the stem ends in a consonant, the ending will be 습니다 instead of ㅂ

니다, or 으십시오 instead of 십시오. For example,

있 + 습니다 → 있습니다
앉 + 으십시오 → 앉으십시오

Dictionary form of a verb : When verbs are cited or listed, the form STEM+다 is used. We may call it the "dictionary form," because it is used almost exclusively for dictionary entry. It is useful to learn this form to be able to look up a verb in the dictionary. Following are the dictionary forms of some of the verbs you have learned:

가다	to go	없다	not to exist
오다	to come	기다리다	to wait for

Location involving an event : A phrase denoting place takes the suffix equivalent to "in," "at," "on," and so forth. For example,

김 선생님 어디 계십니까?　　　　　Where is Mr. Kim ?

식당에 계십니다.　　　　　He is at the dining hall.

The above is true, however, only when the phrase denotes the place where existence is involved. In other words, the phrase above merely indicates where Mr. Kim is at, since the verb is 계시ㅡ, "to exist."

When a phrase denotes the place where an event or action (as opposed to existence) is involved, it takes an additional suffix, ㅡ서. For example,

김 선생님 어디서 일하세요?　　　Where is Mr. Kim working ?

수원에서 일하세요.　　　He is working in Suwon.

여기서 기다리십시오.　　　Please wait here.

However, 에 in 에서 is often dropped if 에서 is placed after a word ending with a vowel. For example,

여기에서 → 여기서　　　어디에서 → 어디서

Exercises

A. What Do You Hear ?

Cover the Han-gŭl text below. The model voice will say the two sets of verbal exchanges in Korean, each set voiced twice. As you listen, put the Korean exchange into English.

Exchange I	Exchange II
A : 저는 총무과에서 일합니다.	A : 한국말 어렵습니까 ?
B : 저는 비서실에 있습니다.	B : 네, 어려워요. 영어 하세요 ?
A : 선생님은 어느 나라 분이세요 ?	A : 영어요 ? 잘 못합니다.
B : 프랑스 사람입니다.	B : 영어도 어려워요.

B. What Do You Say ?

Work with your instructor or classmate in the following series of role-playing.

1. You have encountered one of your co-workers at the lounge. Ask that person if he/she works in the organization.
2. You have been asked by one of your co-workers if you work in the same organization. Respond to him/her by stating your own section.
3. Suppose your co-worker is evidently a foreigner, how would you ask him/her to find out what nationality he/she is.
4. When asked of your nationality, state that you are (a) an American, (b) a Frenchman, or (c) a German. Say one at a time.
5. Introduce yourself by stating your name, and then ask your listener what his/her name is.
6. Your new acquaintance has stated his/her name. Make an interesting remark on his/her name, such as "We have a person with that name in our office, too."
7. Now you know your foreigner-acquaintance's name. Ask an interesting question on his/her name, such as "Are there many people with that name in your country ?"

8. Respond to the above by saying that (a) "There are some." (b) "There are very many." or (c) "There aren't so many."
9. You wish to compliment your foreigner-acquaintance on his/her Korean. How would you say ?
10. You have been complimented on your Korean. Tell your acquaintance that (a) you don't speak it very well, or (b) you speak it poorly.

C. Vacabulary Exercise

Each of the following model sentences is accompanied by a list of cues. After reading to each sentence, say a new one it by replacing the appropriate word with the Korean equivalent of each cue.

> *Example* : You read : 서울에 갑니다.
>   Cue : America
>   You say : 미국에 갑니다.

1. 저는 존스입니다.
    Cues : (a) an American (b) Ki-t'ae Han (c) a Korean

2. 저는 미국 대사관에서 일합니다.
    Cues : (a) Personnel office (b) Seoul City Hall
           (c) Public Relations Office

3. 저는 영어 잘 못합니다.
    Cues : (a) can't speak it at all (b) speak it well
           (c) speak it a little

4. 미국에 존스 씨가 많아요.
    Cues : (a) There aren't so many Joneses.
           (b) There are some Joneses.
           (c) There are very many Joneses.

5. 한국말 어려워요.
    Cues : (a) English (b) German (c) French

D. Grammar Exercise

1. Convert the following long verb forms into short forms.

> *Example* : If you read 있습니다, say 있어요.

(a) 갑니다   (d) 기다립니다

(b) 합니다   (e) 아닙니다

(c) 없습니다   (f) 옵니다

2. Convert the honorific verb forms in the following expressions into short honorific forms.

> *Example* : If you read 앉으십시오, say 앉으세요.

(a) 안녕하십니까?   (d) 안녕히 가십시오.

(b) 김 선생님 계십니까?   (e) 영어 하십니까?

(c) 어디 가십니까?   (f) 이분 아십니까?

3. Convert the short verb foms in the following expressions into long forms.

> *Example* : If you read 가세요? say 가십니까?

(a) 어디서 일하세요?   (d) 커피 한잔 하세요.

(b) 저분 아세요?   (e) 잠깐 기다리세요.

(c) 안녕히 계세요.   (f) 한국말 하세요?

4. Convert the following verb forms into honorific forms.

> *Example* : If you read 갑니다, say 가십니다.

(a) 옵니까?   (d) 기다려요.

(b) 해요?   (e) 앉아요.

(c) 미스 김 있습니까?   (f) 여기서 일합니다.

5. Answer the following questions, using the cues given.

> *Example* : Question : 어디서 일합니까?
> Cue : 총무과
> Answer : 총무과에서 일합니다.

Questions : (a) 어디서 기다립니까?   (c) 화장실 어디 있습니까?
            Cue : 휴게실   Cue : 이층
           (b) 김 선생님 어디 계세요? (d) 어디서 일 하세요?
            Cue : 화장실   Cue : 홍보과

Reading and Writing

1. Shifting Consonant

The Han-gŭl spelling does not always reflect the way words and phrases are pronounced. There are many reasons for the discrepancies between spelling and pronunciation. In this lesson you will learn one important feature of pronunciation in Korean that creates some spelling problems, namely those resulting from connecting words and suffixes.

For example, when 이것 is followed by the suffix —이, the consonant ㅅ is shifted from the second syllable to the third. Listen to your instructor and repeat with each of the following examples, paying particular attention to the shifting consonant.

Spelled	but	Pronounced	Spelled	but	Pronounced
이것이		이거시	한국에		한구게
무엇이		무어시	이분이		이부니
수원에		수워네	선생님이		선생니미

The same is true of verb phrases. If the stem ends in a consonant and the consonant is followed by a vowel (ending), then that consonant is shifted to the next syllable.

Spelled	but	Pronounced	Spelled	but	Pronounced
앉으세요		안즈세요	있어요		이써요
없어요		업써요	들어가다		드러가다

2. Read aloud the following phrases, paying particular attention to the shifting consonants.

미스 한이 가요. 지금 여기 없어요.

이리 앉으세요. 타자기 있어요?

들어가세요. 어느 나라 분이세요?

한국에 가요.

3. Read aloud the lines identified by the letters below.

Summary of Verb Forms

일하다 ("to work")

STATEMENT	LONG	SHORT
HON	일하십니다	일하세요
PLN	일합니다	일해요

QUESTION	LONG	SHORT
HON	일하십니까 ?	일하세요 ?
PLN	일합니까 ?	일해요 ?

REQUEST	LONG	SHORT
HON	일하십시오	일하세요
PLN	(not introduced)	

근무하다 ("to work, serve")

STATEMENT	LONG	SHORT
HON	근무하십니다	근무하세요
PLN	근무합니다	근무해요

QUESTION	LONG	SHORT
HON	근무하십니까 ?	근무하세요 ?
PLN	근무합니까 ?	근무해요 ?

REQUEST	LONG	SHORT
HON	근무하십시오	근무하세요
PLN	(not introduced)	

Words and Phrases

가십니다.	(One) is going. (honorific)
그러세요?	Really?; Is that so?
근무하세요?	Do you work...(in an organization)?
나라	country
독어	German (language)
독일 사람	German (person)
못하다	cannot (do)
미국 사람	American
분	person (honorific)
사람	person
아주	very
어려워요.	It's difficult.
어렵습니까?	Is...difficult?
영국 사람	Englishman
영어	English
이름	name
일하세요?	Do...work?
일합니다.	(One) works (at)....
잘	well
전혀	not at all; never
프랑스 사람	Frenchman
프랑스어	French
—하다	to do; to speak (a language); to eat or drink

Having Social Engagements

Lesson Objectives

1. Carry on a conversation with regard to social engagements. Specifically you will:
   (a) Ask your friend what his/her plans are in the evening.
   (b) Invite him/her to lunch or dinner.
   (c) Discuss with him/her on some activities for the evening.

2. As a person being invited to social occasions, respond as needed to questions/invitations listed above.

3. Use appropriately the following grammatical forms:
   (a) The verb ending indicating suggestion/invitation
   (b) The "stative" verbs in long and short forms
   (c) Short phrases with the suffix—요

4. Read and write in Han-gŭl:
   (a) Selected words from lesson material.
   (b) Selected phrases and sentences from lesson material.

Cultural Notes
Korean Hospitality

Koreans are well known for their hospitality to guests—particularly foreign guests. Inviting out their guests to lunch or dinner is a common practice among Korean men. Few Koreans would invite their foreign guests to dinner at home because Koreans have never been accustomed to that. If you are a fresh acquaintance, your Korean host will mostly likely take you to an impressive eating place. Once the acquaintance develops into an intimate friendship, your Korean host could tour with you many different places, where the taste of food is more important than its appearance.

Having social engagements with persons of the opposite sex is not a traditional part of Korean culture, but it is becoming more popular with the younger generation of Koreans.

Korean women tend not to be open in accepting a dating offer. When offered such a chance, they usually show unwillingness. This may sometimes make it difficult for a Western male to see whether they really are reluctant to accept or whether they are only ritually turning you down.

Communicative Exchanges

FRAME 1

Inviting Someone out to Lunch

Mr. Han wishes to take Mr. Jones out to a Korean restaurant for lunch.

한 : 존스 선생, <u>점심 식사</u>¹ 하셨습니까?	Have you had lunch, Mr. Jones?
존스 : 아직 안 했어요.	Not yet.
한 : 그럼, 우리 점심 식사 같이 하실까요?	Then, shall we have lunch together?
존스 : 그럽시다.	Let's do that.
한 : <u>한국 음식</u>² 좋아하세요?	Do you like Korean food?
존스 : 네, 아주 좋아합니다.	Yes, I like it very much.

SUBSTITUTION
1. 아침 식사   breakfast
   저녁 식사   dinner
2. 미국 음식   American food
   중국 음식   Chinese food
   일본 음식   Japanese food

FRAME 2

Inviting Someone out to the Movies

Mr. Jones asks Mr. Han if he is willing to go to see the movies with him. Accepting his offer, Mr. Han now turns to Miss Yun and asks her if she is willing to go, too.

존스 : 한 선생, 오늘 저녁[1]에 무엇하세요?   What do you do this evening?

한   : 글쎄요, 별로 할 일 없어요.   Well, nothing particular.

존스 : 우리 영화 구경[2] 같이 가실까요?   Shall we go to see the movies together?

한   : 좋아요. 같이 갑시다.   Fine. Let's go.

   (Mr. Han then turns to Miss Yun, his co-worker.)

한   : 미스 윤, 오늘 저녁에 영화 구경 같   Shall we go to see the movies
     이 가실까요?   together this evening, Miss Yun?

윤   : 오늘 저녁은 바쁩니다. 죄송해요.[3]   I'm busy this evening. Sorry.

```
SUBSTITUTION
1. 오늘 밤              tonight
   내일 아침            tomorrow morning
2. 미술관              art museum
   음악회              concert
3. 미안합니다.          (I'm) sorry.
```

FRAME 3

Making a Dinner Appointment

Mr. Han wants to make a dinner appointment with Mr. Jones, but Mr. Jones just cannot give an answer right away.

한	: 존스 선생, 내일 저녁에 시간 있으세요?	Are you free tomorrow evening, Mr. Jones?
존스	: 글쎄요, 봅시다.	Well, let me see.
한	: 저녁 식사 같이 합시다.	Let's have dinner together.
존스	: 그럽시다. <u>몇 시에</u>[1] 만날까요?	Let's do that. At what time shall we meet?
한	: 여섯 시[2] 어떻습니까?	How about six o'clock?
존스	: 나중에 제가 연락드리지요.	I'll be in touch with you later.
한	: 좋습니다. 그럼 제 사무실 전화 번호 드리지요.	That's fine. Then I'll give you my office phone number.

SUBSTITUTION

1. 언제   when
   어디서   (at) where
2. 한 시   one o'clock
   다섯 시   five o'clock
3. 알려 드리지요.   I will let you know.

Grammar and Usage

1. Making a Proposition : ―실까요 ?

You have learned so far three types of expression: statement, question, and request. For example,

Statement : 한국말 잘 하십니다.   You speak Korean well.
Question : 한국말 하십니까 ?   Do you speak Korean ?
Request   : 한국말로 하십시오.   Please speak in Korean.

These sentences can also be made with short verb forms (STEM+어요).

There is another type of expression: proposition. A proposition is often expressed in English as "Shall we ...?" or "Shall I ...?" In Korean this expression is obtained by adding the suffix ―(을)까요? to the verb stem. If the subject is "we" and the social relationship between the two persons requires some degree of respect, the honorific marker ―시 may be added.

저녁 식사 같이 하실까요 ?   Shall we have dinner together ?

같이 가실까요 ?   Shall we go together ?

If the verb stem ends with a consonant, an extra vowel 으 is inserted:

여기 앉으실까요 ?   Shall we sit down here ?

If the subject of such a sentence is "I," the honorific marker is not used.

지금 갈까요 ?   Shall I go now ?

2. Typical Responses to a "Proposition" Question

Three typical responses to a "proposition" question are (1) to accept, (2) to decline, and (3) to evade the proposition. The "accepting" answer usually has the verb ending ―시다 (for the plain form) or ―십시다 (for the honorific form), meaning in English "Let us ...." For example,

Question : 같이 가실까요 ?   Shall we go together ?
Answer   : 네, 같이 갑시다.   Yes, let's go together.

The "declining" answer may vary, but it usually consists of some expressions of regret and excuse for not accepting the proposition. For example,

> Question : 같이 가실까요 ?　　　　　　Shall we go together ?
> Answer　 : 미안합니다. 지금 못 갑니다.　　Sorry, but I can't go now.

The "evading" answer may vary also, but it often can be simply 글쎄요 equivalent to the English interjection "Well."

> Question : 같이 가실까요 ?　　　　　Shall we go together ?
> Answer　 : 글쎄요.　　　　　　　　　Well.

3. The "Stative" Verb

In English, predicate adjectives are generally preceded by the verb "to be," as in "The car is big." or "It is good."

In Korean, we have a single word, placed at the end of a sentence, functioning as both verb and adjective to express a "state" or "quality" of being. Because of its singular role, we call the word a "stative" verb as opposed to an ordinary verb. So far you have learned stative verbs such as:

> 좋아요.　　　　　　　(It is) good.
> 괜찮아요.　　　　　　(It is) okay.
> 바쁘세요 ?　　　　　 (Are you) busy ?

The question verb 어떻습니까 ? is a stative verb. "How is ...?", "How about ...?", "What do you think of ...?" are all possible English translations of it.

Various forms of the following stative verbs are irregular:

Dictionary form		Short form	Long form
좋다	to be good	좋아요	좋습니다
바쁘다	to be busy	바빠요	바쁩니다
괜찮다	to be all right	괜찮아요	괜찮습니다
어떻다	to be how	어때요 ?	어떻습니까 ?

Note that ㅎ at the end of the stem is not pronounced, but still the stem is considered to end with a consonant. The long forms of such verbs take the ending —습니다.

The honorific forms of the four verbs listed above may then be classified into short and long forms as follows:

Short form	Long form
좋으세요.	좋으십니다.
바쁘세요.	바쁘십니다.
어떠세요?	어떠십니까?
괜찮으세요?	괜찮으십니까?

4. How to Mix Abbreviated Conversation with "Polite" Tone

In conversation, we do not always use complete sentences; many things are understood and therefore not explicitly expressed. Look at the following conversation in English:

	Full meaning
A : Shall we go ?	Shall we go to the place we talked about ?
B : Where ?	Which place do you mean ?
A : To Suwon.	I meant to go to Suwon.
B : When ?	When do you want us to go to Suwon ?
A : Tomorrow.	I meant to suggest that we go to Suwon tomorrow.

The same type of abbreviated conversation can be carried out in Korean. However, Korean is a "politeness-conscious" language, and any such short phrases without a verb would sound too abrupt and blunt. To make such phrases sound reasonably "polite," the suffix —요 is added to the end of them, as in the following exchange.

A : 갈까요?	Shall we go ?
B : 어디요?	Where ?
A : 수원에요.	To Suwon.
B : 언제요?	When ?
A : 내일요.	Tomorrow.

Exercises

A. What Do You Hear?

Cover the Han-gŭl text below. The model voice will say the two sets of verbal exchanges in Korean, each set voiced twice. As you listen, put the Korean exchanges into English.

Exchange Ⅰ	Exchange Ⅱ
A : 저녁 식사 하셨습니까?	A : 몇 시에 만날까요?
B : 아직 안 했어요.	B : 여섯 시 어떻습니까?
A : 저녁 식사 같이 하실까요?	A : 나중에 알려드리지요.
B : 그럽시다.	B : 좋습니다.

B. What Do You Say?

Work with your instructor or classmate in the following series of role-playing.

1. Your friend or acquaintance has just asked you if you have had lunch or dinner. Suppose your answer is no. How would you say it?
2. You wish to invite out your friend or acquaintance to lunch/dinner/ movies. How would you say it in a proposition form?
3. You are willing to accept your friend's proposition such as above. What would be your typical response like?
4. What if you wish to decline such an offer?
5. You wish to find out whether your friend likes a certain kind of food (e.g., Korean, Chinese, American, or Japanese). How would you say?
6. Say to your friend that you like or don't like a certain kind of food such as above.
7. You have already expressed your willingness to accept your friend's invitation to lunch/dinner/movies. Now you wish to set up the time for it. Propose a certain time in a proposition question, such as one o'clock or six o'clock.
8. Suppose you are not ready to give a final answer to your friend's

proposed time and you wish to let him know some time later, how would you put it?

9. Your friend says that he will let you know later about the appointment. Then he might need your phone number. How would you respond?

C. Vocabulary Exercise

Each of the following model sentences is accompanied by a list of cues. After reading each sentence, say a new one by replacing the appropriate word with the Korean equivalent of each cue.

> *Example* : You read : 신문 있어요?
>   Cue : coffee
>   You say : 커피 있어요?

1. 내일 시간 있어요?
   Cues : (a) now (b) today (c) this evening

2. 한국 음식 좋아하세요?
   Cues : (a) American food (b) Japanese food (c) Chinese food

3. 영화 구경 같이 가실까요?
   Cues : (a) concert (b) art museum (c) Seoul Station

4. 식사 같이 하실까요?
   Cues : (a) coffee (b) dinner (c) lunch

5. 오늘 저녁에 무엇 하십니까?
   Cues : (a) tomorrow (b) weekend (c) tomorrow evening

D. Grammar Exercise

1. Convert each of the following questions into a proposition form, using —(오)실까요? at the end of the sentence.

> *Example* : You read : 가십니까?
>   You say : 가실까요?

   (a) 점심 식사 하십니까?   (d) 언제 가십니까?
   (b) 영화 구경 가십니까?   (e) 커피 하십니까?
   (c) 여기 앉으십니까?   (f) 내일 가십니까?

2. Convert each of the following questions into a proposition form, using
   ─(을)까요? at the end of the sentence.

> *Example* : You read : 갑니까?
>   You say : 갈까요?

   (a) 이리 앉습니까?   (d) 무엇 합니까?
   (b) 거기 갑니까?   (e) 어디 앉습니까?
   (c) 기다립니까?   (f) 언제 갑니까?

3. Convert each of the following stative verbs into the long form:

   (a) 좋아요.   (c) 어때요?
   (b) 바빠요.   (d) 괜찮아요?

4. Convert each of the following stative verbs into the short form:

   (a) 어떻습니까?   (c) 좋습니다.
   (b) 괜찮습니다.   (d) 바쁩니다.

5. Read each of the following sentences, and repeat back the first phrase as
   you would do to ascertain what you heard.

> *Example* : You read : 오늘 저녁에 무엇 하세요?
>   You say : 오늘 저녁에요?

   (a) 저녁 식사 하실까요?   (e) 조선 호텔이 어딥니까?
   (b) 내일 시간 있어요?   (f) 주말에 어디 가세요?
   (c) 영어 하세요?   (g) 휴게실에 갔습니다.
   (d) 옆방에 있습니다.   (h) 여섯 시 어떻습니까?

Reading and Writing

1. Discrepancies between spelling and pronunciation

    Several phrases you have learned in this lesson are spelled in one way but pronounced in another. This can be well explained by the general rules of sound changes in Korean. At this point of learning, you do not have to learn all of the general rules. All you have to do is simply learn the spelling while remembering the proper pronunciation. Some of the rules of sound change are given below for your information.

Spelled	Pronounced	General rules
같이	가치	(1) Consonant shift (See Lesson 8) : ㅌ goes to the next syllable.
		(2) ㅌ before 이 is pronounced ㅊ.
어떻습니까?	어떠씀니까?	(3) ㅎ before ㅅ makes the following ㅅ pronounced ㅆ.
좋아요	조아요	(4) ㅎ between two vowels is normally not pronounced.
연락	열락	(5) ㄴ before ㄹ is pronounced ㄹ.

2. Read aloud the following phrases, keeping the above rules in mind.

(a) 밭이	field (as subject)	(e) 훈련	training
(b) 좋습니다.	It's good.	(f) 붙이다	to attach
(c) 닿습니다.	(One) arrives.	(g) 하얗습니다.	It's white.
(d) 놓아요.	Put (it) down.	(h) 편리	convenience

3. Read aloud the lines identified by the letters below.

Summary of Verb Forms

좋다("to be good")

STATEMENT	LONG	SHORT
HON	(not introduced)	
PLN	좋습니다	좋아요

QUESTION	LONG	SHORT
HON	(not introduced)	
PLN	좋습니까?	좋아요

끝나다("to end")

STATEMENT	LONG	SHORT
HON	(not applicable)	
PLN	끝납니다	끝나요

QUESTION	LONG	SHORT
HON	(not applicable)	
PLN	끝납니까?	끝나요?

어떻다("to be how")

QUESTION	LONG	SHORT
HON	어떠십니까?	어떠세요?
PLN	어떻습니까?	어때요?

Note : Stative verbs are usually not used in request forms.

Words and Phrases

같이	together
그럽시다.	Let's do that.
글쎄요.	Well.
나중에	later
내일	tomorrow
몇 시에	at what time
미술관	art museum
미안합니다.	(I'm) sorry.
밤	night
별로 할 일 없어요.	I've nothing to do particularly.
봅시다.	Let me see.
—시	o'clock
시간	time
시간 있으세요?	Do you have spare time?
식사	meal
식사하다	to take a meal; to dine
아직	(not) yet
아침	morning
알려 드리지요.	I'll let you know.
언제	when
연락드리지요.	I'll be in touch with you.
영화 구경	seeing the movies
음식	food and drink
음악회	concert
저녁	evening
전화 번호	telephone number
점심 식사	lunch
좋습니다.	It's good; that's fine.
좋아요.	It's good; that's fine.
좋아하다	to like; to be fond of

죄송해요.	(I'm) sorry. (honorific)
한 시	one o'clock
할 일	things to do

Small Talk during a Break   **10**

Lesson Objectives

1. Carry on a conversation with an intimate co-worker of yours over daily events and activities, mutually-shared interests, etc. Specifically you will:
   (a) Ask your co-worker about the interesting activities he/she had during the weekend.
   (b) Tell that person of a party you had at home in the evening.
   (c) Ask that person what his/her ordinary after-work activities are.
   (d) Exchange information on mutually-shared interests.

2. When asked about your activities, respond as needed to questions listed above.

3. Use appropriately the following grammatical forms:
   (a) The past forms of verbs
   (b) The object-marking suffix

4. Read and write in Han-gŭl:.
   (a) Selected words from lesson material.
   (b) Selected phrases and sentences from lesson material.

Cultural Notes
Birthday Celebrations in Korea

Americans celebrate someone's birthday regardless of his or her age, but Koreans tend to celebrate birthdays with less enthusiasm than Americans do. For example, while American adults love to talk about (and celebrate) the birthdays of their own or of their family members, Koreans consider the birthdays of children and older people more important than those of the other adults.

The two most important birthdays in the life of a Korean are his first and his sixtieth. (It is true that as more people live to a greater age, the sixtieth birthday tends to lose its ritualistic significance.)

On his first birthday the Korean child, dressed in traditional costume, sits before the table loaded with a variety of fruits, cakes, and other foods. Official photographs are taken. Guests and family members offer presents and enjoy the feast.

The sixtieth birthday is an occasion for great celebration because it marks the completion of the 60-year cycle, a symbol of fullness and maturity in life. Again, there is a feast for all family members and guests.

Communicative Exchanges

FRAME 1

A Talk over Weekend Activities

Mr. Han and his co-worker Miss Yun have a talk over some of the activities that the latter had during the weekend.

한 : 미스·윤, 주말¹ 잘 지냈어요 ?

Did you have a good weekend, Miss Yun ? (Literally, ·"Did you fare well over the weekend ?")

윤 : 네. 아주 재미있었어요. 친구들 하고 같이 산²에 갔어요.

Yes. It was great fun. I went up the mountain with my friends.

한 : 어느 산에요 ?

Which mountain ?

윤 : 도봉산에요. 날씨³가 아주 좋았 어요.

Mt. Tobong. The weather was so beautiful.

한 : 도봉산 좋지요 !

I know Mt. Tobong is beautiful.

SUBSTITUTION

1. 휴가   vacation
   추석   Ch'usŏk (Korean Thanksgiving Day)
   크리스마스   Christmas
2. 바닷가   beach
   시골   countryside
3. 경치   scenery

FRAME 2

Talking about Last Night's Birthday Party

Miss Yun gives an account of the birthday party they had for her niece last night.

윤 : 어젯밤 우리 집에서 생일 파티¹
했어요.

We had a birthday party at our house last night.

한 : 그래요? 누구 생일이었어요?

Really? Whose birthday was it?

윤 : 우리 조카 보라의 생일이었어요.

It was my niece Pora's birthday.

한 : 파티에 누가 왔어요?

Who came to the party?

윤 : 우리 오빠² 친구들이 오셨어요.

My brother's friends came.

SUBSTITUTION	
1. 잔치	feast
2. 언니	elder sister (of a girl)
누나	elder sister (of a boy)
형	elder brother (of a boy)

FRAME 3

Talking about Evening Activities at Home

Mr. Jones asks Mr. Park what he usually does at home in the evening.

존스 : 박 선생, 저녁에 보통 무엇 하세요? 　 What do you usually do in the evening, Mr. Park?

박　 : 보통 가족¹하고 같이 시간을 보냅니다. 　 I usually spend time with my family.

존스 : 주로 무엇을 하세요? 　 What do you do mainly?

박　 : 주로 텔레비전을 봅니다. 이따금 맛있는 음식²도 만듭니다. 　 Mainly I watch TV. Once in a while we fix delicious food, too.

존스 : 음식은 주로 누가 만듭니까? 　 Who mainly fixes the food?

박　 : 우리 아내³가 만듭니다. 　 My wife does.

SUBSTITUTION

1. 동생　　　　　　　　　younger brother／sister
2. 빵　　　　　　　　　　bread
   과자　　　　　　　　　pastry, cakes, sweets
   떡　　　　　　　　　　Korean rice cakes
3. 집사람　　　　　　　　wife (humble form)

FRAME 4

Talking about Your Favorite TV Programs

Mr. Jones and Mr. Park go on talking about some of the TV programs they both like.

존스 : 텔레비전 프로 중에서 어떤 것을 자 주 보세요?

Among the TV programs which one do you watch often ?

박   : 뉴스와 음악¹ 프로를 자주 봅니다.

I often watch news and music programs.

존스 : 저도 뉴스와 음악 프로를 많이 봅니 다. 그러나 이따금 스포츠 프로도 봅니다.

I also watch news and music programs a lot. But occasionally I watch sports programs, too.

박   : 스포츠 프로 중에서 어떤 것을 제 일² 좋아하세요?

Among the sports programs which one do you like best ?

존스 : 야구³ 프로요.

The baseball program.

SUBSTITUTION

1. 교육   education
   과학   science
2. 더   more
   가장   most
3. 농구   basketball
   배구   volleyball
   축구   football

Grammar and Usage

1. The Past Tense

The past tense of a Korean verb is formed when we add the suffix —었 to the verb stem, as in 먹었어요 ("ate"). Let us use the verb 읽다 ("to read"), to illustrate the general rule for forming the past tense.

Honorific form	Plain form
STEM + (으)시 + 었 + ENDING	STEM + 었 + ENDING

읽으시었어요
↓
contracted
↓

Short form :	읽으셨어요	읽었어요
Long form :	읽으셨습니다	읽었습니다

If the suffix —었 is directly preceded by a stem containing the vowel 아 or 오, it changes to —았. For example, in the plain forms of such verbs as 가다 ("to go"), 오다 ("to come"), 보다 ("to see"), the past suffix is —았.

Honorific form	Plain form	
오셨어요	오았어요	"came"
	↓	
	contracted	
	↓	
	왔어요	
보셨어요	보았어요	"saw"
	↓	
	contracted	
	↓	
	봤어요	
가셨어요	가았어요	"went"
	↓	
	contracted	
	↓	
	갔어요	

The verb 하 다 ("to do; to have (a meal or drink); to speak (a language)"), is irregular. The combination of the stem 하— and the past suffix results in 했.

Honorific form	Plain form	
하셨어요	했어요	"did"
하셨습니다	했습니다	

When the verb stem ends with a vowel, the combination of the vowel and 어 is generally contracted. The following are general rules of such contractions:

이	plus	어	→	are generally contracted as	→	여
우	plus	어	→		→	워
오	plus	아	→		→	와
BUT						
으	plus	어	→	must always be contracted as	→	어

Honorific form	Plain form		
기다리셨어요	기다리었어요	→	기다렸어요
쓰셨어요	(쓰었어요)	→	썼어요
보셨어요	보았어요	→	봤어요
오셨어요	(오았어요)	→	왔어요

> NOTE: The forms in parentheses are never actually used even though they are alleged to be generic forms.

The rules for formation of the past tense also apply to the negative forms of verbs, including those expressing existence and identity.

여기가 호텔입니다.	여기가 호텔이었습니다.
연필이 있습니까?	연필이 있었습니까?
봉투가 없습니다.	봉투가 없었습니다.
저는 안 갑니다.	저는 안 갔습니다.

2. How to Accurately Translate Korean Tenses into English

The present tense in Korean is equivalent to many tense forms in English; for example, 가요 can be translated "I go," "I am going," or "I will go." Likewise, the past tense in Korean is equivalent to more than one form in English, most typically the simple past and the present perfect. For example, 먹었어요 can be translated "I ate" (simple past) or "I have eaten" (present perfect). Many problems of this nature can be solved if you understand the contextual relationships of sentences.

3. The Object of a Verb

You have learned a number of verbs expressing actions, such as 먹다 ("to eat"), 보다 ("to see" or "to look at"), 읽다 ("to read"), and 쓰다 ("to write"). These verbs usually require two nouns: one that performs the action and another which receives it. The former is called the SUBJECT and the latter the OBJECT. So far, you have seen the object unmarked, that is, with no suffix added to it, as in the following examples:

Object	Verb	
커피	하셨어요?	Did you have <u>coffee</u>?
점심	하셨어요?	Did you have <u>lunch</u>?
책	읽습니다	I read <u>books</u>.
편지	씁니다	I write <u>a letter</u>.
텔레비전	봅니다	I watch <u>television</u>.

In conversation, it is perfectly all right not to use an object-marking suffix; it is the normal way of speaking in Korean. However, an object-marking suffix will be used when one writes or when the object is stressed in speaking. This suffix is —을 (if it is after a consonant) and —를 (if it is after a vowel.)

커피를 하셨어요?　　　Did you have coffee?
점심을 잡수셨어요?　　Did you have lunch?

In a word, the object-marking suffix is not absolutely necessary in conversation, but it is important to recognize it in someone's speech.

Exercises

A. What Do You Hear ?

Cover the Han-gŭl text below. The model voice will say the two sets of verbal exchanges in Korean, each voiced twice. As you listen, put the Korean exchange into English.

Exchange Ⅰ

A : 주말 잘 지냈어요 ?

B : 아주 재미있었어요.

　　친구들하고 시골에 갔어요.

A : 어느 시골에요 ?

B : 음성에요.

Exchange Ⅱ

A : 저녁에 주로 무엇을 하세요 ?

B : 주로 텔레비전 봅니다.

A : 어떤 것 많이 보세요 ?

B : 스포츠 프로를 제일 좋아해요.

B. What Do You Say ?

Work with your instructor or classmate in the following series of role-playing.

1. You are talking to an intimate co-worker of yours. Ask your friend if he/she had a nice weekend (or vacation).
2. Respond to such a greeting as above by saying that the weekend (or vacation) was great fun. Give details of your weekend (or vacation) activities.
3. Tell your co-worker or friend that you had a birthday party at home on the previous night.
4. Respond to such a statement as above by asking whose birthday party it was and who was invited to the party.
5. Give details of what went on in the party.
6. Ask your co-worker or friend what kind of evening activities he/she usually has at home.
7. Respond to such a question as above by stating specific activities: watching TV or fixing food and cakes.
8. Ask further details of such activities as above: what kind of TV programs

your friend often watches, what kind of TV sports programs he/she likes best, etc.

C. Vocabulary Exercise

Each of the following model sentences is accompanied by a list of cues. After reading each sentence, say a new one by replacing the appropriate word with the Korean equivalent of each cue.

> *Example* : You read : 주로 텔레비전을 봅니다.
> Cue : occasionally
> You say : 이따금 텔레비전을 봅니다.

1. 크리스마스 잘 지냈어요 ?
   Cues : (a) vacation (b) weekend (c) Ch'usŏk

2. 우리 오빠 친구들이 왔어요.
   Cues : (a) older brother's (b) older sister's (c) younger ·brother's

3. 맛있는 음식 만듭니다.
   Cues : (a) (Korean rice) cakes (b) cakes and sweets (c) bread

4. 뉴스 프로를 자주 봅니다.
   Cues : (a) sports (b) music (c) science

5. 친구들하고· 산에 갔어요.
   Cues : (a) beach (b) countryside (c) Mt. Tobong

D. Grammar Exercise

1. Cover the text below. The model voice will say each of the following present tense verbs in the long form. As you listen, say aloud its counterpart in the past tense.

(a) 합니다	→	했습니다	(f) 없습니다 → 없었습니다	
(b) 갑니다	→	갔습니다	(g) 만듭니다 → 만들었습니다	
(c) 옵니다	→	왔습니다	(h) 보냅니다 → 보냈습니다	
(d) 봅니다	→	봤습니다	(i) 좋습니다 → 좋았습니다	
(e) 있습니다	→	있었습니다	(j) 지냅니다 → 지냈습니다	

2. Cover the text below. The model voice will say each of the following present tense verbs in the short form. As you listen, say aloud its counter-

part in the past tense.

(a) 해요	→	했어요	(f) 없어요	→	없었어요
(b) 가요	→	갔어요	(g) 만들어요	→	만들었어요
(c) 와요	→	왔어요	(h) 보내요	→	보냈어요
(d) 봐요	→	봤어요	(i) 좋아요	→	좋았어요
(e) 있어요	→	있었어요	(j) 지내요	→	지냈어요

3. Cover the text below. The model voice will say each of the past tense verbs in the short-plain form. As you listen, say aloud the past tense, short-honorific form of the verb.

(a) 했어요	→	하셨어요	(f) 없었어요	→	안 계셨어요
(b) 갔어요	→	가셨어요	(g) 만들었어요	→	만드셨어요
(c) 왔어요	→	오셨어요	(h) 보냈어요	→	보내셨어요
(d) 봤어요	→	보셨어요	(i) 좋았어요	→	좋으셨어요
(e) 있었어요	→	계셨어요	(j) 지냈어요	→	지내셨어요

4. After reading each of the following utterances, say a new one it by converting the present tense form of the verb into the past tense form.

> *Example* : You read : 잘 지내요.
> You say : 잘 지냈어요.

(a) 아주 재미있어요.
(b) 날씨가 아주 좋아요.
(c) 우리 집에서 생일 파티 해요.
(d) 우리 오빠 친구들이 와요.
(e) 저녁에 무엇을 해요?

Reading and Writing

1. Some Spelling Peculiarities

Among a number of verbs you have spelling peculiarities.

읽 다 ("to read") has two consonants at the end of the stem. The stem of this verb 읽— does not change regardless of what ending may be attached. Both ㄹ and ㄱ are pronounced when a vowel directly follows, but ㄹ is not pronounced when a consonant immediately follows. For example,

Spelled	Pronounced
읽다	익따
읽습니다	익씀니다

When a vowel follows the verb stem 읽, ㄹ is the first to be pronounced after 이 but ㄱ is pronounced in the next syllable by the rule of shifting consonants. For example,

Spelled	Pronounced
읽어요	일거요
읽었습니다	일거씀니다

쓰다 ("to write") drops the vowel—both in spelling and pronunciation.

	Spelled & Pronunciation
쓰+었습니다	썼습니다

Read aloud the following, paying particular attention to the silent consonants.

(a) 닭   chicken
(b) 흙도   soil also
(c) 밝아요.   It's bright.
(d) 맑습니다. It's clear.
(e) 늙었습니다. He is old.
(f) 낡았습니다. It's worn out.

2. Read aloud the lines identified by the letters below.

유효기간/EXPIRES

9406 9010

ⓐ 국민카드 The CNB Credit Card 매 출 전 표

국민카드

판 매 원 CASHIER	사 업 자 등록번호	
	상 호 대표자성명	
24 30 90 11	주 소	

ⓑ 판매일자/TRANS.DATE   ※매출취소시 당초매출일

890413

년 월 일   년 월 일

판 매 내 역 DESCRIPTION	수 량 Q.N.T.	단 가 UNIT COST	ⓒ 금 액 OUNT OF PURCHASE

부(分割)   리 보 払 い REVOLVING

개월

승인번호/ CREDIT APPROVAL

서명/SIGNATURE

본인은 거래금액을 확인하여 이에 서명함.

세금/TAX	
봉사료/TIP	
합 계 ₩ TOTAL $	

사용하실 수 있읍니다.
할 수 없읍니다.

공급받는자의 주민등록번호 또는 사업자등록번호

문의전화 : 서울(02) 753 – 3100

회원용(영수증) Ⓓ

간이세금계산서   (공급받는자용)

No.   귀하

공	영업자 납세번호	**101 – 81 – 18640**		
ⓓ	상 호	**㈜한림출판사**	성 명	**임 인 수** ㊞
급	영업장 소재지	**서울 • 종로구 관철동 14〜5**		
자	업 태	**제조업**	종 목	**출판물**

작성년월일	금 액	비 고
198 . . .		

위 금액을 영수(청구)함.

ⓔ 품 목	수량	단가	금 액	비고

Summary of Verb Forms

하다("to do")

STATEMENT
Present

	LONG	SHORT
HON	하십니다	하세요
PLN	합니다	해요

Past

	LONG	SHORT
HON	하셨습니다	하셨어요
PLN	했습니다	했어요

QUESTION
Present

	LONG	SHORT
HON	하십니까?	하세요?
PLN	합니까?	해요?

Past

	LONG	SHORT
HON	하셨습니까?	하셨어요?
PLN	했습니까?	했어요?

REQUEST

	LONG	SHORT
HON	하십시오	하세요
PLN	(not introduced)	

SUGGESTION

HON	하실까요?
PLN	할까요?

먹다("to eat")

STATEMENT
Present

	LONG	SHORT
HON	잡수십니다	잡수세요
PLN	먹습니다	먹어요

Past

	LONG	SHORT
HON	잡수셨습니다	잡수셨어요
PLN	먹었습니다	먹었어요

QUESTION
Present

	LONG	SHORT
HON	잡수십니까?	잡수세요?
PLN	먹습니까?	먹어요?

Past

	LONG	SHORT
HON	잡수셨습니까?	잡수셨어요?
PLN	먹었습니까?	먹었어요?

REQUEST

	LONG	SHORT
HON	잡수십시오	잡수세요
PLN	(not introduced)	

SUGGESTION

HON	잡수실까요?
PLN	먹을까요?

Note: Request forms and suggestion forms are not used in past tense.

보다("to watch; to see")

STATEMENT		
Present		
	LONG	SHORT
HON	보십니다	보세요
PLN	봅니다	봐요
Past		
	LONG	SHORT
HON	보셨습니다	보셨어요
PLN	봤습니다	봤어요
QUESTION		
Present		
	LONG	SHORT
HON	보십니까?	보세요?
PLN	봅니까?	봐요?
Past		
	LONG	SHORT
HON	보셨습니까?	보셨어요?
PLN	봤습니까?	봤어요?
REQUEST		
	LONG	SHORT
HON	보십시오	보세요
PLN	(not introduced)	
SUGGESTION		
HON	보실까요?	
PLN	볼까요?	

읽다("to read")

STATEMENT		
Present		
	LONG	SHORT
HON	읽으십니다	읽으세요
PLN	읽습니다	읽어요
Past		
	LONG	SHORT
HON	읽으셨습니다	읽으셨어요
PLN	읽었습니다	읽었어요
QUESTION		
Present		
	LONG	SHORT
HON	읽으십니까?	읽으세요?
PLN	읽습니까?	읽어요?
Past		
	LONG	SHORT
HON	읽으셨습니까?	읽으셨어요?
PLN	읽었습니까?	읽었어요?
REQUEST		
	LONG	SHORT
HON	읽으십시오	읽으세요
PLN	(not introduced)	
SUGGESTION		
HON	읽으실까요?	
PLN	읽을까요?	

쓰다("to write")

STATEMENT

	Present			Past	
	LONG	SHORT		LONG	SHORT
HON	쓰십니다	쓰세요	HON	쓰셨습니다	쓰셨어요
PLN	씁니다	써요	PLN	썼습니다	썼어요

QUESTION

	Present			Past	
	LONG	SHORT		LONG	SHORT
HON	쓰십니까?	쓰세요?	HON	쓰셨습니까?	쓰셨어요?
PLN	씁니까?	써요?	PLN	썼습니까?	썼어요?

REQUEST

	LONG	SHORT
HON	쓰십시오	쓰세요
PLN	(not introduced)	

SUGGESTION

HON	쓰실까요?
PLN	쓸까요?

Words and Phrases

가장	most (adverbial use)
경치	scenery
과자	cakes; sweets
과학	science
교육	education
날씨	weather
농구	basketball
누나	elder sister (of a boy)
동생	younger brother / sister
더	more
떡	Korean rice cake
만들다	to fix (a meal); to make
맛있는	delicious
바닷가	beach
배구	volleyball
보다	to see, watch
보통	usually; generally
빵	bread
산	mountain
생일	birthday
스포츠	sports
쓰다	to write
아내	wife
야구	baseball
언니	elder sister (of a girl)
오빠	elder brother (of a girl)
음악	music
이따금	occasionally
읽다	to read
잔치	feast; party
잡수셨어요?	Did you eat...? (honorific)

재미있었어요.	It was fun.
제일	best (adverbial use)
조카	niece; nephew
좋았어요.	It was good; It was fine.
주로	mainly
지내다	Did you have a (good) time?
집	house; home
집사람	my wife (a husband's humble use)
책	book
축구	football
텔레비전	TV
파티	party
편지	letter
프로	program; short form of 프로그램
형	older brother (of a boy)
휴가	vacation

Up to Lesson 10 verb forms were introduced as they appear in actual phrases and sentences, from Lesson 11 on, however, verb forms will be introduced in stems(or dictionary forms) only. The same is true of all verb forms introduced in the index columns.

Meeting Out-of-town People

Lesson Objectives

1. Carry on a conversation with a new acquaintance you meet on a trip. Specifically you will:
   (a) Ask that person about his/her travel experiences and plans, namely, whether this trip to Korea is his/her first one, what the purpose of the trip is, and how long he/she intends to stay in Korea.
   (b) Ask that person about his/her occupations, namely, what he/she does for a living and how long he/she was engaged in that occupation.
   (c) Ask that person about his/her language learning experience, namely, how he/she learned Korean, who helped him/her with his/her lessons, and how long he /she has studied the language.
   (d) Answer properly each of the questions listed above, as needed.

2. Understand fully some general rules about:
   (a) The word order for place and time specification.
   (b) The singular and plural forms of Korean nouns.
   (c) Numbers expressing calendar units.
   (d) The use of —에서 in the sense of "from."

3. Read and understand written Korean. Specifically you will:
   (a) Read and write Korean words involving the syllable 의.
   (b) Write contractions of two successive vowels.

Cultural Notes
International Understanding

In spite of the increasing number of foreigners visiting Korea, many Koreans still find meeting foreigners, particularly Westerners, a novel experience. Hearing a foreigner speak Korean is even more of a pleasant surprise for them.

To Koreans, this means that the foreigner is very much interested in Korea and its culture. Naturally Koreans are increasingly interested in knowing about the foreigner's country and culture. The initial conversation would usually cover matters of a personal nature, such as one's travel experiences and plans, one's occupations, and one's language learning experience.

In such circumstances, the mere fact that you are able to express yourself, however skimpily, in Korean can be an advantage and head start toward making friends with native Koreans.

Communicative Exchanges

FRAME 1

Coming to Korea

While waiting for their baggage to roll in, Mr. Baker and his new Korean acquaintance, Mr. Hong, have a friendly talk.

홍	: 한국에 처음 오십니까?	Is this your first trip to Korea?
베이커	: 아니오, <u>작년 가을</u>[1]에 왔었습니다.	No. I was here once last fall.
홍	: <u>무슨 일로</u>[2] 오셨어요?	What has brought you here?
베이커	: 사업 때문에 왔습니다.	I've come for business purpose.
홍	: 얼마 동안 한국에 계십니까?	How long will you be in Korea?
베이커	: 약 <u>이 주일</u>[3] 있습니다.	I'll be here for about two weeks.

SUBSTITUTION

1.	금년 가을	this/past fall
	작년 봄	last spring
2.	무슨 용무로	on what business
	무슨 목적으로	for what purpose
3.	일 주일	one week
	일 개월	one month

FRAME 2

Talking about One's Occupations

The topic is now changed to each other's places of departure and occupations abroad.

홍 : 미국 <u>어디서</u>¹ 오셨어요?	Where in America are you from?
베이커 : 뉴욕주 버팔로에서 왔습니다.	I'm from Buffalo, New York.
홍 : 아, 그러세요? 저는 뉴욕에서 왔습니다.	Oh, is that so? I'm coming from New York.
베이커 : 거기서 뭐 하셨어요?	What did you do there?
홍 : <u>대학</u>²에 다녔습니다, 4년 동안요.	I went to college—for four years.
베이커 : 뭐 공부하셨어요?	What did you study?
홍 : <u>경제학</u>³을 했습니다.	I studied economics.

SUBSTITUTION
1. 어느 주에서   from what state
   어느 지방에서   from what region
2. 회사   business firm
   은행   bank
3. 정치학   political science
   의학   medical science
   화학   chemistry

FRAME 3

Talking about One's Foreign Language Experience

Impressed with Mr. Baker's fluent Korean, Mr. Hong brings up the subject of language learning.

홍   : 한국말을 어디서 배우셨어요? | Where did you learn Korean?

베이커 : 미국에서 <u>혼자서</u>[1] 배웠어요. 저 희 회사에 한국인 직원이 계십니 다. 그분이 많이 도와 주셨어요. | I learned it by myself in America. We have a Korean employee in our firm. He helped me a lot.

홍   : 얼마 동안 배우셨어요? | How long have you learned it?

베이커 : 약 이 년 배웠습니다. | I've learned for about two years.

홍   : 한국말 아주 잘 하십니다. | You speak Korean very well.

베이커 : 감사합니다. 아직도 더 많이 <u>배 워야 합니다.</u>[2] | Thank you. I still have to learn a lot more.

SUBSTITUTION	
1. 학교에서	at (in) school
학원에서	at a (private) institute
2. 공부해야 합니다.	(One) has to study.
읽어야 합니다.	(One) has to read.

Grammar and Usage

1. The Word Order for Place and Time Specification

When you specify a place or a time by two or more words in English, you would start from a more specific description and then proceed to add a less specific (larger) category. For example, Buffalo (city), New York (state) or the 24th (day) of April (month), etc.

In Korean, the word order in similar instances is the reverse of the English way: it moves from a large category to a smaller one. See the following for comparison.

Place Specification:	
Suwon Kyŏnggi-do	경기도 수원
Time Specification:	
summer last year	작년 여름

Note that the adjectives "this" and "last" in "this winter" and "last night" are not used in Korean. Earlier, you learned the sentence:

어제 저녁에 뭐 하셨어요?   What did you do last night?

The phrase 어제 저녁 starts with the specification of the day (어제) followed by the part of the day (저녁). The same principle applies to a phrase like "this winter," which starts with 금년 ("this year") followed by 겨울 ("winter").

Other examples are as follows:

금년 봄	this spring (this year spring)
금년 여름	this summer (this year summer)
작년 가을	last fall (last year fall)
작년 겨울	last winter (last year winter)

2. The Singular and Plural of Nouns

The Korean noun does not generally carry a plural suffix to indicate more than one item. Note the following sentence that you have already seen.

의자가 있습니다 can mean
$\left\{ \begin{array}{l} \text{There is a chair.} \\ \text{There are chairs.} \end{array} \right.$

Whether the sentence denotes the existence of a single chair or many chairs is usually determined by the context. The Korean verb does not change its form whether the subject is singular or plural. So, there again, the full meaning of a sentence may be determined by the context. For example,

갑니다 can mean
$\left\{ \begin{array}{l} \text{I am} \\ \text{We are} \\ \text{You are} \\ \text{He is} \\ \text{She is} \\ \text{They are} \end{array} \right\}$ going.

However, when the noun in a sentence indicates some specific person(s), the plural marker —들 is required. (By "specific" or "definite," we mean something or somebody specifically referred to by the speaker and understood by the listener. In this instance, the English speaker would use "the" in English.) For example,

this person	이 사람	these persons	이 사람들
that gentleman	그분	those gentlemen	그분들
the student	그 학생	the students	그 학생들

3. Numbers Expressing Days, Weeks, Months and Years

The number (e.g., 일 "one," 이 "two," 삼 "three," 사 "four," 오 "five") is followed by the appropriate noun (e.g., 일 "day," 주일 "week," 월 "month," 년 "year"). Thus,

Days	Weeks	Months	Years
일 일	일 주일	일 개월	일 년
이 일	이 주일	이 개월	이 년
삼 일	삼 주일	삼 개월	삼 년
사 일	사 주일	사 개월	사 년
오 일	오 주일	오 개월	오 년

In the case of month numeration, 개 (meaning "individual item") is inserted between the number and the noun 월. Without 개 inserted, 일월 means "January," 이월 "February," etc.

4. Words or Phrases Expressing Quantity

A word or phrase which expresses quantity such as 다 ("all"), 한잔 ("one cup,") etc., follows the noun which it quantifies. For example,

커피 한잔 하십시오.
Please have a cup of coffee.

선생님들이 다 한국분입니다.
All the teachers are Koreans.

책상이 몇이 있습니까?
How many desks are there?

학생들 둘이 여기 왔습니다.
Two students have come here.

5. The Use of —에서 in the Sense of "from"

The suffix —에서 was introduced earlier as a suffix indicating the location of an event. The same suffix is also used to denote the origin of an event (equivalent to "from"). As in the first usage, —에서 is usually shortened to 서 after short place words, such as:

어디에서, 여기에서, 저기에서, 거기에서 → 어디서, 여기서, 저기서, 거기서

어디서 오셨습니까?
Where are you from?

뉴욕에서 왔습니다.
I am (=have come) from New York.

서울에서 편지가 왔어요.
A letter has come from Seoul.

Exercises

A. Short Exchanges: Listening and Speaking

Beginning with this lesson, a reinforced exercise in listening and speaking is provided. Follow the steps given below as you work on each exercise question.

> Step 1. Cover the Han-gŭl portion, and repeat after the model voicing as you look at the English equivalent.
>
> Step 2. Now cover the English portion, and again repeat after the model voicing, making sure you pronounce each word and phrase correctly and you understand them fully.
>
> Step 3. Now cover the Han-gŭl text. As you look at the English equivalent, say the Korean version of it.
>
> Step 4. Keep the Han-gŭl text covered. Aided by the English text, carry on the exchange in Korean with your instructor or classmate.

1. 오셨어요 ?   Has he come ?
    안 왔어요.   No, he has not.
2. 스미스 선생 왔어요 ?   Has Mr. Smith come ?
    네, 왔어요.   Yes, he has.
3. 언제 오셨어요 ?   When did you come ?
    작년 봄에 왔어요.   I came last spring.
4. 작년 봄에 왔어요 ?   Did you come last spring ?
    아니오, 금년 봄에 왔어요.   No, I came this spring.
5. 한국에 처음 왔어요 ?   Have you come to Korea for the first time ?

    네, 처음 왔어요.   Yes, for the first time.
6. 어디서 오셨어요 ?   Where are you from ?
    미국에서 왔어요.   I am from America.
7. 미국 어디서 오셨어요 ?   Where in America are you from ?
    뉴욕에서 왔어요.   I am from New York.

8. 거기서 뭐 하셨어요?   What did you do there?
   대학에 다녔어요.   I went to college.
9. 거기가 고향입니까?   Is that your hometown?
   네, 고향입니다.   Yes, it's my hometown.
10. 선생님 고향이 어딥니까?   Where is your hometown?
    뉴욕입니다.   It's New York.
11. 한국에서 배우셨어요?   Did you learn (it) in Korea?
    아니오, 미국에서 배웠어요.   No, I learned (it) in America.
12. 미국 어디서 배우셨어요?   Where in America did you learn (it)?
    학교에서 배웠어요.   I learned (it) at school.
13. 그 학교가 어디 있어요?   Where is that school?
    뉴욕에 있습니다.   It's in New York.
14. 얼마 동안 배우셨어요?   How long have you learned it?
    약 이 년 배웠어요.   I've learned for about 2 years.
15. 한국말 잘 하십니다.   You speak good Korean.
    감사합니다. 아직도 더   Thank you. I still have to learn more.
    배워야 합니다.

B. What Do You Say?

Work with your instructor or classmate in the following series of role-playing.

1. Ask the foreign acquaintance whom you just met whether the trip he/she is taking to Korea is his/her first one.
2. Ask that person what the purpose of his/her trip is.
3. Ask that person how long he/she is going to stay in Korea.
4. Supposing you are the foreign traveler in question, answer questions 1, 2 and 3 above, properly.
5. Ask your foreign acquaintance what he/she does for a living.
6. Ask that person how long he/she has been engaged in that occupation.
7. Taking the role of the foreign traveler, answer questions 5 and 6, properly.
8. Ask your foreign acquaintance how he/she learned Korean.
9. Ask that person who helped him/her with his/her lessons.
10. Ask that person how long he/she has studied the Korean language.
11. Taking the role of the foreign acquaintance, answer questions 8, 9 and

10, properly.

12. Your new acquaintance compliments your fluency in the foreign language. Tell your new acquaintance that you still have to learn a lot more.

C. Vocabulary Exercise

Follow the steps given below as you work on each exercise question.

Step 1. Cover the English portion on the right. Your instructor will read to you a key Korean word or phrase and then an exchange in Korean containing the same word or phrase.

Step 2. Try to understand what your instructor says. Uncover the English portion and see if your knowledge is correct.

Step 3. Now cover the Han-gŭl portion on the left, and say correctly the Korean equivalent of the English exchange listed under the cue.

Step 4. Uncover the Han-gŭl portion and see if your answer is correct.

---

1. You hear : 금년   this year
  금년에 오셨어요?   Did you come this year?
  한국에 금년에 오셨어요? Did you come to Korea this year?
  Cue : When did you come?
    I came here this year.

2. You hear : 작년 last year
  작년에 오셨어요? Did you come last year?
  금년에 왔어요. I came this year.
  Cue : Did you come to Korea last year?
    No, I came to Korea in the spring of this year.

3. You hear : 처음 for the first time
  그거 처음 봤어요. I saw it for the first time.
  이거 처음입니다. This is the first time for me.
  Cue : Did you come to Korea for the first time?
    Yes, I came for the first time.

4. You hear : 이번 this time
  이번이 처음입니까? Is this the first time?
  이번이 처음 아닙니다. This is not the first time.

    Cue : Did you come to Korea for the first time ?
        Yes, this is the first time.

5. You hear : 얼마 동안   how long
   얼마 동안 여기에 계십니까?   How long will you be here ?
   일 주일 동안 있습니다.   I will be here for a week.
   Cue : How long will you be in the States ?
      I'll be there for two weeks.

6. You hear : —(에)서   from
   미국 어디서 오셨어요?   Where in America have you come from ?
   뉴욕에서 왔어요.   I've come from New York.
   Cue : Where are you from ?
      I am from San Francisco.

7. You hear : 배우다   to learn, study
   한국말 배웠어요.   I studied Korean.
   한국말 어디서 배우셨어요?   Where did you study Korean ?
   Cue : Did you study Korean in Korea ?
      No, I studied it in America.

8. You hear : —야 합니다.   have to (do)
   더 배워야 합니까?   Do I have to learn more ?
   네, 더 배워야 합니다.   Yes, you have to learn more.
   Cue : Do you have to go now ?
      Yes, I have to.

D. Grammar Exercise

Answer the following questions, using the English cues.

> *Example* : Question : 언제 한국에 오셨습니까?
>   Cue : last spring
>   Answer : 작년 봄에 왔습니다.

1. 언제 한국에 오셨어요?
   Cue : this summer
2. 언제 미국에 가십니까?
   Cue : this fall
3. 언제 집에 가십니까?
   Cue : tonight

4. 미국 어디서 오셨어요?
   Cue : State of California, U.S.A.
5. 얼마 동안 여기에 계십니까?
   Cue : for one week

Reading and Writing

1. Pronunciation of 외, 뵈, 되

The pronunciation of 외 varies depending on the speaker's regional background. To the foreign speaker's ear, 외 might sound almost like 웨.

Spelled	Pronounced	
왼쪽으로	왼쪼그로	to the left
외국어	외구거	a foreign language
또 뵙겠습니다.	또 뵙께씀니다.	See you again.

Read aloud the following phrases, paying particular attention to the pronunciation of 외, 되, 쇠, and 회.

(a) 외국 사람 foreigner (d) 쇠 iron
(b) 해외 overseas (e) 쇠고기 beef
(c) 되다 to become (f) 회사 company

2. Contraction Exercise

As you have already learned, two successive vowels are often contracted into one syllable. This often happens when the past tense is formed. Unite the contracted form of each of the following.

> *Example* : 이+아=야

(a) 오+아= (f) 가시었어요=
(b) 우+어= (g) 보아요   =
(c) 우+이= (h) 배우었어요=
(d) 이+어= (i) 내리어요 =
(e) 이+오= (j) 오았습니다=

3. Read aloud the lines identified by the letters a, b, c, d, e, below.

황 · 소 · 식 · 당 ⓐ
- ● 특색있는 갈비와 불고기
- ● 곱창구이와 삼겹살
- ● 각종 별미 찌개 전문 ⓑ

영업시간 : 오전9시 ~ 오후9시
주　　소 : 서울 종로구 관철동
전　　화 : 735-7500/2

한 남 관 광
—국내 여행에서 세계 일주까지—
- ● 단체행사 특별우대 ⓒ
- ● 각급학교 수학여행
- ● 꿈과 낭만의 신혼여행

♣ 귀하를 정중히 초대합니다. ⓓ

시사영어학원 ⓔ
- ＊ 30 여개의 다양한 강좌
- ＊ 체계적이고도 성의있는 강의
- ＊ 최고 수준의 강사와 현대적 설비
- ＊ 오랜 전통의 외국어 학습의 선구자

전화상담 : 734 – 2442

Summary of Verb Forms

배우다 ("to learn")

	STATEMENT					
	Present				**Past**	
	LONG	SHORT			LONG	SHORT
HON	배우십니다	배우세요		HON	배우셨습니다	배우셨어요
PLN	배웁니다	배워요		PLN	배웠습니다	배웠어요

	QUESTION					
	Present				**Past**	
	LONG	SHORT			LONG	SHORT
HON	배우십니까?	배우세요?		HON	배우셨습니까?	배우셨어요?
PLN	배웁니까?	배워요?		PLN	배웠습니까?	배웠어요?

	REQUEST	
	LONG	SHORT
HON	배우십시오	배우세요
PLN	(not introduced)	

	SUGGESTION
HON	배우실까요?
PLN	배울까요?

Words and Phrases

가을	fall
개월	(number of) month(s)
겨울	winter
경제학	economics
고향	hometown
공부하다	to study
금년	this year
一년	year
대학	college; university
一때문에	for; because
목적으로	for the purpose (of)
배우다	to learn, study
봄	spring
약	about
얼마 동안	how long
여름	summer
외국어	foreign language
외국 사람	foreigner
용무	business; errand
은행	bank
의학	medical science
이번	this time
작년	last year
정치학	political science
주	state
一주일	(number of) week(s)
지방	region
직원	employee
학원	(private) institute
화학	chemistry
혼자서	by oneself
회사	business firm

Taking a Taxi

Lesson Objectives

1. Discuss, on the Korean taxi, your needs with the taxi driver. Specifically you will:
   (a) State your destination to the taxi driver.
   (b) Ask the driver if he/she is willing to go to a certain place or area.
   (c) Tell him/her exactly where you want to get off.
   (d) Give him/her some necessary directions before reaching the destination.
   (e) Ask him/her what the fare is.

2. Understand fully some general rules about:
   (a) The verb-ending expressing a proposition, —읍시다/—ㅂ시다.
   (b) The suffix 겠 expressing the speaker's intention or confirming the hearer's intention.
   (c) The suffix 까지 expressing the spacial extent.

3. Read and write Korean words and phrases involving the consonant ㄹ in order to understand the peculiar characteristics of the consonant in spelling and pronunciation.

Cultural Notes
Short Travels by Taxi

In densely populated areas such as downtown Seoul, getting around can be a problem. The best means of transportation for visitors is a taxi. However, unless you are familiar with local customs and conditions, even getting a taxi may prove to be a difficult task.

There are two kinds of taxis: the "call" taxi and the regular taxi. The "call" taxi is a medium-sized sedan. It usually cruises about the major hotels, or it may be available on call. (A number of tourist hotels operate their own taxis, which are available only to hotel guests.)

The regular taxi is of two kinds: a compact size and a medium size. Some of the medium-sized taxis are also called the "88 taxi"; however, it is not available on call. You can catch regular taxis at pre-designated taxi stands, or at any convenient stop in the street.

In Seoul and other major Korean cities, taxi stands are generally located near subway exits, major hotels, department stores, and other large buildings. A taxi stand is marked by the sign, which reads 택시.

When there are no designated taxi stands available, you need to catch taxis by shouting "Taxi!" or waving your hand. When the cab slows down or pulls over, you should approach it quickly because others may cut in.

For various reasons the cab drivers are often selective about the destinations. So you should ask the driver, before you get in, if he could go in the direction of your own destination.

During the rush hour, you may have to share a taxi with other passengers going in the same direction. This practice is called 합승 ("ride-together").

Tipping is not customary, but it is often done when the cab driver helps you with your baggage.

Communicative Exchanges

FRAME 1

Stating Your Destination after Getting in

At the taxi stand, Mr. Baker gets into a cab. Then follows a talk between him and the cab driver.

운전기사 : 어디까지 가세요?	How far are you going, sir?
베이커 : 용산¹ 갑시다.	Take me to Yongsan, please. (Literally, "Let's go to Yongsan.")
운전기사 : 네. 용산 어디까지 가세요?	Okay. Where in Yongsan are you going?
베이커 : 용산역 앞까지² 갑니다.	I'm going up to the front of Yongsan Station.
운전기사 : 네, 알겠습니다.	I see.

```
SUBSTITUTION
1. 종로               Chongno
   명동               Myŏng-dong
   영동               Yŏngdong
2. 이태원까지          up to Itaewon
   서울역 앞까지        up to the front of Seoul Station
```

FRAME 2

Stating Your Destination before Getting in

Mr. Baker hails a cab and gets in.

베이커 : 택시!	Taxi!

(The taxi pulls over.)

세종로[1] 가요?	Can you go to Sejongno?
운전기사 : 세종로 어디까지 가세요?	Where are you going on Sejongno?
베이커 : 미국 대사관 앞까지[2] 갑시다.	Take me to the front of the U.S. Embassy, please.
운전기사 : 네, 타세요.	Okay, get in, please.

SUBSTITUTION

1. 잠실	Chamshil
서대문	Sŏdaemun
김포 공항	Kimp'o Airport
2. 신라 호텔까지	up to Shilla Hotel
덕수궁 앞까지	up to the front of Tŏksugung Palace

FRAME 3

Telling the Driver Where to Get off

As the taxi approaches the destination, the driver asks Mr. Baker exactly where he wants to get off.

운전기사 :	손님, 여기가 용산입니다. 어디서 내리시지요?	Sir, we're in Yongsan now. Where would you like to get off?
베이커 :	앞으로 곧장¹ 가세요. 그리고 다음 네거리에서 내려주세요.	Go straight ahead, and let me off at the next intersection, please.
운전기사 :	네, 다음 네거리에 택시 정류장²이 있습니다. 거기서 내리세요.	Sure. There's a taxi stand off the next intersection. You can get off there.
베이커 :	좋습니다.	That's fine.

SUBSTITUTION	
1. 오른쪽으로	to the right
왼쪽으로	to the left
2. 버스 정류장	bus stop
전철 입구	subway entrance

FRAME 4

Getting out of the Taxi

The taxi slowly pulls over as it reaches Mr. Baker's destination.

베이커	: 조금만 더 가 주세요.	Could you go a little farther, please ?
운전기사	: 네, 그러지요.	Sure, I'll.
베이커	: 됐습니다. 여기 세워 주세요. 요금 얼맙니까?	Okay. Stop here, please. How much is the fare ?
운전기사	: 이천이백 원[1]입니다.	2,200 won, sir.
베이커	: 자, 여기 있습니다.	Here, Mr. !
운전기사	: 감사합니다.	Thank you.
베이커	: 수고하세요.	Good-bye. (Literally, "May you have good hard work!")

SUBSTITUTION	
1. 천칠백 원	1,700 won
삼천육백 원	3,600 won
사천이백 원	4,200 won

Grammar and Usage

1. How to Make a Proposition

You have already learned a verb form to make a suggestion with: STEM + (을)까요 ? which is generally equivalent to "Shall we...?"

저녁 식사 같이 하실까요 ?   <u>Shall we</u> have dinner together ?

There is another form very similar to the above, but a little more positive in making a proposition. For example, 저녁 식사 같이 합시다. "<u>Let's</u> have dinner together." We will call this the proposition form. The general formula for making a proposition form is as follows:

> It will be ㅂ시다, when the verb stem ends with a vowel.

덕수궁에 갑시다.   Let's go to Tŏksugung Palace.

> It will be 읍시다, when the verb stem ends with a consonant.

여기 앉읍시다.   Let's sit down here.

Like the suggestion form, the proposition form is often used with the honorific suffix to make it even more polite. For example,

커피 한잔 하십시다.   Let's have a cup of coffee.
내일 가십시다.   Let's go tomorrow.

There is another meaning to the proposition form, though somewhat limited in usage. In this usage, the "I" (speaker) makes his desire or intention known to one next to him.

그 책 좀 봅시다.   Let me take a look at the book. (or May I take a look at the book ?)

여기 좀 앉읍시다.   Let me sit down here for a moment. (or Allow me to sit down...)

> CAUTION : The proposition form is not used when you are speaking to either your senior or superior. In such cases, you should use STEM+ 을까요? rather than STEM+읍시다.

2. How to Express One's Intention with 겠

When the speaker states his own intention, the suffix 겠 is added to the verb stem.

이 책 읽겠어요.   I'm going to read this book.

Also when the speaker asks the listener of his/her intention, the suffix 겠 is added to the verb stem.

이 책 읽겠어요?   Are you going to read this book ?

When the speaker's listener is a person who deserves honorific treatment, the suffix 겠 is preceded by the honorific suffix 으시 or 시.(으시 is used when the verb stem ends with a consonant and 시 is used when the verb stem ends with a vowel.)

이 책 읽으시겠어요?   Would you like to read this book ?
지금 가시겠어요?   Would you like to go now ?

3. Suffix Denoting an Extent: 까지

In directing the taxi driver, the customer used (in Frames 1 and 2) 용산역 앞까지 ("up to") instead of 용산역 앞에 ("to").

In this case, the difference between 까지 and 에 is slight, but it is more common to use the former when one's directions involve a spacial extent. This suffix 까지 is also used in time expressions, but those may be translated differently in English.

다섯 시까지 기다렸습니다.   I waited <u>until</u> five o'clock.
두 시 반까지 오십시오.   Please come <u>by</u> two thirty.

Exercises

A. Short Exchanges: Listening and Speaking

This is a reinforced exercise in listening and speaking. Follow the steps given below as you work on each exercise question.

> Step 1. Cover the Han-gŭl portion, and repeat after the model voicing as you look at the English equivalent.
>
> Step 2. Now cover the English portion, and again repeat after the model voicing, making sure you pronounce each word and phrase correctly and you understand them fully.
>
> Step 3. Now cover the Han-gŭl text. As you look at the English equivalent, say the Korean version of it.
>
> Step 4. Keep the Han-gŭl text covered. Aided by the English text, carry on the exchange in Korean with your instructor or classmate.

1. 가세요?　　　　　　　　　Are you going?
   네, 가요.　　　　　　　　　Yes, I am going.

2. 누가 가요?　　　　　　　　Who is going?
   제가 가요.　　　　　　　　I am going.

3. 김 선생님 가세요?　　　　Is Mr. Kim going?
   안 가세요.　　　　　　　　He is not going.

4. 어디 가세요?　　　　　　　Where are you going?
   용산 가요.　　　　　　　　I am going to Yongsan.

5. 용산 갑시다.　　　　　　　Let's go to Yongsan.
   네, 갑시다.　　　　　　　　Yes, let's go.

6. 어디 가세요?　　　　　　　Where are you going?
   용산에 가요.　　　　　　　I am going to Yongsan.

7. 지금 가세요?　　　　　　　Are you going now?
   네, 지금 가요.　　　　　　Yes, I am going now.

8. 탈까요?　　　　　　　　　Shall I get in?
   네, 타세요.　　　　　　　　Yes, get in.

9. 어디까지 가십니까?   How far are you going?
　세종로까지 갑시다.   Let's go to Sejongno.
10. 세종로 어디까지 가세요?   Where in Sejongno are you going?
　미국 대사관 앞까지 갑니다.   Going to the front of the U.S. Embassy.
11. 내리시겠어요?   Would you like to get off?
　네, 내리겠어요.   Yes, I'd like to get off.
12. 어디서 내리시겠어요?   Where do you want to get off?
　다음 네거리에서 내려 주세요.   Let me off at the next intersection.
13. 전철 입구에서 내리시겠어요?   Would you like to get off at the subway entrance?
　네, 거기서 내려 주세요.   Yes, let me off there, please.
14. 조금만 더 가 주세요.   Could you go a little farther, please?
　네, 그러지요.   Sure, I'll.
15. 얼맙니까?   How much is it?
　천팔백 원입니다.   1,800 won.

B. What Do You Say?

Work with your instructor or classmate in the following series of role-playing.

1. Tell the taxi driver that you want to go to Myŏng-dong.
2. Tell the taxi driver to go to the front of the American Embassy.
3. A taxi comes to a stop. Ask the driver if he can go to Sejongno.
4. Tell the driver to let you off at the next intersection
5. Ask the driver what the fare is.
6. What do you say as you hand the fare to the driver?

C. Vocabulary Exercise

Follow the steps given below as you work on each exercise question.

Step 1. Cover the English portion on the right. Your instructor will read to you a key Korean word or phrase and then an exchange in Korean containing the same word or phrase.

Step 2. Try to understand what your instructor says. Uncover the English portion and see if your knowledge is correct.

Step 3. Now cover the Han-gŭl portion on the left, and say correctly the

Korean equivalent of the English exchange listed under the cue.

Step 4. Uncover the Han-gŭl portion and see if your answer is correct.

1. You hear : —읍시다   let's
   학교에 갑시다.   Let's go to school.
   여름에 부산 갑시다.   Let's go to Pusan in summer.
   Cue : Let's go home.
       Yes, let's go.

2. You hear : 타다   to take (a taxi); to get in (a car)
   택시 탈까요?   Shall we take a taxi?
   네, 탑시다.   OK, let's do.
   Cue : Let's go to Chosun Hotel.
       OK, then, let's take a taxi.

3. You hear : —까지   to (destination); up to
   어디까지 가십니까?   How far are you going? (Up to where
                                         are you going?)
   김포 공항까지 갑시다.   Let's go to the Kimp'o Airport.
   Cue : How far are you going?
       I'm going (up) to Shilla Hotel.

4. You hear : 곧장   straight (adv.)
   앞으로 곧장 가세요.   Go straight ahead.
   뒤로 곧장!   Straight back!
   Cue : Can I go straight ahead here?
       Yes, you can (go straight ahead).

5. You hear : 내리다   to get off (from a car)
   그분 언제 내렸어요?   When did he get off?
   지금 내리겠어요?   Would you like to get off now?
   Cue : Where would you like to get off?
       I want to get off in front of that hotel.

6. You hear : 내려 주다   to let someone off
   저기서 내려 주세요.   Let me off over there.
   미국 대사관 앞에서 내려 주세요.   Let me off in front of the American
                                         Embassy.

Cue : Would you like to get off here ?

No, let me off in front of that house.

7. You hear : 정류장　　　　　　　　　(taxi) stand; (bus) stop

버스 정류장이 가까이에 있어요 ?　Is there any bus stop nearby ?

저기가 택시 정류장입니까 ?　　　Is that a taxi stand over there ?

Cue : Let's meet at the taxi stand.

There's a coffee shop in front of the taxi stand.

8. You hear : 세워 주다　　　　　　　to stop (a car) for someone

여기서 세워 주세요.　　　　　　Please stop (your car) here.

저 건물 앞에서 세워 주세요.　　Please stop in front of that building.

Cue : Where would you like to get off ?

Please stop at the intersection over there.

D. Grammar Exercise

1. Respond affirmatively to the following questions, using the proposition form.

> *Example* : Question : 택시 탈까요 ?
> Respond : 택시 탑시다.

(a) 이리 앉을까요 ?　　　　　(f) 전철 탈까요 ?

(b) 책 읽을까요 ?　　　　　　(g) 여기서 내릴까요 ?

(c) 편지 쓸까요 ?　　　　　　(h) 잠깐 기다릴까요 ?

(d) 영어 배울까요 ?　　　　　(i) 점심 잡수실까요 ?

(e) 길 건너갈까요 ?　　　　　(j) 텔레비전 볼까요 ?

2. Respond affirmatively to the following questions, using the suffix 겠.

(a) 잠깐 기다리시겠어요 ?　　(f) 한국말 배우시겠어요 ?

(b) 집에 가시겠습니까 ?　　　(g) 오늘 일하시겠어요 ?

(c) 부산에 가시겠어요 ?　　　(h) 여기서 내리시겠어요 ?

(d) 신문 읽으시겠어요 ?　　　(i) 여기 계시겠어요 ?

(e) 길 건너가시겠어요 ?　　　(j) 커피 한잔 하시겠어요 ?

Reading and Writing

1. The peculiar case of the Korean ㄹ

The consonant ㄹ has peculiar characteristics in Korean. First of all, you must have noticed that ㄹ does not generally occur in the beginning of a word (except in loan words). There are also the following peculiarities:

(a) ㄹ is pronounced like "l" in English at the end of a syllable.

길	street	일	work
서울	Seoul	날	day
내일	tomorrow	겨울	winter

(b) ㄹ is pronounced like "r" when followed by a vowel (and is shifted to the next syllable).

Spelled		Pronounced	
길이	→	기리	street
서울에	→	서우레	to Seoul

(c) ㄹ changes to ㄴ in pronunciation when preceded by another consonant (other than another ㄹ or ㄴ).

Spelled		Pronounced	
세종로	→	세종노	Sejongno (street)
청량리	→	청냥니	Ch'ŏngnyangni (district)

(d) Combinations of ㄹ and ㄴ (ㄹ+ㄴ or ㄴ+ㄹ) are pronounced ㄹ+ㄹ.

Spelled		Pronounced	
연락	→	열락	contact
권리	→	궐리	right(s)

2. Read aloud the following phrases, paying attention to the pronunciation of

(a)	달이	moon (subject)	(d)	등록	registration
(b)	정리	arrangement	(e)	승리	victory
(c)	종로	(name of a street)	(f)	강릉	Kangnŭng

3. Read aloud the lines identified by the letters a, b, c, d and e, below.

Summary of Verb Forms

내리다 ("to get off")

타다 ("to get on")

STATEMENT		
Present		
	LONG	SHORT
HON	내리십니다	내리세요
PLN	내립니다	내려요

Past		
	LONG	SHORT
HON	내리셨습니다	내리셨어요
PLN	내렸습니다	내렸어요

QUESTION		
Present		
	LONG	SHORT
HON	내리십니까?	내리세요?
PLN	내립니까?	내려요?

Past		
	LONG	SHORT
HON	내리셨습니까?	내리셨어요?
PLN	내렸습니까?	내렸어요?

REQUEST		
	LONG	SHORT
HON	내리십시오	내리세요
PLN	(not introduced)	

SUGGESTION	
HON	내리실까요?
PLN	내릴까요?

STATEMENT		
Present		
	LONG	SHORT
HON	타십니다	타세요
PLN	탑니다	타요

Past		
	LONG	SHORT
HON	타셨습니다	타셨어요
PLN	탔습니다	탔어요

QUESTION		
Present		
	LONG	SHORT
HON	타십니까?	타세요?
PLN	탑니까?	타요?

Past		
	LONG	SHORT
HON	타셨습니까?	타셨어요?
PLN	탔습니까?	탔어요?

REQUEST		
	LONG	SHORT
HON	타십시오	타세요
PLN	(not introduced)	

SUGGESTION	
HON	타실까요?
PLN	탈까요?

Words and Phrases

갑시다.	Let's go.
건너가다	to cross (a street)
그러지요.	I'll do so.
길	street; road
내려 주다	to let someone off
내리다	to get off (from a car)
네거리	intersection
다음	next
세우다	to stop
손님	customer; passenger
알았습니다.	I understand.
앞까지	up to the front of
얼맙니까?	How much is it?
여기 있습니다.	Here you are.
오른쪽으로	to the right
왼쪽으로	to the left
요금	fare
원	won (Korean monetary unit)
입구	entrance
전철	subway
정류장	bus stop; taxi stand
타다	to get in (a car)
택시	taxi

Shopping

Lesson Objectives

1. Carry on a conversation with your friend or acquaintance to seek advice on shopping. Specifically you will:
   (a) Ask your friend where the best place to shop is.
   (b) Comment on the merchandise your friend has bought.
   (c) Ask your friend where that particular merchandise is sold.
   (d) Take the role of your friend and provide him/her with appropriate information on shopping, as needed.

2. Carry on a conversation with the salesperson as you shop in a store. Specifically you will:
   (a) Respond to the salesperson's greetings and his/her offer to help.
   (b) Ask for merchandise you are looking for and understand the salesperson's responses.
   (c) Ask for prices and understand the shopkeeper's responses.
   (d) Ask whether credit cards are accepted.
   (e) Converse with the salesperson on a variety of things related to buying.

3. Master the following grammatical features. Specifically you will correctly use:
   (a) The verb phrase 갔다 오다.
   (b) The short form of 입니다.
   (c) Different verb forms of the L verbs (stems ending with ㄹ).

4. Read and understand written Korean. Specifically you will:
   (a) Read Korean words and phrases involving the combinations of ㅎ and another consonant.

(b) Read familiar sentences in Han-gŭl and translate them into English.

(c) Answer questions in written Korean, using your comprehension of the reading material.

(d) Find the meaning of simple words, using a Korean-English dictionary.

Cultural Notes
Shopping in Korea

For foreigners visiting Korea, the most convenient shopping places are the gift shops near tourist hotels as well as foreigners' commissaries. There are also various specialty shops in tourist shopping centers or arcades where salespersons speak some English. However, prices in specialty stores may be slightly higher than in ordinary stores. Therefore, you may wish to shop at stores where ordinary Korean shoppers go. In such places it is to your advantage to speak a little Korean.

In most Korean cities, there are two kinds of shopping areas for natives: department stores and various independent stores located in downtown, and markets in various neighborhoods. The downtown shopping districts, such as Seoul's Myŏng-dong area, have fashionable department stores where prices are fixed, and shopping is generally no different from what one does in America except, of course, the language. In various neighborhood shopping areas and open markets, people often haggle prices. In this lesson, you will learn not how to haggle but the minimum essential expressions used in shopping.

Popular buys in Korea for foreign visitors include silk brocade, leather goods, clothing, brassware, lacquer ware, ceramic articles, traditional chests, jewelry of gold and semi-precious stones, and others.

Communicative Exchanges

FRAME 1

Seeking Advice on Shopping

Mr. Baker, who wishes to go shopping, seeks advice from Miss Kim, a new Korean acquaintance.

베이커 : 미스 김, 저는 오늘 쇼핑 좀 하겠습니다.	Miss Kim, I'd like to do shopping today.
김　　: 아, 그러세요?	Oh, is that right?
베이커 : 어느 상가가[1] 제일 좋아요?	Which shopping area is best?
김　　: 무엇을 사시겠어요?	What are you buying?
베이커 : 선물[2] 좀 사겠어요.	I'll buy some gift items.
김　　: 그럼, 아마 백화점이 제일 좋겠지요.	Then, maybe a department store would be best.

SUBSTITUTION
1. 상점이　　　　　　　store
   양복점이　　　　　　tailor's shop
   보석상이　　　　　　jewelry store
2. 구두　　　　　　　　shoes
   골동품　　　　　　　antique
   도자기　　　　　　　chinaware

FRAME 2

Getting an Idea about a Shopping Site

Mr. Baker meets with Miss Kim carrying a shopping bag. Mr. Baker is curious to know what she has bought.

베이커 : 미스 김, 어디 갔다 오세요?

Miss Kim, where have you been to?

김   : 옷 가게에요. 옷 좀 샀어요.

To the clothing store. I bought some clothes.

베이커 : 좀 보여 주세요. <u>참 좋아</u> <u>요!</u>[1] 이런 옷 어디서 <u>팔아</u> <u>요?</u>[2]

Please show me those. Oh, very nice! Where do they sell this kind of clothes?

김   : 저기 파출소가 보이지요? 그 바로 옆에 옷 가게가 있어요.

You see a police box over there? Right next to it is a clothing store.

SUBSTITUTION

1. 참 예뻐요!

   참 멋있어요!

   참 싸요!

2. 구할 수 있어요?

Oh, very pretty!

Oh, very elegant!; Oh, very stylish!

Oh, very cheap!; Oh very reasonable!

Can you get...?

FRAME 3

Asking for Merchandise

Mr. Baker enters a luggage store and a salesperson welcomes him.

점원	: 어서 오세요.	Please come right in.
	뭐 찾으십니까?	May I help you? (Literally, "What are you looking for?")
베이커	: <u>가방 있어요?</u>[1]	Do you have luggage?
점원	: 여행 가방이요?	Do you mean a suitcase?
베이커	: 네. 튼튼하고 <u>값이 좀 싼 것</u>[2] 있어요?	Yes. Do you have something sturdy and fairly inexpensive?
점원	: <u>있고말고요.</u>[3]	Of course, we do.

SUBSTITUTION

1. 가방 좀 보여 주세요.   Show me some luggage, please.
2. 너무 비싸지 않은 것   something not too expensive
   품질이 좋은 것   something good in quality
3. 물론 있지요.   Of course, we have.

FRAME 4

Asking Prices

Mr. Baker points at items and asks the prices in a necktie shop.

베이커 : 이 넥타이 얼마여요?   How much is this necktie?

점원   : 만 이천 원입니다.   12,000 won.

베이커 : 저 넥타이는 얼마여요?   How much is that tie?

점원   : 그건 이만 팔천 원입니다.   That's 28,000 won.

베이커 : 왜 그렇게 <u>비싸요</u>?[1]   Why is that so expensive?

점원   : 그건 외국산입니다. 한국산은   That's foreign-made. A Korean-
         좀 쌉니다. 품질은 거의 <u>같습</u>   made tie is less expensive. Their
         <u>니다</u>.[2]   qualities are almost the same.

베이커 : 한국산 주세요.   I'll take the Korean-made tie.

점원   : 네.   All right, sir.

SUBSTITUTION	
1. 싸요?	(Is it) cheap?
무거워요?	(Is it) heavy?
2. 마찬가집니다.	(It is) the same.
비슷합니다.	(It is) similar.

FRAME 5

Paying at the Store

Mr. Baker picks up several items and is now ready to pay.

베이커 : 전부 얼맙니까?   How much is it all together?

(The salesperson adds them up.)

점원   : 전부 십이만 오천삼백 원입니   125,300 won all together.
다.

베이커 : <u>미국 돈[1]</u> 받아요?   Do you accept American money?

점원   : 죄송합니다만 미국 돈은 안   I'm sorry, but we don't accept Amer-
받습니다. 크레디트 카드는   ican money. We do accept credit
받습니다.   cards.

(Baker looks in his purse.)

베이커 : 아, 한국 돈 있어요. <u>현금으</u>   Oh, I do have Korean money. I'll pay
<u>로[2]</u> 내겠어요.   in cash.

점원   : 네, 좋습니다.   That's fine.

SUBSTITUTION
1. 자기앞 수표   cashier's check
크레디트 카드   credit card
2. 수표로   in check

Grammar and Usage

1. To Have Been to a Place: 갔다 오다

In Korean, there is a special verb phrase construction available to express the notion of "having been to a place": 갔다 오다.

Literally, it means "to go to a place and come back from there," and the English equivalent is "to have been to..."

어디 갔다 오세요?	Where <u>have</u> you <u>been</u> (to)?
	("Where are you <u>coming</u> <u>back</u> <u>from</u>?")
학교에 갔다 옵니다.	I <u>have</u> <u>been</u> to school.

This phrase is used in the present-tense form as above when someone has just come back from a place. It may be used in the past-tense form (갔다 왔어요) if someone has been back for some time, as in:

아침에 백화점에 갔다 왔습니다. I have been to a department store in the morning.

2. Asking Someone to Agree

In English, a little tag question is added when the speaker asks if the listener would agree, as in:

It's a nice day, <u>isn't it?</u>
You know him, <u>don't you?</u>

In Korean, this is done by replacing the verb ending with 지요 (with a rising tone of voice).

서울에 가시지요?	You are going to Seoul, aren't you?
한국분이시지요?	You are a Korean, aren't you?
김 선생님 계시지요?	Mr. Kim is in, isn't he?

The suffix is also used with the past tense.

점심 잡수셨지요?	You ate your lunch, didn't you?

그분 서울에 갔지요 ?   He went to Seoul, didn't he ?

The 지요 ending may be used negatively, too; but note that the tag question in the English counterpart turns out in the affirmative form.

김 선생님 안 계시지요 ?   Mr. Kim is not in, is he ?

봉투가 없지요 ?   You don't have envelopes, do you ?

3. Short Form of —입니다

The short form of —입니다 is written—이어요 as expected, but in standard speech, it is normally pronounced —이에요, as in:

저분은 한국분이에요.   He is a Korean.

저것이 당신 책이에요 ?   Is that your book ?

거기가 고향이에요.   That's my hometown.

여가가 용산이에요 ?   Is this Yongsan ?

In this course, we will write this form as it is pronounced (i.e. —이에요). Sometimes, —이에요 is further shortened as —예요. However, it is necessary for you to know that the standard writing regards —이어요 to be "correct" and, therefore, it is spelled that way in many writings.

4. The L Verbs

You have learned two verbs whose stems end in ㄹ. These verbs drop the final consonant ㄹ from their stems when followed by some endings. For now, what you need to know is:

Drop ㄹ everywhere except before 어/아 or ㄷ, ㅈ, ㄱ.

Dictionary form	Drop ㄹ	Keep ㄹ
	압니다	알아요
알다 ("to know")	아십니다	알았습니다
	아세요 ?	알지요 ?
	팝니다	팔아요
팔다 ("to sell")	파십니다	팔았습니다
	파세요 ?	팔지요 ?

5. Expression of Visibility

The expression of visibility such as "I see a policeman there." or "Do you see a restaurant?" takes a unique construction, in which the thing being seen is the subject, as in:

NOUN $\begin{Bmatrix} 이 \\ 가 \end{Bmatrix}$ 보입니다.	NOUN is visible or I see NOUN.

파출소가 보입니까?	Do you see the police box?
안 보입니다.	I don't see it.
저기 택시가 보이지요?	You see a taxi there, don't you?
박 선생님이 안 보입니다.	I don't see Mr. Park.

Exercises

A. Short Exchanges: Listening and Speaking

This is a reinforced exercise in listening and speaking. Follow the steps given below as you work on each exercise question.

Step 1. Cover the Han-gŭl portion, and repeat after the model voicing as you look at the English equivalent.
Step 2. Now cover the English portion, and again repeat after the model voicing, making sure you pronounce each word and phrase correctly and you understand them fully.
Step 3. Now cover the Han-gŭl text. As you look at the English equivalent, say the Korean version of it.
Step 4. Keep the Han-gŭl text covered. Aided by the English text, carry on the exchange in Korean with your instructor or classmate.

1. 어디 갔다 오세요?   Where have you been to?
   백화점에요.   To the department store.
2. 뭐 샀어요?   What did you buy?
   구두 샀어요.   I bought shoes.
3. 좀 보여 주세요.   Please show me those.
   여기 있어요.   Here they are.
4. 팔아요?   Do they sell them?
   네, 팔아요.   Yes, they sell them.
5. 어디서 팔아요?   Where do they sell them?
   저기 구두 가게에서 팔아요.   At the shoe store over there.
6. 뭐 찾으세요?   What are you looking for?
   여름 모자 있어요?   Do you have summer hats?
7. 값이 싼 것 있어요?   Do you have something inexpensive?
   네, 있습니다.   Yes, we do.
8. 품질이 좋은 것 있어요?   Do you have something good in quality?
   있고말고요.   Of course, we do.

9. 어디 있어요?	Where is it?
여기 있어요.	It's here.
10. 가방 많이 있어요?	Do you have many suitcases?
네, 많이 있어요.	Yes, we have a lot (of them) here.
11. 이거 얼마입니까?	How much is this one?
칠천오백 원입니다.	7,500 won.
12. 저건 얼마입니까?	How much is that one?
그건 만 원입니다.	That one is 10,000 won.
13. 비싸요.	It's expensive.
그래요?	Is that right?
14. 왜 그렇게 비싸요?	Why is it so expensive?
외국산입니다.	It's foreign-made.
15. 한국산 있어요?	Do you have a Korean-made item?
네, 있습니다.	Yes, we do.

B. What Do You Say?

Work with your instructor or classmate in the following series of role-playing.

1. Ask your friend which shopping area is best.
2. Your friend asks what you intend to buy. Tell him/her you want to buy a few gift items.
3. You have seen the shoes that your friend bought. Ask where this/that kind of shoes are sold.
4. Ask the salesperson if the store carries suitcases.
5. Ask the salesperson if the store carries something fairly inexpensive.
6. Ask the salesperson why this/that merchandise is more expensive.
7. Tell the salesperson you would like to have a Korean-made item.
8. Ask the salesperson if the store accepts American money/credit card.
9. Tell the salesperson you want to pay in cash.
10. Assuming the role of the friend/salesperson, respond to the questions given above.

C. Vocabulary Exercise

Follow the steps given below as you work on each exercise question.

> Step 1. Cover the English portion on the right. Your instructor will read to you a key Korean word or phrase and then an exchange in Korean containing the same word or phrase.
>
> Step 2. Try to understand what your instructor says. Uncover the English portion and see if your knowledge is correct.
>
> Step 3. Now cover the Han-gŭl portion on the left, and say correctly the Korean equivalent of the English exchange listed under the cue.
>
> Step 4. Uncover the Han-gŭl portion and see if your answer is correct.

1. You hear : 도자기   chinaware
   이 도자기 얼맙니까?   How much is this chinaware ?
   이만 오천원입니다.   25,000 won.
   Cue : Do you have chinawares ?
          We have lots of them here.

2. You hear : 사다   to buy
   뭐 샀어요?   What did you buy ?
   구두 샀어요.   I bought a pair of shoes.
   Cue : Did you buy a necktie ?
          Yes, I bought one.

3. You hear : 찾다   to look for
   뭐 찾으십니까?   What are you looking for ?
   가방 찾습니다.   I am looking for a briefcase.
   Cue : What are you looking for ?
          I am looking for my credit card.

4. You hear : 주다   to give
   저거 둘 주세요.   Give me two of those.
   이거 친구에게 주세요.   Give this to your friend.
   Cue : Give me it.
          Give me two of those.

5. You hear : 모두   all; all together
   모두 얼맙니까?   How much is it all together ?
   모두 이천 원입니다.   2,000 won all together.

Cue : How much is it all together ?

2,000 won all together.

6. You hear : 갔다 오다   to have been to...

어디 갔다 오세요?   Where have you been to ?

상점에 갔다 와요.   I have been to the store.

Cue : Where have you been to ?

I have been to my house.

7. You hear : 많이 있다   there are many

상점이 어디 많이 있어요?   Where do they have many stores ?

종로에 많이 있어요.   There are many on Chongno Street.

Cue : Are there many ties ?

There are many ties.

8. You hear : 팔다   to sell

저 상점에서 뭐 팔아요?   What do they sell in that store ?

골동품 팝니다.   They sell antiques.

Cue : Do they sell clothes at that store ?

No, they don't sell clothes.

D. Grammar Exercise

1. Answer the following questions, using the English cues.

> *Example* : Question : 어디 갔다 오세요?   Where have you been to ?
> Cue : school
> Answer : 학교 갔다 와요.   I have been to school.

(a) department store   (e) Seoul

(b) coffee shop   (f) rest room

(c) tailor's shop   (g) restaurant

(d) jewelry store   (h) home

2. The verb phrase 갔다 오다 may also be used to express your intention. Answer the following questions, using the cues.

> *Example* : Question : 어디 가세요?   Where are you going ?
> Cue : home
> Answer : 집에 갔다 오겠어요.   I am going home, and will be back.

(a) Pusan   (e) department store

(b) restaurant   (f) store

(c) rest room   (g) Seoul Station

(d) school   (h) U.S. Embassy

3. Listen and repeat after each voicing, paying particular attention to different forms of the L verbs.

(a) The verb 알다 ("to know")

> ㄹ is retained when the ending begins 아/어 or the consonant ㄷ, ㅈ, or ㄱ.

알아요.	I know.
알았어요.	{ I know. I understand.
알았지요?	You got it, didn't you?
알지요?	You know, don't you?
알겠어요.	I understand. (idiomatic)

> Otherwise ㄹ is dropped.

압니까?	Do you know?
아십니까?	Do you know? (honorific)
아세요?	Do you know? (honorific)
아시지요?	You know, don't you? (honorific)
아셨어요?	Did you get it? (honorific)
아셨지요?	You got it, didn't you? (honorific)

(b) The verb 팔다 ("to sell")

> ㄹ is retained.

팔아요.	They sell it.
팔았어요.	I sold it.
팔았지요?	You sold it, didn't you?
팔지요?	They sell it, don't they?
팔겠어요.	I will sell it.
팔까요?	Shall we sell it?

ㄹ is dropped.

팝니다.	They sell it.
파십니다.	He sells it. (honorific)
파세요.	He sells it. (honorific)
파십시오.	Please sell it. (honorific)
파십시다.	Let's sell it. (honorific)
파셨어요.	He sold it. (honorific)
파시겠어요?	Would you like to sell it? (honorific)

4. Answer the following quesitons, using Long forms (non-honorific) only.

> *Example* : Question : 아세요?   Do you know it?
>   Answer : 압니다.   I know it.

(a) 아십니까?   (d) 파세요?

(b) 아셨습니까?   (e) 파셨어요?

(c) 아시지요?   (f) 파시겠어요?

5. Answer the following questions, using Short forms (non-honorific) only.

> *Example* : Question : 아세요?
>   Answer : 알아요.

(a) 아십니까?   (d) 파세요?

(b) 아셨습니까?   (e) 파셨어요?

(c) 아시지요?   (f) 파시겠어요?

Reading and Writing

1. Aspiration by ㅎ

As you know, there are four aspirated consonants in Korean represented by ㅊ, ㅋ, ㅌ, and ㅍ. There are, however, other cases where the same aspirated sounds are obtained through combinations of two consonants. If an unaspirated consonat (ㄱ, ㄷ, ㅅ, ㅂ or ㅈ) is preceded or followed by ㅎ, the consonant is aspirated. For example, the combination of ㅎ and ㄱ in 백화점 is pronounced like ㅋ:

Spelled		Pronounced
백화점	→	배콰점

Read aloud the following, paying particular attention to the aspirated consonants.

(a) 좋지요?	Isn't it nice?
(b) 무엇 해요?	What are you doing?
(c) 어떻게	how
(d) 급해요.	It's urgent.
(e) 시작합니다.	We'll start.
(f) 그렇게	in that way
(g) 낙하산	parachute
(h) 그렇지요?	Isn't that right?
(i) 국화	chrysanthemum

2. Read and translate the following into English.

한 선생은 오늘 명동에 갔다 왔다. 명동에는 백화점과 상점들이 많다. 한 백화점에 들어가서 그는 구두하고 국화를 좀 샀다.

3. Answer in written Korean the following questions in line with the contents of the reading material provided above.

(a) 한 선생이 어디 갔다 왔어요?

(b) 언제요?

(c) 명동에 무엇이 많이 있어요?

(d) 무엇을 샀어요?

(e) 모자도 샀어요?

4. Look up each of the following words in a Korean-English dictionary and write in English the first meaning you find.

(a) 바다   (d) 소리

(b) 나무   (e) 지리

(c) 가구

Summary of Verb Forms

팔다 ("to sell")

STATEMENT
Present

	LONG	SHORT
HON	파십니다	파세요
PLN	팝니다	팔아요

Past

	LONG	SHORT
HON	파셨습니다	파셨어요
PLN	팔았습니다	팔았어요

QUESTION
Present

	LONG	SHORT
HON	파십니까?	파세요?
PLN	팝니까?	팔아요?

Past

	LONG	SHORT
HON	파셨습니까?	파셨어요?
PLN	팔았습니까?	팔았어요?

REQUEST

	LONG	SHORT
HON	파십시오	파세요
PLN	(not introduced)	

SUGGESTION

HON	파실까요?
PLN	팔까요?

사다 ("to buy")

STATEMENT
Present

	LONG	SHORT
HON	사십니다	사세요
PLN	삽니다	사요

Past

	LONG	SHORT
HON	사셨습니다	사셨어요
PLN	샀습니다	샀어요

QUESTION
Present

	LONG	SHORT
HON	사십니까?	사세요?
PLN	삽니까?	사요?

Past

	LONG	SHORT
HON	사셨습니까?	사셨어요?
PLN	샀습니까?	샀어요?

REQUEST

	LONG	SHORT
HON	사십시오	사세요
PLN	(not introduced)	

SUGGESTION

HON	사실까요?
PLN	살까요?

찾다 ("to look for")

STATEMENT
Present

	LONG	SHORT
HON	찾으십니다	찾으세요
PLN	찾습니다	찾아요

Past

	LONG	SHORT
HON	찾으셨습니다	찾으셨어요
PLN	찾았습니다	찾았어요

QUESTION
Present

	LONG	SHORT
HON	찾으십니까?	찾으세요?
PLN	찾습니까?	찾아요?

Past

	LONG	SHORT
HON	찾으셨습니까?	찾으셨어요?
PLN	찾았습니까?	찾았어요?

REQUEST

	LONG	SHORT
HON	찾으십시오	찾으세요
PLN	(not introduced)	

SUGGESTION

HON	찾으실까요?
PLN	찾을까요?

갔다 오다 ("to have been to")

STATEMENT
Present

	LONG	SHORT
HON	갔다 오십니다	갔다 오세요
PLN	갔다 옵니다	갔다 와요

Past

	LONG	SHORT
HON	갔다 오셨습니다	갔다 오셨어요
PLN	갔다 옵니다	갔다 왔어요

QUESTION
Present

	LONG	SHORT
HON	갔다 오십니까?	갔다 오세요?
PLN	갔다 옵니까?	갔다 와요?

Past

	LONG	SHORT
HON	갔다 오셨습니까?	갔다 오셨어요?
PLN	갔다 왔습니까?	갔다 왔어요?

REQUEST

	LONG	SHORT
HON	갔다 오십시오	갔다 오세요
PLN	(not introduced)	

SUGGESTION

HON	갔다 오실까요?
PLN	갔다 올까요?

Words and Phrases

가게	store
가구	furniture
가방	bag; luggage; briefcase; suitcase
값이 싼	inexpensive
갔다 오다	to have been to...
골동품	antique
구두	shoes
구하다	to get
급하다	to be urgent
나무	tree
낙하산	parachute
내다	to pay
도자기	chinaware
돈	money
둘	two
마찬가지이다	(It is) the same
멋있다	to be elegant, stylish
모두	all together
모자	hat; cap
무거운	heavy
바다	sea
받다	to accept
백화점	department store
보석상	jewelry store
보여 주다	to show
비슷하다	to be similar
비싸다	to be expensive
사다	to buy
상가	shopping area
상점	store
소리	sound

쇼핑	shopping
수표로	in check
시작하다	to start
싸다	to be cheap
아마	maybe
알다	to know
양복점	tailor's shop
어서 오세요.	Please come right in.
옆에	next to
예쁘다	to be pretty; charming
옷	clothes (generic)
외국산	foreign-made
있고말고요.	Of course; It's available.
자기앞 수표	cashier's check
저	that
전부	all together
제일 좋다	to be best
주다	to give
지리	geography
찾다	to look for
크레디트 카드	credit card
튼튼한	sturdy
팔다	to sell
품질	quality
한국산	Korean-made
현금으로	in cash

Social Talk

Lesson Objectives

1. Carry on a short conversation typically occurring among friends in a social gathering. Specifically you will:
   (a) Apologize for being late or respond to such an apology.
   (b) Greet an acquaintance or friend, using common expressions.
   (c) Respond to common greetings with appropriate expressions.
   (d) Discuss matters of common interest such as traffic congestion and quitting of cigarette smoking.

2. Understand fully some general rules about:
   (a) 그렇다, the form used in agreeing with the speaker.
   (b) Other verb forms whose stems end with ㅎ.
   (c) The noun suffix —도 that is used with the subject (or object) of a sentence.

3. Read and understand written Korean. Specifically you will:
   (a) Read Korean words and phrases involving the aspirated consonants.
   (b) Read familiar sentences in Han-gŭl and translate them into English.
   (c) Answer questions in written Korean, using your comprehension of the reading material.
   (d) Find the meaning of simple words, using a Korean-English dictionary.

Cultural Notes
The *Tabang* Culture

In cities, Koreans often use teahouses or tearooms for business or personal meetings. Called 다방, this establishment serves various non-alcoholic beverages—coffee, tea, ginseng tea, juices, soda drinks, and the like. (Unlike the coffee shop in the U.S., the *tabang* does not serve any snacks or foods.) People spend time in the *tabang,* drinking coffee (or other beverages), talking, or waiting as long as they want. Some tearooms have comfortable, sofa-like chairs—so comfortable that it's almost like being in the living room of your own home. Music is turned on all day long. These tea rooms are found almost everywhere in a city.

Communicative Exchanges

FRAME 1

Meeting at the *Tabang*

Mr. Baker and two of his Korean friends meet in a tearoom.

윤	: 베이커 선생, 늦어서 <u>미안합</u> <u>니다.</u>[1]	I'm sorry for being late, Mr. Baker.
베이커	: 괜찮아요.	It's okay.
윤	: 오래 기다리셨지요?	You've been waiting long, haven't you?
베이커	: 아니오, 나도 <u>조금 전에</u>[2] 왔어요. 교통이 꽤 혼잡하지요?	No, I got here just a while ago, too. The traffic is quite congested, isn't it?
윤	: 네, 정말 혼잡해요. 서울엔 차가 너무 많아요.	Oh, yes. It's really heavy. There're too many cars in Seoul.

SUBSTITUTION	
1. 죄송합니다.	I'm sorry. (a politer form)
2. 방금	just a moment ago
지금 막	just now

FRAME 2

Greeting Each Other

The minute they sit down, they exchange greetings.

윤 : 조 선생 아시지요, 베이커 선생?	Mr. Baker, you know Mr. Cho, don't you?
베이커 : 네, <u>얼마 전에 만나 뵈었어요.</u>[1]	I met him some time ago.
요즘 어떻게 지내셨어요?	How have you been lately?
조 : 네, 잘 지냈습니다.	Well, I've been fine.
어떻게 지내세요?	How are you getting on?
베이커 : 잘 지냅니다.	I am (doing) fine.
윤 : 우리 <u>차</u>[2]를 시킵시다.	Let's order some tea (or drinks).
베이커 선생, 뭘 드시겠어요?	Mr. Baker, what would you like to drink?
조 선생은 뭘 드시겠어요?	Mr. Cho, what would you like to have?
조 : 전 인삼차 하겠어요.	I'll have ginseng tea.
베이커 : 전 커피 하겠어요.	I'll have coffee.

SUBSTITUTION
1. 처음 뵙네요.   This is the first time I see him.
2. 마실 것   something to drink

FRAME 3

Offering/Declining a Cigarette

Mr. Yun offers his friends cigarettes, and it brings on something to talk about.

윤　：자, 담배 한대 피우시지요.　Well, please have a cigarette.

베이커：저 이젠 담배 안 피웁니다.　I don't smoke any more.

윤　：아, 그러세요? 언제 담배 끊　Oh, is that right? When did you quit
　　으셨어요?　smoking?

베이커：약 삼 개월 전에요.　About three months ago.

윤　：조 선생도 끊었어요?　Did you quit, too, Mr. Cho?

조　：저는 아직 담배를 끊지 않았　I haven't quit smoking yet. I don't
　　어요. 요즘 <u>감기 들어서</u>[1] 안　smoke because I've got a cold these
　　피웁니다.　days.

베이커：그런 때 끊는 것이 제일 좋습　It's best to quit smoking at a time
　　니다.　like that.

SUBSTITUTION	
1. 건강이 안 좋아서	because of ill health
속이 안 좋아서	because of ill digestion

Grammar and Usage

1. How to Agree

There are two Korean verbs used to express one's agreeing to what has been said. They are 그렇다 ("to be so") and 그러다 ("to do so"). You have already seen either of these:

(1) 커피 한잔 하실까요?   Shall we have a cup of coffee?
     <u>그러세요.</u>   Let's do that.

(2) 저 담배 안 피웁니다.   I don't smoke.
     아, <u>그러세요?</u>   Oh, is that right?

The two verbs, with the 어요 ending, result in the same form in most cases; so their meanings are determined by the context:

그러세요?   Is that right? (stative verb)
그러세요.   Let's <u>do</u> that. (action verb)

그래요?   Is that right? (stative verb)
그래요.   He <u>does</u> so. (action verb)

However, when the long form ending —습니다 or —지요 is added, they have different forms.

<u>Stative verb</u>   <u>Action verb</u>
그렇습니다. That's right.   그럽니다. He does so.
그렇지요? Isn't that right?   그러지요? Does he do so?

2. The H Verbs

Among the verbs you have learned so far are two stative verbs whose stems end in ㅎ and are irregular in conjugation. They are 그렇다 ("to be so") and 어떻다 ("to be how"). They have three stem forms as follows:

ㅎ is retained before certain consonants.

그렇습니까?   Is that right?
어떻습니까?   How is it?

그렇지요?	Isn't that right?

> ㅎ is dropped before 시 or 세.

그러세요?	Is that right? (honorific)
그러십니까?	Is that right? (honorific)
어떠세요?	How are you? (honorific)
어떠십니까?	How are you? (honorific)

> ㅎ is dropped and the stem vowel changes to 애 vowel in short forms.

그래요?	Is that right?
어때요?	How is it? / What do you think of it?

However, the verb 좋다 ("to be good, fine"), which has only one syllable in the stem, is not irregular. It retains ㅎ in all cases.

좋습니다.	It's fine. (or It looks good.)
좋아요.	It's fine.
좋지요?	Good, isn't it?
좋으십니다.	It's fine. (or It looks fine.) (honorific)

3. "Also" as Noun Suffix

In Korean, 도 ("also") may be used as a noun suffix. When it is attached to a noun or noun phrase, any subject or object suffixes <u>must</u> be removed. Examine the following:

나는 조금 전에 왔어요. → 나도 조금 전에 왔어요. (Subject marker)
BUT NOT: 나는도 조금 전에 왔어요.

그는 한국말을 합니다. → 그는 한국말도 합니다. (Object marker)
BUT NOT: 그는 한국말을도 합니다.

Other times, 도 ("also") may be used along with an adverb or adverbial phrase. In that case, simply add 도 to the adverbial element.

다방이 <u>거기에</u> 있어요.   →   다방이 <u>거기에도</u> 있어요.
영화를 <u>아홉시에</u> 합니다.   →   영화를 <u>아홉시에도</u> 합니다.

Exercises

A. Short Exchanges: Listening and Speaking

This is a reinforced exercise in listening and speaking. Follow the steps given below as you work on each exercise question.

> Step 1. Cover the Han-gŭl portion, and repeat after the model voicing as you look at the English equivalent.
>
> Step 2. Now cover the English portion, and again repeat after the model voicing, making sure you pronounce each word and phrase correctly and you understand them fully.
>
> Step 3. Now cover the Han-gŭl text. As you look at the English equivalent, say the Korean version of it.
>
> Step 4. Keep the Han-gŭl text covered. Aided by the English text, carry on the exchange in Korean with your instructor or classmate.

1. 늦어서 미안합니다.   I'm sorry for being late.
   괜찮아요.   It's okay.
2. 오래 기다렸어요?   Did you wait long?
   아뇨, 오래 안 기다렸어요.   No, I didn't wait long.
3. 언제 오셨어요?   When did you come?
   조금 전에 왔어요.   I came a little while ago.
4. 조 선생도 조금 전에 왔어요. Mr. Cho came a little while ago, too.
   아, 그래요?   Oh, is that right?
5. 교통이 꽤 복잡하지요?   The traffic is quite congested, isn't it?
   네, 정말 복잡해요.   Oh, yes. It's really congested.
6. 조 선생님 아시지요?   You know Mr. Cho, don't you?
   네, 전에 만나 뵈었어요.   Yes, I met him before.
7. 요즘 어떻게 지내셨어요?   How have you been lately?
   잘 지냈습니다.   I've been fine.
8. 선생님은 어떻게 지내세요?   How are you getting on?
   잘 지냅니다.   I'm doing fine.

9. 조 선생님 아십니까?   Do you know Mr. Cho ?
   네, 잘 압니다.   Yes, I know him well.
10. 차를 시킵시다.   Let's order some tea.
   저는 커피를 하겠습니다.   I'll have coffee.
11. 담배 피우세요 ?   Do you smoke ?
   네, 피웁니다.   Yes, I smoke.
12. 담배 피우시지요.   Please have a cigarette.
   저 담배 안 피웁니다.   I don't smoke.
13. 담배 언제 끊으셨어요 ?   When did you quit smoking ?
   약 일 년 전에요.   About a year ago.
14. 선생님도 담배를 끊으셨어요 ?   Did you quit smoking, too ?
   저는 아직 끊지 않았어요.   I haven't quit smoking yet.
15. 저는 요즘 감기 들었어요.   I've got a cold these days.
   그래서 담배 안 피웁니까 ?   Is that why you don't smoke ?

B. What Do You Say ?

Work with your instructor or classmate in the following series of role-playing.

1. Apologize to your friend for being late.
2. Tell your friend he/she must have been waiting for long.
3. Say that the traffic is quite congested.
4. You have been introduced to someone. Say that you met him/her some time ago.
5. Ask your friend or acquaintance how he/she has been lately.
6. Say that you would like to have ginseng tea.
7. Say that you don't smoke any more.
8. Say that you quit smoking three months ago.
9. Say that you don't smoke because you've got a cold.
10. Say that it's a good idea to quit smoking.

C. Vocabulary Exercise

Follow the steps given below as you work on each exercise question.

Step 1. Cover the English portion on the right. Your instructor will read to you a key Korean word or phrase and then an exchange in Korean containing the same word or phrase.

Step 2. Try to understand what your instructor says. Uncover the English portion and see if your knowledge is correct.

Step 3. Now cover the Han-gŭl portion on the left, and say correctly the Korean equivalent of the English exchange listed under the cue.

Step 4. Uncover the Han-gŭl portion and see if your answer is correct.

1. You hear : 늦어서   because (one/it) is late
   늦어서 미안합니다.   I'm sorry for being late.
   너무 늦어서 못 옵니다.   He can't come because it's too late.
   Cue : We can't do it because it is late.
          Let's do it tomorrow.

2. You hear : —도   also; too
   김 선생님도 오셨어요.   Mr. Kim came, too.
   저도 갑니다.   I am going, too.
   Cue : Mr. Kim, do you also know this person ?
          Yes, I know him, too.

3. You hear : 조금 전에   a little while ago
   조금 전에 갔어요.   He went a little while ago.
   조금 전에 여기 있었어요.   He was here a little while ago.
   Cue : When did you come ?
          I came a little while ago.

4. You hear : 만나 보다   to meet
   김 선생님 만나 뵈었어요?   Have you met Mr. Kim ?
   네, 얼마 전에 만나 뵈었어요.   Yes, I met him some time ago.
   Cue : Have you met that gentleman ?
          Yes, I've met him once.

5. You hear : 지내다   to get along; to fare
   어떻게 지내세요 ?   How are you getting along ?
   잘 지냅니다.   I am doing fine.

Cue : How is your wife doing ?
　　　She is doing fine.

6. You hear : 시키다　　　　　　　to order (food, drink)
　　마실 것 시켰어요?　　　　　Did you order something to drink ?
　　네, 지금 시키겠습니다.　　　Sure, I'm going to order now.
　　Cue : We can't order meals here.
　　　　　We can't order meals ?

7. You hear : 담배 피우다　　　　to smoke
　　담배 피우세요?　　　　　　Do you smoke ?
　　저 담배 안 피워요.　　　　 I don't smoke.
　　Cue : Please have a cigarette.
　　　　　I smoked just a moment ago.

8. You hear : 감기 들다　　　　　to catch cold
　　감기 들어서 아파요.　　　　I'm sick because I caught cold.
　　언제 감기 들었어요?　　　　When did you catch cold ?
　　Cue : He's ill today.
　　　　　Why ? Has he got a cold ?

D. Grammar Exercise

1. Write the long form (with the ending 습니까) of the following three verbs
　그렇다, 어떻다 and 좋다, respectively.

　＿＿＿＿＿＿＿＿＿＿　　Is that right ?　　　　(honorific)

　＿＿＿＿＿＿＿＿＿＿　　How is everything ?　　(honorific)

　＿＿＿＿＿＿＿＿＿＿　　Is that OK ?　　　　　(honorific)

2. Write the short honorific form (with the ending —세요) of the same three
　verbs, respectively.

　＿＿＿＿＿＿＿＿＿＿　　Is that right ?　　　　(honorific)

　＿＿＿＿＿＿＿＿＿＿　　How is everything ?　　(honorific)

　＿＿＿＿＿＿＿＿＿＿　　Is that OK ?　　　　　(honorific)

3. Write the short non-honorific form (with the ending —어요) of the same
　three verbs, respectively.

_____	Is that right ?	(non-honorific)
_____	How is everything ?	(non-honorific)
_____	Is that OK ?	(non-honorific)

4. Respond to the following sentences, using the verb 그렇다 in both short and long forms.

   (a) 저는 영어 못합니다.　　　　　(d) 이거 아주 좋습니다.

   (b) 저는 담배 안 피웁니다.　　　　(e) 저분 미국에서 오셨어요.

   (c) 저는 한 선생님을 잘 알아요.　　(f) 고향이 뉴욕입니다.

5. Add the noun suffix 도 ("also") to the underlined word or phrase in each sentence.

> _Example_ : You read : <u>구두</u>를 샀어요.　I bought a pair of shoes.
> 　　　　　 You say　: <u>구두</u>도 샀어요.　I bought a pair of shoes also.

   (a) <u>가방</u>이 있어요?　　　　　(d) 그분 <u>한국말</u>을 하세요?

   (b) <u>모자</u>를 찾아요.　　　　　(e) 집에서 <u>텔레비전</u> 봐요.

   (c) <u>자동차</u> 많이 있어요.

Reading and Writing

1. Read aloud the following words, paying particular attention to the aspirated consonants.

   (a) 그렇게   (e) 어떻게
   (b) 무엇 합니까?   (f) 많이
   (c) 백화점   (g) 국화
   (d) 좋지요.   (h) 입학

2. Read aloud the following, paying particular attention to the varying sounds of ㄹ.

   (a) 연락을   (e) 달리
   (b) 훈련을   (f) 물이
   (c) 종로에서   (g) 정리가
   (d) 승리를   (h) 소리는

3. Read and translate the following into English.

   강 선생님이 윤 선생님 집에 갔다. 그런데 윤 선생님이 집에 없었다. 윤 선생님 부인은 집에 있었다. 강 선생님은 방에 앉아서 윤 선생님을 기다렸다.

4. Answer in written Korean the following questions in line with the contents of the reading material above.

   (a) 강 선생님이 어디 갔어요?   (d) 누가 누구를 기다렸어요?
   (b) 윤 선생님이 집에 있었어요?   (e) 어디서 기다렸어요?
   (c) 누가 집에 있었어요?

5. Look up each of the following words in a Korean-English dictionary and write in English the first meaning you find.

   (a) 지루하다   (d) 나누다
   (b) 버리다   (e) 머리
   (c) 아프다

Summary of Verb Forms

지내다 ("to fare")

STATEMENT
Present

	LONG	SHORT
HON	지내십니다	지내세요
PLN	지냅니다	지내요

Past

	LONG	SHORT
HON	지내셨습니다	지내셨어요
PLN	지냈습니다	지냈어요

QUESTION
Present

	LONG	SHORT
HON	지내십니까?	지내세요?
PLN	지냅니까?	지내요?

Past

	LONG	SHORT
HON	지내셨습니까?	지내셨어요?
PLN	지냈습니까?	지냈어요?

REQUEST

	LONG	SHORT
HON	지내십시오	지내세요
PLN	(not introduced)	

SUGGESTION

(not applicable)

담배 피우다 ("to smoke")

STATEMENT
Present

	LONG	SHORT
HON	피우십니다	피우세요
PLN	피웁니다	피워요

Past

	LONG	SHORT
HON	피우셨습니다	피우셨어요
PLN	피웠습니다	피웠어요

QUESTION
Present

	LONG	SHORT
HON	피우십니까?	피우세요?
PLN	피웁니까?	피워요?

Past

	LONG	SHORT
HON	피우셨습니까?	피우셨어요?
PLN	피웠습니까?	피웠어요?

REQUEST

	LONG	SHORT
HON	피우십시오	피우세요
PLN	(not introduced)	

SUGGESTION

HON	피우실까요?
PLN	피울까요?

Words and Phrases

감기 들다	to catch cold
교통	traffic
그러세요?	Is that right?
그런 때	at a time like that
끊다	to quit
너무	too
늦다	to be late
담배 피우다	to smoke
―대	piece (counter for cigarettes)
들다	to drink; to eat
마실것	something to drink
만나 보다	to meet
방금	just a moment ago
속이 안 좋다	to have ill digestion
시키다	to order (drinks, meals)
아프다	to be sick
오래	for long
요즘	lately
이젠 안 하다	not to do any more
입학	entrance into a school
―전에	ago
정말	really
조금 전에	a little while ago
지금 막	just now
차	car
혼잡하다	to be congested

Dining out

Lesson Objectives

1. Carry on a conversation with your friend about your eating out at a restaurant. Specifically you will:
   (a) Suggest that you and your friend eat out.
   (b) Discuss kinds of restaurants to eat at.

2. Carry on communication in the restaurant. Specifically you will:
   (a) Respond to the waiter's (or waitress's) questions.
   (b) Understand, or ask, directions to the table.
   (c) Discuss, with your companion, the food to be ordered.
   (d) Order the food for you and your companion.
   (e) Ask for an additional service; for instance, ask for more water.

3. Understand fully some general rules about:
   (a) The ending 지요 to express the speaker's intention.
   (b) The verb phrase 갖다 주다.

4. Read and understand written Korean. Specifically you will:
   (a) Read Korean words and phrases involving the vowel 의 and understand the characteristics of the vowel in spelling and pronunciation.
   (b) Read familiar sentences in Han-gŭl and translate them into English.
   (c) Answer questions in written Korean, using your comprehension of the reading material.
   (d) Complete Korean sentences by filling in appropriate words or phrases in Han-gŭl.

Cultural Notes
Korean Restaurants

Restaurants in Korea can be divided into four kinds in terms of the foods they serve: Korean, Chinese, Japanese, and Western. Food is served by a waiter or waitress in most eating places no matter whether you are having a full meal or just a snack. (In certain areas of Seoul such as Itaewon, Chongno and Yŏngdong, fast-food places are available, where you serve youself. In buffet restaurants of major tourist hotels, you serve yourself, too.)

Tipping is not customary in Korea, but you may tip a waiter or waitress if you wish. At establishments for American service personnel or foreign tourists, things work much the same way as in the States, and you are expected to tip.

Communicative Exchanges

FRAME 1

Going out to Lunch

Mr. Baker offers his Korean friends to go out to lunch.

베이커 : 점심 하러 나가실까요?	Shall we go out for lunch?
윤 : 네, <u>그러십시다.</u>[1]	Yes, let's do so.
베이커 : 어디가 좋을까요?	Where do you think is a good place?
조 : 글쎄요, 한일관이 어떨까요?	Well, how about Hanilgwan?
베이커 : 한일관 좋지요, <u>깨끗하고</u>[2] 음식이 맛있어요.	Hanilgwan is good. The place is clean, the food is tasty.
윤 : 그럼, 한일관 갑시다.	Then, let's go to Hanilgwan.

SUBSTITUTION
1. 좋은 생각입니다. That's a good idea.
2. 친절하고 (They're) friendly and...
   조용하고 (It's) quiet and...

FRAME 2

Being Seated at the Restaurant

The three men enter the Hanilgwan restaurant.

여종업원 : 어서 오세요.
　　　　몇 분이세요?

Please come right in.
How many people?

베이커　 : 세 사람이오.

Three people.

여종업원 : 이리 오세요. 여기 앉으세요.

Come this way. Please be seated here.

윤　　　 : 위층¹에도 자리가 있지요?

You have the dining space up-stairs, too, don't you?

여종업원 : 네, 있어요. 위층이 <u>더 조용해
　　　　요.</u>²

Yes, we do. It's quieter upstairs.

조　　　 : 위층에 올라갈까요?

Shall we go upstairs?

베이커　 : 그러십시다.

Let's do so.

SUBSTITUTION	
1. 삼 층	3rd floor
오 층	5th floor
2. 더 혼잡해요.	(It is) more crowded.
더 시원해요.	(It is) cooler.
더 따뜻해요.	(It is) warmer.

FRAME 3

Ordering Food

The waitress takes orders from Mr. Yun, Mr. Cho and Mr. Baker.

여종업원 : 뭐 하시겠어요?	What would you like to have?
베이커 : 글쎄요, 저는 <u>불고기백반</u>[1] 하지요.	Well, I'll have *pulgogi* & rice.
윤 : 저는 갈비 시키지요.	I'll order *kalbi*.
조 : 저는 냉면 하겠어요.	I'll have *naengmyŏn*.
여종업원 : 불고기백반 하나, 갈비 하나, 냉면 하나요. 음료수는요?	One *pulgogi* & rice, one *kalbi*, one *naengmyŏn*. Anything to drink?
베이커 : 맥주 좀 하실까요?	Shall we have some beer?
조 : 좋습니다.	That's fine.
여종업원 : 맥주 한 병이오. 감사합니다.	One bottle of beer. Thank you.

SUBSTITUTION
1. 비빔밥   *pibimpap* (mixed vegetables & meat on rice)
   만두국   *mandukuk* (Korean won-ton soup)
   설렁탕   *sŏllŏngt'ang* (beef & noodle soup with rice)
   갈비탕   *kalbit'ang* (beef ribs soup with rice)

FRAME 4

Asking for Additional Service

Mr. Baker calls the waitress for more water, Mr. Yun for more *kimch'i*.

베이커 : 여보세요, 아가씨[1]! 물[2] 좀 더 주세요.
Hello, young Miss! Give (us) some more water, please.

여종업원 : 네, 곧 갖다 드리지요.
Yes, sir. I'll bring it right away.

윤 : 아가씨! 김치도 좀 더 갖다 주세요.
Miss! Bring (us) some more *kimch'i*, too.

여종업원 : 네, 그러지요.
Sure, I'll.

조 : 김치 맛이 어떻습니까?
How does this *kimch'i* taste?

베이커 : 다른 식당 김치보다 더 맛이 있어요.
It tastes better than *kimch'i* in other restaurants.

SUBSTITUTION

1. 아주머니 — woman (middle-aged)
   아저씨 — man (middle-aged)
   젊은이 — young man
2. 밥 — (steamed) rice
   간장 — soy sauce

Grammar and Usage

1. How to State Your Intention with —지요

You already learned to state your intention by using —겠:

가시겠어요?	<u>Would</u> you <u>like to</u> go?
네, 가겠어요.	Yes, I <u>would</u>.

There is another verb form used frequently to express the speaker's intention: STEM＋지요.

제가 가지요.	I <u>will</u> go.
그거 시키지요.	I <u>would</u> order that.
곧 갖다 드리지요.	I'<u>ll bring</u> it over to you right away.

This means that the ending —지요 has two usages: one with a sharp rising intonation to ask the hearer to agree (Lesson 13), and one to state the speaker's intention with a statement intonation (either an even or falling tone).

2. Two Forms of the Verb "to Bring"

The Korean verb 갖다 주다 ("to bring") is a compound of two verbs and the last half 주다, as you notice, means "to give." In this case, the verb 주다 expresses doing a service for someone.

물 좀 갖다 주세요.	Please <u>bring</u> me some water.
그거 둘 주세요.	Please <u>give</u> me two of those.

> CAUTION: The verb 갖다 주다 ("to bring") may not be used for "bringing a person."

The verb 주다 has a unique characteristic of changing its stem entirely when you offer a service or something to someone to show your respect. In other words, the stem 주— changes to 드리— to show the speaker's respect to the recipient (but not to the subject).

이것 드리지요.	I'll give you this.

곧 갖다 드리지요.   I'll bring it (to you) right away.

To aid your memory in distinguishing the two forms, associate the form 주다 with simply "to give" and 드리다 with "to give respectfully."

There are three situations when this distinction plays important roles:

(1) Requesting a service for yourself (speaker)
주세요.   <u>Give</u> it to me.
갖다 주세요.   <u>Bring</u> it to me.

(2) Stating your service for the hearer
드리지요.   I'll <u>give</u> it (respectfully) to you.
갖다 드리지요.   I'll <u>bring</u> it (respectfully) to you.

(3) Doing a service for a third person respectfully
드리세요.   <u>Give</u> it (respectfully) to him.
갖다 드리세요.   <u>Bring</u> it (respectfully) to him.

3. Comparative Expressions

In English, adjectives often change their forms as in <u>good</u>—<u>better</u>, <u>bad</u>—<u>worse</u>, etc. In other adjectives you either add the suffix—er, as in <u>fast</u>—<u>faster</u>, or add <u>more</u> before an adjective, as in <u>more beautiful</u>.

In Korean, the comparative expressions are made uniformly by adding 더 ("more") before an adjective or adverb.

더 조용해요.   It's quieter.
더 쌉니다.   It's cheaper.
더 비쌉니다.   It's more expensive.

Exercises

A. Short Exchanges: Listening and Speaking

This is a reinforced exercise in listening and speaking. Follow the steps given below as you work on each exercise question.

Step 1. Cover the Han-gŭl portion, and repeat after the model voicing as you look at the English equivalent.

Step 2. Now cover the English portion, and again repeat after the model voicing, making sure you pronounce each word and phrase correctly and you understand them fully.

Step 3. Now cover the Han-gŭl text. As you look at the English equivalent, say the Korean version of it.

Step 4. Keep the Han-gŭl text covered. Aided by the English text, carry on the exchange in Korean with your instructor or classmate.

1. 점심 잡수셨어요? — Did you have lunch?
   네, 먹었습니다 — Yes, I did.

2. 점심 잡수실까요? — Shall we have lunch?
   네, 그러십시다. — Yes, let's do so.

3. 점심 하러 나가실까요? — Shall we go out for lunch?
   그러십시다. — Let's do so.

4. 어디 가실까요? — Where shall we go?
   한일관 어떻습니까? — How about Hanilgwan?

5. 한일관에 가실까요? — Shall we go to Hanilgwan?
   그러십시다. — Let's do so.

6. 어서 오세요. 몇 분입니까? — Please come right in. How many?
   두 사람이오. — Two.

7. 이리 오세요. — Please come this way.
   네. — Yes.

8. 위층에도 자리 있어요? — Do you have any (dining) space upstairs, too?

   네, 위층에도 있습니다. — Yes, we have the space upstairs, too.

9. 어디 앉을까요?   Where shall we sit ?
  여기 앉으세요.   Please be seated here.

10. 위층이 조용해요?   Is it quiet upstairs ?
  네, 더 조용해요.   Yes, it's quieter.

11. 뭐 하시겠어요?   What would you like to have ?
  불고기 하겠어요.   I will have *pulgogi*.

12. 맥주 좀 하실까요?   Shall we have some beer ?
  좋습니다.   That's fine.

13. 물 좀 더 갖다 주세요.   Please bring me some more water.
  네, 갖다 드리지요.   Yes, I'll bring it over to you.

14. 김치도 좀 더 갖다 주세요.   Please bring some more *kimch'i*, too.
  네, 그러지요.   Yes, I'll.

15. 김치 맛이 어떻습니까?   How does the *kimch'i* taste ?
  다른 식당의 김치보다 더   It tastes better than the *kimch'i* in other
  맛이 있어요.   restaurants.

B. What Do You Say ?

Work with your instructor or classmate in the following series of role-playing.

1. Suggest that you and your friend go to Hanilgwan.
2. Ask your friend what's a good place for lunch.
3. Agree to your friend's suggestion to do something.
4. Ask the waiter/waitress if it is quieter upstairs.
5. Say that you'd like to have *pulgogi* dinner.
6. Say that you'd like to order the same dish.
7. Order two *pulgogi* dinners.
8. Order two bottles of beer.
9. Ask the waitress for more water.
10. Ask your companion how the *kimch'i* tastes.

C. Vocabulary Exercise

Follow the steps given below as you work on each exercise question.

Step 1. Cover the English portion on the right. Your instructor will read to you a key Korean word or phrase and then an exchange in Korean containing the same word or phrase.

Step 2. Try to understand what your instructor says. Uncover the English portion and see if your knowledge is correct.

Step 3. Now cover the Han-gŭl portion on the left, and say correctly the Korean equivalent of the English exchange listed under the cue.

Step 4. Uncover the Han-gŭl portion and see if your answer is correct.

1. You hear : 나가실까요?   Shall we go out?
   지금 나가실까요?   Shall we go out now?
   조금 후에 나가실까요?   Shall we go out a little later?
   Cue : Shall we go out for dinner?
         That's a good idea.

2. You hear : 그러십시다.   Let's do so.
   점심 여기서 하실까요?   Shall we have lunch here?
   그러십시다.   Let's do so.
   Cue : Shall we sit here?
         Let's do so.

3. You hear : 더 조용해요.   It's quieter.
   위층이 조용해요?   Is it quiet upstairs?
   위층이 더 조용해요.   It's quieter upstairs.
   Cue : Is this restaurant quieter?
         Yes, it is.

4. You hear : 불고기   *pulgogi* (grilled beef)
   뭘 하실까요?   What would you like to have?
   불고기 주세요.   Give me *pulgogi*.
   Cue : Do you serve *pulgogi*?
         Yes, we do.

5. You hear : 아가씨   young lady
   아가씨, 오늘 불고기 있어요?   Hello, young Miss, do you have *pulgogi* today?
   아가씨, 여기가 명동입니까?   Young lady, is this Myŏng-dong?

Cue : Hello, Miss, bring me some *pulgogi*.

　　Miss, where's the rest room, please ?

6. You hear : 갖다 주세요. 　　　　　Please bring it to me.

그거 지금 갖다 주세요. 　　　　Please bring it to me now.

물 좀 갖다 주세요. 　　　　　　Please bring me some water.

Cue : Please bring us some tea.

　　I'm sorry we don't have tea today.

7. You hear : 갖다 드리지요. 　　　　I (We) will bring it to you.

간장 좀 더 갖다 주세요. 　　　　Please bring us some more soy sauce.

네, 곧 갖다 드리지요. 　　　　　Yes, I'll bring it right away.

Cue : Please bring us some more *kimch'i*.

　　Yes, I'll bring it right now.

8. You hear : 맛있어요. 　　　　　It's tasty.

김치 맛있어요 ? 　　　　　　　Is the *kimch'i* tasty ?

이 냉면이 더 맛있어요. 　　　　This *naengmyŏn* tastes better.

Cue : How is your *kalbit'ang* ?

　　It tastes good.

D. Grammar Exercise

1. Listen and repeat, paying particular attention to the falling intonation.

(a) 제가 하지요. 　　　　　　　I'll do it.

(b) 이거 하나 사지요. 　　　　　I'll buy one of these.

(c) 또 오지요. 　　　　　　　　I'll come again.

(d) 그러지요. 　　　　　　　　　I'll do that.

(e) 기다리지요. 　　　　　　　　I'll wait.

2. Respond to the following questions, using the ending ㅡ지요.

> *Example*: Question : 가세요 ? / 가시겠어요 ?
> 　　　　　Answer 　: 가지요.

(a) 집에 가세요 ? 　　　　　　　Are you going home ?

(b) 여기서 내리시겠어요 ? 　　　Are you going to get off here ?

(c) 불고기 잡수시겠어요 ? 　　　Would you like to have *pulgogi* ?

(d) 여기 앉으시겠어요 ? 　　　　Would you like to sit down here ?

(e) 기다리시겠어요?　　　　　　　　Would you like to wait?

3. Listen to the following requests and respond affirmatively:

> *Example*: Request　: 물 갖다 주십시오.
> 　　　　　 Response　: 네, 갖다 드리지요.

(a) 김치 갖다 주십시오.
(b) 불고기 갖다 주십시오.
(c) 계산서 갖다 주십시오.
(d) 담배 갖다 주십시오.
(e) 가방 갖다 주세요.

4. Using each of the cues listed below, make a polite request to bring something to you.
　　(a) water　(b) cigarette　(c) hat　(d) books　(e) coffee

5. Using each of the cues listed above, make a polite request (with 드리세요) to bring something to a third person.

Reading and Writing

1. The pronunciation of 의

   The vowel 의 is pronounced in several ways, depending on the environment.

   (a) In careful speech, 의 is pronounced as though the vowel 으 and 이 are pronounced fast in one breath. In the first syllable of a word, 으 is stronger than 이, as in:

의자	chair
의미	meaning
의사	physician

   However, in the second syllable, 이 is stronger and 으 is almost dropped, as in:

회의	conference
거의	almost

   (b) In fast speech, 의 is further reduced to a simple vowel. It is almost pronounced 으 in the first syllable of a word, and is almost pronounced 이 in the second syllable, as in:

Spelled		Pronounced
의자	→	으자
의미	→	으미
의사	→	으사
회의	→	회이
거의	→	거이

   (c) 의 is pronounced 에 when it is a possessive suffix.

Spelled		Pronounced
김 선생의 집	→	김 선생에 집
·23의 4892	→	23에 4892

   (d) Read aloud the following, paying particular attention to the pronunciation of 의.

(1) 회의
(2) 거의
(3) 의자
(4) 의미

(5) 논의
(6) 의복
(7) 27의 2314
(8) 박 선생의 자동차

2. Read and translate the following into English.

오늘 장 선생은 밖에서 점심을 먹었다. 장 선생은 한일관에 갔다. 박 선생도 한일관에 갔다. 한일관에서 두 분은 불고기와 냉면을 시켰다. 한 일관에는 사람들이 많이 있었다.

3. Answer in written Korean the following questions in line with the contents of the reading material above.

(a) 장 선생은 어디 갔어요?
(b) 박 선생은 어디 갔어요?
(c) 점심을 집에서 먹었어요?

(d) 한일관에서 무엇을 시켰습니까?
(e) 어디에 사람이 많이 있었어요?

4. Complete the sentences by filling in the blanks. Each Korean sentence should express the idea contained in the English sentence.

(a) 뭐 _____겠어요?
   What would you like to order?
(b) 어디 _____?
   Where do you think is a good place?
(c) 어디 _____?
   Where shall we sit?
(d) 맥주 좀 _____?
   Shall we have some beer?
(e) 김치 맛이 _____?
   How does the *kimch'i* taste?

5. Translate the following sentences into English, using a Korean-English dictionary.

(a) 점심 밖에서 잡수셨어요?

   _____

(b) 갈비탕이 더 맛이 있어요.

_____

(c) 만두국 둘 시켰습니다.

_____

(d) 간장 좀 갖다 주세요.

_____

(e) 삼 층에도 자리가 있지요?

_____

Summary of Verb Forms

시키다 ("to order")

STATEMENT

Present

	LONG	SHORT
HON	시키십니다	시키세요
PLN	시킵니다	시켜요

Past

	LONG	SHORT
HON	시키셨습니다	시키셨어요
PLN	시켰습니다	시켰어요

QUESTION

Present

	LONG	SHORT
HON	시키십니까?	시키세요?
PLN	시킵니까?	시켜요?

Past

	LONG	SHORT
HON	시키셨습니까?	시키셨어요?
PLN	시켰습니까?	시켰어요?

REQUEST

	LONG	SHORT
HON	시키십시오	시키세요
PLN	(not introduced)	

SUGGESTION

HON	시키실까요?
PLN	시킬까요?

PROPOSITION

HON	시키십시다
PLN	시킵시다

주다 ("to give")

STATEMENT

Present

	LONG	SHORT
HON	주십니다	주세요
PLN	줍니다	주어요(줘요)

Past

	LONG	SHORT
HON	주셨습니다	주셨어요
PLN	주었습니다	주었어요

QUESTION

Present

	LONG	SHORT
HON	주십니까?	주세요?
PLN	줍니까?	주어요(줘요)?

Past

	LONG	SHORT
HON	주셨습니까?	주셨어요?
PLN	주었습니까?	주었어요?

REQUEST

	LONG	SHORT
HON	주십시오	주세요
PLN	(not introduced)	

SUGGESTION

HON	주실까요?
PLN	줄까요?

PROPOSITION

HON	주십시다
PLN	줍시다

Words and Phrases

간장	soy sauce
갖다 드리지요.	I'll bring it to you. (honorific)
거의	almost
계산서	check; bill
곧	right away
그러십시다.	Let's do so.
김치	*kimch'i*
깨끗하다	to be clean
나가실까요?	Shall we go out?
다른	other
따뜻하다	to be warm
물	water
밖에서	outside
밥	(steamed) rice
시원하다	to be cool
아가씨	Miss; young lady
아저씨	man (middle-aged)
아주머니	woman (middle-aged)
어떨까요?	How would be ...?; How about...?
여보세요	hello
여종업원	waitress
위층	upstairs
의미	meaning
의사	physician
젊은이	young man
점심 하러	(in order) to have lunch
조용하다	to be quiet
친절하다	to be friendly
회의	conference

Talking about the Time of Events

Lesson Objectives

1. Carry on a conversation with your friend or acquaintance concerning the time of various events. Specifically you will:
   (a) Ask your friend what time it is.
   (b) Ask your friend what time a particular event will start and when it will be over.
   (c) Ask your friend what time he/she leaves his/her office for the day.
   (d) Ask your friend if he/she works on weekends, too.
   (e) Respond properly to each of the questions listed above, as needed.

2. Understand fully some general rules about:
   (a) The adjective expressing a great quantity.
   (b) Noun phrases expressing the duration of an action, with or without a suffix.
   (c) The three noun suffixes (-만, -도, -는) expressing the notions of "only," "also," and "at least."

3. Read and understand written Korean. Specifically you will:
   (a) Read Korean words and phrases involving nasal sounds and understand the characteristics of the nasalization in Korean.
   (b) Read familiar sentences in Han-gŭl and translate them into English.
   (c) Answer questions in written Korean, using your comprehension of the reading material.
   (d) Complete Korean sentences by filling in appropriate words or phrases in Han-gŭl.

Cultural Notes
Days of Work and Rest

Koreans work five and a half days a week—Monday through Friday and a half day (morning hours) Saturday. Downtown Seoul is, therefore, most crowded Saturday afternoons because people who leave their offices and people who go out for shopping are all out in streets at the same time.

The number of work hours is "officially" the same as in America, but the general work habit of both white-collar and blue-collar workers is to put in one or two hours more than the "official" eight hours. For that reason, the evening rush hours are extended more than in America: five to eight p.m., rather than five to six.

The holidays are, of course, different from those in the U.S. The followings are some of the most important ones in Korea:

New Year's Day
(January 1)

Lunar New Year's Day
(January 1 on the lunar calendar)

Independence Movement Day
(March 1)

Arbor Day
(April 5)

Buddha's Birthday
(April 8 on the lunar calendar)

Children's Day
(May 5)

Memorial Day
(June 6)

Constitution Day
(July 17)

Independence Day
(August 15)

Harvest Moon Day
(August 15 on the lunar calendar)

Armed Forces Day
(October 1)

National Foundation Day
(October 3)

Han-gŭl Day
(October 9)

Christmas
(December 25)

Communicative Exchanges

FRAME 1

Asking What Time It Is

Mr. Baker wants to know what time the meeting begins.

베이커 : <u>회의</u>[1] 몇 시부터 시작합니까?   What time does the meeting begin ?

윤   : 아홉 시 반부터 시작해요.   It begins at 9 : 30.

베이커 : 지금 몇 십니까?   What time is it now ?

윤   : 여덟 시 이십오 분입니다.   It's twenty-five minutes after eight.

베이커 : 그럼, 약 <u>한 시간</u>[2] 더 있군요.   Then, we have about an hour to spare.

윤   : 네, 시간 많아요.   Yes, we have plenty of time.

SUBSTITUTION	
1. 영화	movies
훈련	training
음악회	concert
2. 한 시간 반	one hour and a half

FRAME 2

Asking What Time One Gets off

Mr. Baker and Mr. Yun talk about the time they each go home from work.

베이커 :	윤 선생, 보통 몇 시에 <u>퇴근</u> 하세요 ?[1]	Mr. Yun, what time do you usually leave your office ?
윤 :	보통 여섯 시 반에 합니다.	Usually at 6 : 30.
베이커 :	왜 그렇게 늦게 합니까 ?	Why so late ?
윤 :	우리 사무실은 오후에 <u>할 일</u>[2] 이 많아요. 베이커 선생은 몇 시에 퇴근하세요 ?	In our office we get a lot of work to do in the afternoon. What time do you go home from work, Mr. Baker ?
베이커 :	우리는 다섯 시 반에 일이 끝 납니다.	Our work is over at 5 : 30.

```
SUBSTITUTION
1.  출근하세요 ?            Do you go (come) to the office ?
    일어나세요 ?            Do you get out of bed ?
    주무세요 ?             Do you go to bed ? (honorific)
2.  남은 일               leftover work
    잡무                 odds and ends to do
```

FRAME 3

Asking about Work Hours

Mr. Baker comes across Mr. Yun, who is going to work on Saturday morning.

베이커 : 윤 선생, 이렇게 일찍 어디 가세요? / Mr. Yun, where are you going this early?

윤　　: 회사에 나갑니다. / Going to work.

베이커 : 토요일에¹도 일하세요? / Do you work on Saturdays, too?

윤　　: 네, 오전에²만 일합니다. / Yes. Only in the morning

베이커 : 몇 시간 근무하세요? / How many hours do you work?

윤　　: 네 시간 합니다. / Four hours.

베이커 : 일 너무 많이 하지 마세요. / Don't work too hard.

윤　　: 네. 또 뵙시다. / Sure. See you again.

SUBSTITUTION	
1. 일요일에	on Sundays
2. 저녁에	in the evening
오후에	in the afternoon
낮에	in the daytime

Grammar and Usage

1. An Adjective Expressing a Great Quantity: 많다

Earlier, you learned an adverb 많이 expressing a great quantity of things or persons. (Note here that many of Korean adverbs are best translated as adjectives in English.)

구두가 <u>많이</u> 있습니다.	There are <u>many</u> shoes.
학생이 <u>많이</u> 있어요.	There are <u>many</u> students.

In this lesson, you will learn an adjective which also expresses a great quantity. A Korean adjective frequently placed, like a Korean verb, at the end of a sentence. For example,

시간 <u>많아요</u>.	We have <u>a lot of</u> time.
사람이 <u>많습니다</u>.	There are <u>many</u> people.

Obviously the two expressions 많이 and 많다 are closely related. The adverb 많이 is actually derived from the adjective 많다.

2. The Duration Suffix: —을

The duration of time taken in doing something is often marked by —을 in Korean.

몇 시간을 일합니까?	How many hours do you work?
여덟 시간을 일해요.	I work eight hours.

However, as in the case of object marking, the use of —을 is normally restricted to an emphatic expression. Usually, the expression of duration takes no suffix at all, as in:

몇 시간 공부했어요?	How many hours did you study?
두 시간 공부했어요.	I studied two hours.

You need not use a duration suffix (—을) in conversation, but it is important to know that others may sometimes use that form. So make sure that you are able to recognize it.

3. "Only," "Also," and "At Least": —만/—도/—은/는

The parts of speech (such as noun and verb) in English do not always coincide with Korean parts of speech. Expressions such as "only," "also," "at least" are adverbials in English, but in Korean they are noun suffixes.

한국말만 배웁니다.	I am learning <u>only</u> Korean.
한국말도 배웁니다.	I am learning Korean <u>also.</u>
한국말은 배웁니다.	I am learning Korean <u>at least.</u>

There are two points that you must know about these suffixes:

> When they are attached to the SUBJECT or the OBJECT of a sentence, each is attached directly to the noun or noun phrase. In other words, the subject or the object-marking suffix must not be used.

부인도 안녕하세요 ?   BUT NOT   부인<u>이</u>도...
   (부인 as subject)

불고기만 주세요.   BUT NOT   불고기<u>를</u>만...
   (불고기 as object)

> When they are attached to phrases other than the subject or the object, both the role-marking suffix and —만/—도/—는 are used.

학교에서만 공부합니다.	He studies <u>only</u> at school.
일요일에도 일 해요 ?	Do you work <u>on</u> Sundays <u>also</u> ?
두 시까지는 끝나요.	It will be done <u>at</u> <u>least</u> <u>by</u> two.

Note the relative position of the two suffixes. The suffix marking the role of the noun (—에서, —에, etc.) in that sentence always precedes —만/—도/—는.

It is also useful to remember that —이/가 and —을/를 are not critically needed in most sentences, and these are the same suffixes that should be omitted when —만/—도/—는 is attached.

4. How to Turn a Noun into a Verb with 하다

Earlier, you learned the verb 일하다 ("to work"), 근무하다 ("to be on duty"), 전화하다 ("to telephone"). Some (but not all) verbs are made up of a noun (denoting some action) and the verb 하다 ("to do"). In this lesson, you have 시작하다 ("to start, begin").

Noun					Verb	
일	work	+	하다	→	일하다	to work
근무	being on duty	+	하다	→	근무하다	to be on duty
전화	telephone	+	하다	→	전화하다	to telephone
시작	beginning	+	하다	→	시작하다	to begin

When you negate this type of verb, the prefix 안 is placed immediately before 하다, as shown below.

일 <u>안</u> 합니다.	I am not working.
오늘은 근무 <u>안</u> 해요.	I am not on duty today.
아직 시작 <u>안</u> 했어요.	We haven't started yet.

Exercises

A. Short Exchanges: Listening and Speaking

This is a reinforced exercise in listening and speaking. Follow the steps given below as you work on each exercise question.

Step 1. Cover the Han-gŭl portion, and repeat after the model voicing as you look at the English equivalent.

Step 2. Now cover the English portion, and again repeat after the model voicing, making sure you pronounce each word and phrase correctly and you understand them fully.

Step 3. Now cover the Han-gŭl text. As you look at the English equivalent, say the Korean version of it.

Step 4. Keep the Han-gŭl text covered. Aided by the English text, carry on the exchange in Korean with your instructor or classmate.

---

1. 영화 시작해요?   Do they start the movie?
   네, 시작해요.   Yes, they do.
2. 언제 시작해요?   When does it start?
   한 시에 시작해요.   It starts at one.
3. 회의 몇 시에 시작해요?   What time does the meeting begin?
   아홉 시부터 시작합니다. It begins at nine o'clock.
4. 지금 몇 십니까?   What time is it now?
   일곱 십니다.   It's seven.
5. 아직 시간 있어요?   Do we still have time?
   시간 많아요.   We have plenty of time.
6. 몇 시에 퇴근하세요?   What time do you leave your office?
   여섯 시 반에 합니다.   At six-thirty.
7. 몇 시에 일이 끝나요?   What time do you finish your work?
   일곱 시에 끝나요.   At seven.
8. 왜 그렇게 늦게 끝나요?   Why do you finish so late?
   할 일이 많아요.   We have lots of work to do.

9. 몇 시에 출근하세요?	What time do you go to work?
여덟 시 반에 해요.	At eight-thirty.
10. 몇 시에 일어나세요?	What time do you get up?
여섯 시에 일어나요.	I get up at six.
11. 토요일에 뭐 하세요?	What do you do on Saturdays?
토요일에 일해요.	I work on Saturdays.
12. 토요일에도 일하세요?	Do you work on Saturdays, too?
네, 그래요.	Yes, that's right.
13. 몇 시간 일하세요?	How many hours do you work?
네 시간 해요.	I work four hours.
14. 오후에 일하세요?	Do you work in the afternoon?
아뇨, 오전에만 해요.	No, I work only in the morning.
15. 오늘 몇 시간 근무하셨어요?	How many hours did you work today?
네 시간만 했어요.	I worked only four hours.

B. What Do You Say?

Work with your instructor or classmate in the following series of role-playing.

1. Ask your friend what time it is.
2. Ask your friend what time the meeting begins.
3. Respond properly to each of the questions given above, respectively.
4. Ask your friend what time he/she usually leaves his/her office.
5. Say that you get more work in your office in the afternoon.
6. Say that your work is over at 5 : 30.
7. Ask your friend if he/she works on Saturdays, too.
8. Say that you work only in the morning.

C. Vocabulary Exercise

Follow the steps given below as you work on each exercise question.

Step 1. Cover the English portion on the right. Your instructor will read to you a key Korean word or phrase and then an exchange in Korean containing the same word or phrase.

Step 2. Try to understand what your instructor says. Uncover the English portion and see if your knowledge is correct.

Step 3. Now cover the Han-gŭl portion on the left, and say correctly the
Korean equivalent of the English exchange listed under the cue.

Step 4. Uncover the Han-gŭl portion and see if your answer is correct.

1. You hear : 시작하다   to start
    몇 시부터 시작해요?   What time does it start ?
    두 시부터 시작해요.   It starts at two.
    Cue : What time does the concert start ?
          It starts at seven.

2. You hear : 퇴근하다   to leave one's office
    몇 시에 퇴근하세요?   What time do you leave your office ?
    오늘 늦게 합니다.   I finish work late today.
    Cue : Is Mr. Kim in ?
          No, he has left his office for the day.

3. You hear : 보통   usually; generally
    보통 몇 시에 일어나세요?   What time do you usually get up ?
    보통 여섯 시 반에 일어나요.   Usually at 6 : 30.
    Cue : What time do you usually go to bed ?
          Usually at eleven.

4. You hear : 늦게까지   until late
    늦게까지 일하세요?   Do you work until late ?
    네, 오늘은 늦게까지 일해요.   Yes, I work until late today.
    Cue : Where is he now ?
          He's working until late.

5. You hear : 끝나다   to end; to be over; to finish
    일 언제 끝나요?   When will your work be over ?
    내일 끝나요.   It will be over by tomorrow.
    Cue : What time will the meeting be over ?
          It will be over at three o'clock.

6. You hear : 할 일   work to do
    할 일 많아요?   Do you have a lot of work to do ?
    할 일 없어요.   I don't have any work to do.
    Cue : What are you going to do this weekend ?
          I have a lot of work to do during the weekend.

7. You hear : —만   only

    누구 누구 갑니까 ?   Who (and who) are going ?

    저만 갑니다.   Only I am going.

    Cue : Do we do it only today ?

            No, we do it tomorrow, too.

8. You hear : 근무하다   to work; to be on duty

    몇 시간 근무하세요 ?   How many hours do you work ?

    여덟 시간 근무해요.   I work eight hours.

    Cue : Do you work on Saturdays, too ?

            No, I don't.

D. Grammar Exercise

1. Respond affirmatively to the following questions.

    (a) 사람 많습니까 ?   (d) 할 일 많아요 ?

    (b) 시간 많습니까 ?   (e) 남은 일 많아요 ?

    (c) 좋은 영화 많습니까 ?

2. Respond to the following sentences by asking questions on quantity.

    > *Example* : You hear : 상점이 있어요.
    >
    >   You say : 상점이 많아요 ?

    (a) 택시가 있습니다.   (d) 커피 있어요.

    (b) 양복점이 있습니다.   (e) 골동품 있어요.

    (c) 시간 있어요.

3. Respond to the following questions, using the cues. Do not use the suffix —을 in your answers.

	Cues
(a) 몇 시간 일합니까 ?	8 hours
(b) 몇 시간 있었어요 ?	2 hours and 30 minutes
(c) 몇 분 했습니까 ?	30 minutes
(d) 몇 시간 계셨어요 ?	5 hours
(e) 몇 시간 계시겠어요 ?	4 hours

4. Respond affirmatively, using the suffix —도 ("also").

> *Example* : You hear : 토요일에 근무하세요?
>
> You say : 토요일에도 근무해요.

(a) 아침에 회의 있어요?   (d) 집에서 공부하세요?
(b) 책을 사셨어요?   (e) 작년 봄에 오셨어요?
(c) 영어를 배우세요?

5. Respond affirmatively, using the suffix —만 ("only").
   (a) 한국말을 배웁니까?   (d) 설탕을 갖다 드릴까요?
   (b) 오전에 일하세요?   (e) 집에 있어요?
   (c) 불고기를 시킬까요?

6. Respond affirmatively, using the suffix —은/는 ("at least"). The meaning of —은/는 in the sentences below is somewhat vague and it varies, depending on the context. The English equivalent, "at least," is given only to show the implied meaning.
   (a) 다섯 시에 끝나요?   (d) 오후에 시작합니까?
   (b) 시간이 많아요?   (e) 월요일에 옵니까?
   (c) 가방을 샀어요?

7. Respond negatively, using the suffix — 은 / 는. In the following cases, —은/는 has no English translation, but this usage (in negative sentences) is one of the most common of the suffix.

> *Example* : You hear : 오전에 근무하세요?
>
> Do you work in the morning?
>
> You say : 오전에는 근무 안 합니다.
>
> I don't work in the morning.
>
> Implying : At least not in the morning, but I work at other times.

(a) 영어 합니까?   (d) 돈이 많습니까?
(b) 김치 잡수세요?   (e) 자동차가 있어요?
(c) 모자를 사셨어요?

Reading and Writing

1. Nasalization

You have previously learned that 합니다 is pronounced 함니다. In this lesson, you have learned that 끝납니다 ("to end") is pronounced 끈남니다. This kind of sound change (ㅂ → ㅁ, ㅌ → ㄴ) is called "nasalization." The nasalization refers to a sound change occurring between certain combinations of two consonants.

The nasalization rule may be summarized as follows:

(a)	ㅂ, ㅍ —change to ㅁ	
(b)	ㄷ, ㅌ ㅈ, ㅊ }—change to ㄴ ㅅ, ㅆ	when followed by ㄴ or ㅁ.
(c)	ㄱ, ㅋ, ㄲ —change to ㅇ	

For example,

Spelled		Pronounced
주무십니다	→	주무심니다
있나	→	인나
끝나다	→	끈나다

Read aloud the following words, paying special attention to the nasalized consonants.

(a) 끝나다   (f) 학문
(b) 한국말   (g) 입니다
(c) 갑니다   (h) 중국말
(d) 있나   (i) 받는다
(e) 잊는다   (j) 깎는다

2. Read and translate the following into English.

내일은 토요일이다. 김 선생은 토요일에도 일한다. 오전에만 일한다. 일은 오전 여덟 시에 시작하고 열두 시에 끝난다.

3. Answer in written Korean the following questions in line with the contents of the reading material provided above.

(a) 오늘이 토요일이에요, 내일이 토요일이에요?

(b) 김 선생은 토요일에도 일해요?

(c) 몇 시간 일해요?

(d) 토요일에 몇 시까지 일해요?

(e) 오전 몇 시에 일을 시작해요?

4. Complete the sentences by filling in the blanks. Each Korean sentence should express the idea contained in the English sentence.

(a) 나는 _____에 집_____ 일해요.
    I work at home on Saturdays.

(b) 나는 돈이 _____ 있어요.
    I have a lot of money.

(c) 그것은 _____에 _____습니다.
    It was finished in the morning.

(d) 시간 _____지요?
    We have a lot of time, don't we?

(e) ____ 시에 회의가 _____합니까?
    What time does the meeting start?

5. Translate the following sentences into English, using a Korean-English dictionary.

(a) 보내셨어요?   _____

(b) 약속이 있어요.   _____

(c) 학교 다녀요.   _____

(d) 역에 갔다 왔어요.   _____

(e) 물 좀 갖다 주세요.   _____

Summary of Verb Forms

끝나다 ("to be over")

STATEMENT					
	Present			**Past**	
	LONG	SHORT		LONG	SHORT
HON	(not applicable)			(not applicable)	
PLN	끝납니다	끝나요		끝났습니다	끝났어요

QUESTION					
	Present			**Past**	
	LONG	SHORT		LONG	SHORT
HON	(not applicable)			(not applicable)	
PLN	끝납니까?	끝나요?		끝났습니까?	끝났어요?

REQUEST
(not applicable)

SUGGESTION
(not applicable)

Not: 1. 끝나다 is not used with human subjects; therefore, honorific forms are not applicable.

2. All the other verbs with ─ 하다 in this lesson conjugate like 하다 ("to do")

Words and Phrases

골동품	antique
근무하다	to be on duty
낮	daytime
늦게까지	until late
—만	only
—부터	from
오전	a.m.
오후	p.m.
—을	duration-marking suffix
일	work
일어나다	to get out of bed
일요일	Sunday
일찍	early
잊다	to forget
잡무	odds and ends to do
전화	telephone
주무시다	to go to bed (honorific)
중국말	Chinese
출근하다	to go to work
토요일	Saturday
퇴근하다	to leave one's office
학문	learning
훈련	training

Talking about One's Family

Lesson Objectives

1. Initiate a conversation about someone's family. Specifically you will:
   (a) Ask your friend if he/she is married.
   (b) Ask if that person has children.
   (c) Ask whether the children are boys or girls and how old they are.
   (d) Respond properly to each of the questions listed above, as needed.

2. Talk about work activities of family members. Specifically you will:
   (a) Ask your friend what his/her spouse does.
   (b) Say what kind of occupation your spouse has.
   (c) Say your spouse teaches at school.

3. Understand fully some general rules about:
   (a) The past-tense suffix 었 expressing a state of being.
   (b) A "choice" question that requires one answer or another.
   (c) Some nouns in two different forms, the plain and the honorific.

4. Read and understand written Korean. Specifically you will:
   (a) Read Korean words and phrases involving nasal sounds and understand the characteristics of the nasalization in Korean.
   (b) Read familiar sentences in Han-gŭl and translate them into English.
   (c) Answer questions in written Korean, using your comprehension of the reading material.
   (d) Complete Korean sentences by filling in appropriate words and phrases in Han-gŭl.
   (e) Translate familiar Korean sentences into English, using a Korean-English dictionary.

Cultural Notes
The Korean Family

A Korean places great importance on the family just as an American does, but to a Korean the concept of "family" is broader.

When a Korean adult refers to his/her family, it does not only include his/her spouse and children, but also his/her parents, brothers and sisters, and even grandparents. It was not uncommon for these close relatives to live in the same household, though things are now gradually changing in the Korean family system.

This traditional aspect of family life in Korea naturally affects individual thoughts, behaviors, and preoccupations. In making an important decision, a typical Korean generally takes into serious consideration, the opinions of his/her senior members, particularly of the head of the household. When you socialize with a Korean you would naturally inquire about his/her family members. The honorific and plain forms must be carefully distinguished when you speak about someone else's family as well as your own.

Communicative Exchanges

FRAME 1

Talking about One's Famiiy

"Are you married ?" is a good expression to use to start talking about someone's family.

베이커 : 윤 선생, 결혼하셨어요 ?	Are you married, Mr. Yun ?
윤　　 : 그럼요. 아이들이 둘 있어요.	Oh, yes. I've two kids.
베이커 : 조 선생은요 ?	How about you, Mr. Cho ?
조　　 : 저는 아직 <u>미혼입니다.</u>[1] 베이 커 선생은요 ?	I'm still single. How about you, Mr. Baker ?
베이커 : 저는 결혼했어요. <u>아들 하나 있어요.</u>[2]	I'm married. I've a son.

SUBSTITUTION	
1. 결혼 안 했어요.	(I'm) not married.
약혼 중입니다.	(I'm) engaged.
2. 아직 아이들은 없어요.	I've no children yet.

FRAME 2

Talking about One's Children

Mr. Yun and Mr. Baker exchange basic information about their children.

윤   : 베이커 선생, 아드님 몇 살   How old is your son, Mr. Baker ?
      이지요 ?

베이커 : 지금 두 살 됐어요. 윤 선생   He has turned two. Mr. Yun, are your
      아이들[1]은 아들[2]이에요, 딸[3]이   children boys or girls ?
      에요 ?

윤   : 아들 하나, 딸 하납니다.   A boy and a girl.

조   : 아이들 많이 컸지요 ?   They've grown big, haven't they ?

윤   : 네, 아이들은 빨리 커요.   Yes, kids grow fast.

SUBSTITUTION
1. 자녀분들   (someone's) children (honorific)
2. 남자 아이   young boy
3. 여자 아이   young girl

FRAME 3

Talking about One's Spouse

Mr. Yun and Mr. Baker introduce their wives, and Mr. Cho introduces his fiancée, in her absence.

베이커 : 윤 선생, <u>부인</u>¹은 뭐 하세요?	Mr. Yun, what does your wife do?
윤 : 제 아내는 중학교 선생입니다.	My wife is a junior high school teacher.
베이커 : 그러세요? 우리 집사람도 선생입니다. 국민학교에서 가르쳐요. 조 선생, 약혼자는 뭐 하세요?	Really? My wife is a teacher, too. She teaches at an elementary school. Mr. Cho, what does your fiancée do?
조 : <u>은행</u>²에서 일합니다.	She works in a bank.
윤 : 두 분이 같은 은행에서 일하세요.	They both work in the same bank.
베이커 : 네, 그러세요?	Oh, really?

SUBSTITUTION
1. 사모님   someone's wife (honorific)
2. 무역 회사   export-import company
   보험 회사   insurance company
   병원   hospital

Grammar and Usage

1. The Past-tense Suffix for the Present State

The past-tense suffix —었/았 is occasionally used to express the present state. For example,

결혼하셨어요 ?   <u>Are</u> you married ?
네, 결혼했어요.   Yes, I <u>am</u> married.

This usage is generally restricted to certain verbs, such as 결혼하다 ("to get married"), and 앉다 ("to sit down"). In these verbs an action is often associated with a state of being affected by the action. For now, you only need to remember these two verbs for this usage.

Another thing to notice at this time is that expressions of this type can have two interpretations, depending on the context. For example,

앉았습니다 may mean ⟨ "He sat down."   (past action)
                    "He is seated."   (present state)

결혼했어요 may mean ⟨ "He got married." (past event)
                    "He is married."   (present state)

2. How to Ask a "Choice" Question

When you ask a "choice" question (<u>either</u> this <u>or</u> that) in Korean, two questions are placed one after another without any connectives.

아들이에요, 딸이에요 ?   Is it a son or a daughter ?
        Literally :   Is it a son ? Is it a daughter ?

In such cases, intonation is an important feature. The tone of voice at the end of the first question should rise sharply, and the first question is followed immediately by the next one with a falling intonation.

아들이에요, ↗ 딸이에요 ? ↘

Listen and repeat the following examples, paying close attention to the intonation.

갑니까, 안 갑니까?	Are you going or aren't you?
오늘이에요, 내일이에요?	Is it today or tomorrow?
있어요, 없어요?	Is it there or not?
교실에 가요, 강당에 가요?	Are we going to the classroom or to the auditorium?
왼쪽이에요, 오른쪽이에요?	To the left or to the right?
집에서요, 학교에서요?	At home or at school?
저것이 다방이에요, 식당이에요?	Is that a tearoom or a restaurant?

3. Review of Honorific Forms

You have already seen not only verbs but also some nouns change form when they pertain to a person to whom the speaker shows his respect. Here is a summary of the honorific forms of nouns.

> With some nouns indicating titles, the honorific forms are obtained by using the suffix —님.

Plain		Honorific	
김 선생	→	김 선생님	Mr. Kim
박 사장	→	박 사장님	(company) president Park
이 과장	→	이 과장님	section chief Lee

> For some nouns, the addition of —님 brings about a sound change.

아들	→	아드님	son
딸	→	따님	daughter
하늘	→	하느님	God

> In some others, entirely different nouns are used for honorific expressions.

*집사람	→	부인	wife
집	→	댁	home
이름	→	성함	name
남편	→	{ 주인 / 주인 어른 }	husband
이/그/저 사람	→	이/그/저 분	this/that person

(*집사람 is used to refer to the speaker's own wife.)

It is also important to note that there should be agreement between the noun and the verb in honorific expressions.

Plain   : 한 선생 있어요?   Is Mr. Han there ?
Honorific : 한 선생님 계세요?   Is Mr. Han there ?

4. Summary of Kinship Terms

You have learned a handful of words related to the family system. It is now necessary for you to see the general make-up of Korean kinship terms to be able to use them appropriately.

There are three viewpoints that you should acquire in using Korean kinship terms: (1) the seniority (elder or younger), (2) the sex of the person from whose standpoint you speak of a relative, and (3) how polite you should be (plain or honorific).

The terms shown below are largely informational at this stage.

English	Whose Relative ?	Plain	Honorific
father		아버지	아버님
mother		어머니	어머님
husband		남편	주인 어른
wife		아내/집사람	부인/사모님
elder brother	of a male	형	형님
	of a female	오빠	오라버님
elder sister	of a male	누나	누님
	of a female	언니	형님
younger brother	of a male	동생	아우님
	of a female	남동생	남동생분
younger sister	of a male	누이동생	매씨
	of a female	여동생	아우님
son		아들	아드님
daughter		딸	따님
child/children		아이/아이들	자녀분
baby		아기	——

Exercises

A. Short Exchanges: Listening and Speaking

This is a reinforced exercise in listening and speaking. Follow the steps given below as you work on each exercise question.

> Step 1. Cover the Han-gŭl portion, and repeat after the model voicing as you look at the English equivalent.
>
> Step 2. Now cover the English portion, and again repeat after the model voicing, making sure you pronounce each word and phrase correctly and you understand them fully.
>
> Step 3. Now cover the Han-gŭl text. As you look at the English equivalent, say the Korean version of it.
>
> Step 4. Keep the Han-gŭl text covered. Aided by the English text, carry on the exchange in Korean with your instructor or classmate.

1. 결혼했어요?   Are you married?
   저요? 결혼 안 했어요.   Me? I'm not married.
2. 결혼했어요?   Are you married?
   네, 결혼했어요.   Yes, I'm married.
3. 최 선생님 결혼하셨어요?   Is Mr. Ch'oe married?
   그분 미혼이에요.   He is single.
4. 아직 미혼이에요?   Is he still single?
   네, 그래요.   Yes, that's right.
5. 언제 결혼했어요?   When did you get married?
   금년 봄에 결혼했어요.   I got married this spring.
6. 아드님은 몇 살이지요?   How old is your son?
   한 살 됐어요.   He has one turned one.
7. 따님 몇 살이지요?   How old is your daughter?
   두 살입니다.   She's two.
8. 아들이에요, 딸이에요?   A boy or a girl?

아들이에요.	A Boy.
9. 아들이에요, 딸이에요?	Boys or girls?
아들 하나, 딸 둘입니다.	One boy and two girls.
10. 아이들 많이 컸지요?	They've grown big, haven't they?
아이들은 빨리 커요.	Kids grow fast.
11. 부인 뭐 하세요?	What does your wife do?
선생입니다.	She is a teacher.
12. 어느 학교에서 가르치세요?	Which school does she teach in?
중학교에서요.	In a junior high school.
13. 사모님 뭐 하십니까?	What does your wife do?
은행에서 일합니다.	She works at a bank.
14. 어느 은행에서 일하세요?	Which bank does she work in?
한국은행에서요.	In the Bank of Korea.
15. 두 분이 같은 은행에서 일하세요?	Do both of you work in the same bank?
네, 그래요.	That's right.

B. What Do You Say?

Work with your instructor or classmate in the following series of role-playing.

1. Ask your friend if he/she is married.
2. Say that you're single/engaged.
3. Say that you have two children.
4. Ask your friend how old his/her son is.
5. Ask your friend if his/her child is a boy or a girl.
6. Say that you have one boy and two girls.
7. Ask your friend what his wife does.
8. Say that your wife works in a bank.
9. Say that you and your wife work in the same bank.

C. Vocabulary Exercise

Step 1. Cover the English portion on the right. Your instructor will read to you a key Korean word or phrase and then an exchange in Korean containing the same word or phrase.

Step 2. Try to understand what your instructor says. Uncover the English portion and see if your knowledge is correct.

Step 3. Now cover the Han-gŭl portion on the left, and say correctly the Korean equivalent of the exchange in English listed under the cue.

Step 4. Uncover the Han-gŭl portion and see if your answer is correct.

1. You hear : 결혼하다   to be married
     미스터 윤 결혼했어요?   Is Mr. Yun married?
     아뇨, 아직 결혼 안 했어요.   No, he is not married yet.
     Cue : Who got married?
           Mr. Hong got married.

2. You hear : 몇 살   how old
     아드님 몇 살이지요?   How old is your son?
     지금 두 살 됐어요.   He has turned two.
     Cue : How old is your daughter?
           She's five.

3. You hear : 크다   to grow
     아이들 많이 컸지요?   Your children have grown big, haven't they?
     많이 컸어요.   They've grown big.
     Cue : Your son has grown big, hasn't he?
           He's ten years old now.

4. You hear : 자녀분   (someone's) children (honorific)
     자녀분이 몇 분이십니까?   How many children do you have?
     자녀분들 뭐 하십니까?   What do your children do?
     Cue : How many children does Mr. Son have?
           He has three children.

5. You hear : 부인   (someone's) wife
     부인 뭐 가르치세요?   What does your wife teach?
     김 선생 부인이 오십니다.   Mr. Kim's wife is coming.
     Cue : Mr. Lee, is your wife teaching in school?
           Yes, my wife and I teach in the same school.

6. You hear : 집사람   my wife (plain)

집사람이 아픕니다.   My wife is sick.
집사람은 선생입니다.   My wife is a teacher.
Cue : My wife works in a bank.
    Which bank does she work in ?

7. You hear : 약혼자   fiancé; fiancée
제 약혼자입니다.   This is my fiancée.
약혼자가 지금 어디에 계세요? Where is your fiancée now ?
Cue : Who are you going with to Pusan ?
    I'm going to go with my fiancée.

8. You hear : 주인 어른   (someone's) husband (honorific)
주인 어른 계세요?   Is your husband home ?
주인 어른 나가셨어요?   Is your husband out ?
Cue : When is your husband coming home ?
    He is coming home at five o'clock.

D. Grammar Exercise

1. You will be asked two questions: whether you are married and when you got married. Respond to the second question according to each cue.

Example: Question : 결혼하셨어요 ?	Are you married ?
Answer : 네, 결혼했어요.	Yes, I am married.
Question : 언제 결혼하셨어요 ?	When did you get
Cue : last year	married ?
Answer : 작년에 결혼했어요.	I got married last year.

  Cues : (a) last week   (d) last fall
        (b) ten years ago (e) two years ago
        (c) this spring

2. Combine each of the following pairs of questions to form one "choice" question. Pay particular attention to the intonation.
  (a) 아들입니까 ?   (c) 여기서요 ?
      딸입니까 ?   저기서요 ?
  (b) 결혼하셨어요 ? (d) 선생님한테요 ?
      안 하셨어요 ?   박 선생한테요 ?

(e) 종로에 가세요?
  용산에 가세요?

3. Give Korean equivalents of the following questions.
  (a) Are you going to Yongsan or Sejongno ?
  (b) Here or over there ?
  (c) Is he married or not ?
  (d) Is she Mr. Kim's wife or Mr. Song's wife ?
  (e) Did you buy shoes or clothes ?

4. Convert the following sentences to honorific expressions by modifying the underlined words.
  (a) 집에 가요?
  (b) 저 사람이 누구입니까?
  (c) 저 사람의 이름이 무엇니까?
  (d) 미스터 강 있어요?
  (e) 집이 어디에요?

Reading and Writing

1. Read the following words, paying particular attention to the nasalization.

   (a) 한국말   (e) 국민
   (b) 중국말   (f) 십만원
   (c) 앞날   (g) 옵니다
   (d) 끝납니다   (h) 십리

2. Read and translate the following into English.

   미스터 조는 아직 미혼이다. 지금 약혼 중이다. 미스터 최는 작년에 결
   혼했다. 부인도 같은 은행에서 일한다. 아들이 하나 있고, 딸은 없다.

3. Answer in written Korean the following questions in line with the contents of the reading material provided above.

   (a) 미스터 조는 부인이 계십니까?
   (b) 미스터 최는 언제 결혼했어요?
   (c) 미스터 최의 부인은 어디서 근무합니까?
   (d) 미스터 최는 아이가 몇 있어요?
   (e) 딸이에요, 아들이에요?

4. Complete the sentences by filling in the blanks. Each Korean sentence should express the idea contained in the English sentence.

   (a) 미스터 윤은 _____ _____ 안 했어요?
      Isn't Mr. Yun married yet?
   (b) 아드님은 ___ ___이지요?
      How old is your son?
   (c) _____가 있어요, 없어요?
      Does he have a baby or not?
   (d) _____ 뭐 하세요?
      What does your wife do?
   (e) 우리는 _____ 회사에서 일해요.
      We work in the same company.

5. Translate the following sentences, using a dictionary.

   (a) 설탕 갖다 주세요.

   _____

   (b) 아들한테서 편지 받았어요.

   _____

   (c) 결혼식에 갔다 왔어요.

   _____

   (d) 아기가 예쁩니다.

   _____

   (e) 제 딸은 은행에서 일해요.

   _____

Summary of Verb Forms

가르치다 ("to teach")

STATEMENT

	Present		Past	
	LONG	SHORT	LONG	SHORT
HON	가르치십니다	가르치세요	가르치셨습니다	가르치셨어요
PLN	가르칩니다	가르쳐요	가르쳤습니다	가르쳤어요

QUESTION

	Present		Past	
	LONG	SHORT	LONG	SHORT
HON	가르치십니까?	가르치세요?	가르치셨습니까?	가르치셨어요?
PLN	가르칩니까?	가르쳐요?	가르쳤습니까?	가르쳤어요?

REQUEST

	LONG	SHORT
HON	가르치십시오	가르치세요
PLN	(not introduced)	

SUGGESTION

HON	가르치실까요?
PLN	가르칠까요?

PROPOSITION

HON	가르치십시다
PLN	가르칩시다

Words and Phrases

가르치다	to teach
결혼하다	to get married; to be married
국민학교	elementary school
남자 아이	young boy; son
남편	husband
댁	(someone's) home (honorific)
따님	(someone's) daughter (honorific)
딸	daughter
무역 회사	export-import company
미혼이다	to be single, not married
병원	hospital
보험 회사	insurance company
부인	(someone's) wife (honorific)
빨리	fast
一살이다	to be...years old
설탕	sugar
아드님	(someone's) son (honorific)
아들	son
아이들	children
약혼자	fiancé; fiancée
여자 아이	young girl; daughter
자녀분	(someone's) children (honorific)
주인 어른	(my/your) husband (honorific)
중학교	junior high school
크다	to grow big

Taking Short Trips

Lesson Objectives

1. Carry on a conversation related to a short trip. Specifically you will:
    (a) Ask your friend about a good way to take a trip to a certain place.
    (b) Ask that person how long it takes to complete the trip.
    (c) Ask that person about ticketing.
    (d) Ask that person what part of the station a particular train departs from.
    (e) Ask a passenger on the train about the progress of the trip.
    (f) Ask directions to different places on the train.

2. Understand fully some general rules about:
    (a) The compound verb form expressing the notion of obligation ("must," "should," and "have to").
    (b) The noun suffix expressing the means of doing things "by," "in," and "with").

3. (a) Read Korean loan words and write down their English sources, using your best judgment.
    (b) Read familiar Korean sentences in Han-gŭl and translate them into English.
    (c) Answer questions in written Korean, using your comprehension of the reading material.
    (d) Complete Korean sentences by filling in appropriate words or phrases in Han-gŭl.
    (e) Translate familiar Korean sentences into English, using a Korean-English dictionary.

Cultural Notes
Trains and Buses

Trains and buses are the most common means of transportation in Korea. For the majority of Koreans, the two mass transportation systems are both inexpensive and convenient.

The Korean National Railroads(KNR), a government-owned railroads network, connects the entire country. KNR provides superexpress trains (the Saemaŭl-ho) linking Seoul and Pusan in 4 hours and 10 minutes, and Seoul and Mokp'o in 4 hours and 30 minutes. There are several other types of trains, far less speedy than the Saemaŭl-ho.

Comfortable high-speed express buses also transport to and from major areas of the country. There are about ten major bus lines and most of them have their buses depart from the Express Bus Terminal located in Sŏch'o-dong, South Seoul.

Communicative Exchanges

FRAME 1

Getting Travel Information

Mr. Baker gets basic information concerning an overland trip from Seoul to Pusan.

베이커 : 내일 부산에 갑니다. 비행기가 좋아요, 기차가 좋아요?	I'm going to Pusan tomorrow. Which one is better, the plane or the train?
윤 : 기차가 더 안전하고 <u>편하지요.</u>[1]	The train is safer and more comfortable.
베이커 : 부산까지 기차로 얼마나 걸리지요?	How long does it take to go to Pusan by train?
윤 : 새마을호로 네 시간 십 분 걸립니다.	Four hours and ten minutes by the Saemaŭl-ho.
베이커 : 그러면 기차로 가지요. 표는 내일 <u>역에서</u>[2] 살 수 있어요?	Then I'll go by train. Can I buy the ticket at the station tomorrow?
윤 : 네. 출발 삼십 분 전에 가셔야 합니다.	Yes. You have to be there 30 minutes before your departure.

SUBSTITUTION

1. (더) 빠르지요.　　　　　(It is) faster.
2. 여행사에서　　　　　　at the travel agency

FRAME 2

Buying the Ticket at the Station

Mr. Baker seeks information to buy his train ticket and to stand in the right line before boarding.

베이커 : 실례합니다. 부산행 차표 어디서   Excuse me. Where can I buy a
　　　　샵니까?   train ticket for Pusan?

여객 　 : 저기에 표 파는 곳[1]이 있어요.   There's the ticket window over
　　　　　　　　　　　　　　　　　　　　　　there.

베이커 : 감사합니다.   Thank you.

(Baker buys the ticket at the window.)

베이커 : 부산행 기차는 어느 홈에서 출발합   Which platform does the train
　　　　니까?[2]   for Pusan depart from?

매표원 : 1번 플랫폼에서 떠납니다.   It departs from Platform 1.

베이커 : 감사합니다.   Thank you.

매표원 : 천만에요.   Not at all.

SUBSTITUTION	
1. 매표구/매표소	ticket window
2. 떠납니까?	(does it) leave?

FRAME 3

Asking about the Progress of the Trip

Mr. Baker has a talk with a passenger to get some idea about places and distances.

베이커 : 여기가 어디지요?	Where are we now?
여객 : 여기는 대전입니다.	This is Taejŏn.
베이커 : 부산까지 아직 <u>멀었습니까?</u>[1]	Is Pusan still a long way to go?
여객 : 부산이요? <u>멀었지요.</u>[2] 세 시간 더 가야 합니다.	Pusan? It's a long way. You have to go three more hours.
베이커 : 선생님도 부산까지 가십니까?	Are you going to Pusan, too?
여객 : 아니오, 저는 대구까지 갑니다.	No, I'm going to Taegu.

SUBSTITUTION
1. 많이 갑니까?   (Is it) a long way?
2. 많이 갑니다.   (It is) a long way.
   한참 갑니다.   (It is) quite a long way.

FRAME 4

Asking Directions on the Train

Mr. Baker asks the train conductor how he could get to the lavatory and to the dining car.

베이커 : 실례합니다. 화장실 어디에 있습니까?

Excuse me. Where's the lavatory?

승무원 : 이 칸의 저 끝에 있습니다.

It's at the other end of this coach.

베이커 : 식당차는 어디에 있지요?

Where's the dining car?

승무원 : 식당차요? 이 열차의 끝에[1] 있어요. 여기서부터 다섯 칸 지나 가셔야 합니다.

The dining car? It's at the tail end of this train. You have to pass through five coaches from here.

베이커 : 감사합니다.

Thank you.

승무원 : 천만에요.

You're welcome.

SUBSTITUTION	
1. 맨앞에	at the very front of
한가운데	in the middle of

Grammar and Usage

1. How to Express Obligation

Expressions of obligation in Korean are made in a compound verb form as follows:

Korean	English
VERB STEM + 어야 $\left\{\begin{array}{l}되다 \\ 하다\end{array}\right\}$	$\left\{\begin{array}{l}\text{must} \\ \text{have to} \\ \text{should}\end{array}\right\}$

Sound changes: (a) 어야 changes to 아야 when the last vowel of the stem is 오 or 아. (e.g., 와야, 가야)
(b) When the stem ends in a vowel, the combination of two vowels generally results in contraction.

As you notice, the sound changes required in this form are those that you have learned in the past-tense and the short-form (어요) formations.

가야 됩니다 $\left\{\begin{array}{l}\text{must} \\ \text{have to} \\ \text{should}\end{array}\right\}$ go
　(합니다)

가셔야 됩니다 (honorific)
　(합니다)

와야 돼요 $\left\{\begin{array}{l}\text{must} \\ \text{have to} \\ \text{should}\end{array}\right\}$ come
　(해요)

오셔야 돼요 (honorific)
　(해요)

읽어야 돼요 $\left\{\begin{array}{l}\text{must} \\ \text{have to} \\ \text{should}\end{array}\right\}$ read
　(해요)

읽으셔야 돼요 (honorific)
　(해요)

배워야 됩니다 $\left\{\begin{array}{l}\text{must} \\ \text{have to} \\ \text{should}\end{array}\right\}$ learn
　(합니다)

배우셔야 됩니다 (honorific)
　(합니다)

Of the two forms above, the former (STEM+되다) is more common in speech; therefore, you are encouraged to use STEM+어야 되다 in conversation. The latter form (STEM + 하다), however, will be also used here, so that you may be accustomed to it. Read aloud the following carefully.

해야 됩니다 }
해야 합니다 } must do

먹어야 돼요 }
먹어야 해요 } must eat

가야 됩니다 }
가야 합니다 } must go

앉아야 돼요 }
앉아야 해요 } must sit

B. Prounciation of 되 and 돼

The combination of the verb stem 되 and 어 results in 돼 in spelling. For example,

되 + 어요　＝돼요
되 + 었어요＝됐어요

However, both 되 and 돼 are pronounced almost the same in the Seoul region. In most other dialects, both 되 and 돼 sound almost like 뒈.

CAUTION: The meaning of the Korean "obligatory" form is straight-forward, but you might sometimes be misled by the English translation "must" which has two separate meanings: "obligation" and "probability."

(1) You <u>must</u> go.＝You <u>are obliged to</u> go.
(2) He <u>must</u> be an officer.＝He most <u>probably</u> is an officer.

Needless to say, the Korean construction —어야 하다 has nothing to do with the second English use above.

C. Means of Doing Things

There is a postposition attached to a noun, which expresses a means of doing a thing: NOUN + (으)로

Noun		Example
ending in a vowel } ending in ㄹ }	＋로	{ 버스로 by bus 연필로 with a pencil
ending in other consonants}	＋으로	{돈으로 with money

This kind of phrase, as you know, is open to various translations in English, such as "by," "in," and "with." For example,

자동차로 집에 갔습니다.
I went home <u>by car.</u>

한국에 비행기로 갔습니다.
He went to Korea <u>by air/in an airplane.</u>

무엇으로 떠났습니까?
<u>How</u>
<u>By what means</u> } did he depart?

우리는 영어로 배웠습니다.
We learned it <u>in English.</u>

한국말을 한국말로 가르칩니다.
They teach Korean, <u>using Korean.</u>

Exercises

A. Short Exchanges: Listening and Speaking

This is a reinforced exercise in listening and speaking. Follow the steps given below as you work on each exercise question.

Step 1. Cover the Han-gŭl portion, and repeat after the model voicing as you look at the English equivalent.

Step 2. Now cover the English portion, and again repeat after the model voicing, making sure you pronounce each word and phrase correctly and you understand them fully.

Step 3. Now cover the Han-gŭl text. As you look at the English equivalent, say the Korean version of it.

Step 4. Keep the Han-gŭl text covered. Aided by the English text, carry on the exchange in Korean with your instructor or classmate.

1. 내일 광주에 갑니다. I'm going to Kwangju tomorrow.
   아, 그러세요? Oh, really?

2. 기차가 좋아요, 버스가 좋아요? Which is better, the train or the bus?
   기차가 더 안전하지요. The train is safer.

3. 기차로 얼마 걸리지요? How long does it take by train?
   네 시간 반 걸립니다. It takes 4 hours and a half.

4. 차표는 어디서 살 수 있어요? Where can I buy the train ticket?
   내일 역에서 살 수 있어요. You can buy it at the station tomorrow.

5. 역에 얼마나 일찍 나가야 합니까? How early do I have to be at the station?

   출발 30분 전에 가셔야 합니다. You have to be there 30 minutes before your departure.

6. 광주행 차표 어디서 사지요? Where can I buy a ticket for the train for Kwangju?

   매표구에서 사세요. Buy it at the ticket window.

7. 매표구 어디에 있어요?   Where's the ticket window?
   저기 있어요.   It's over there.
8. 광주행 열차는 어느 플랫폼에   Which platform does the train for
   서 출발합니까?   Kwangju depart from?
   4번 플랫폼에서 출발합니다.   It departs from platform No. 4.
9. 여기가 광주행 열차 떠나는 곳   Is this the place where the train for
   입니까?   Kwangju departs from?
   아닙니다. 그건 저깁니다.   No. That's over there.
10. 이것이 광주행 열차입니까?   Is this the train for Kwangju?
    아닙니다. 이건 경주행 열차입   No. This is the train for Kyŏngju.
    니다.
11. 여기가 어디지요?   Where are we now?
    수원입니다.   We're in Suwon.
12. 여기가 수원입니까?   Is this Suwon here?
    아닙니다. 천안입니다.   No. It's Ch'ŏnan.
13. 광주까지 멀었습니까?   Is Kwangju a long way from here?
    아직 멀었어요.   It's a long way yet.
14. 몇 시간 더 가야 합니까?   How many more hours do we have to
                                       go?
    두 시간 더 가야 합니다.   Two more hours.
15. 대전까지 가십니까?   Are you going to Taejŏn?
    아니오, 광주까지 갑니다.   No, I'm going to Kwangju.
16. 화장실 어디 있지요?   Where's the lavatory?
    이 칸의 저 끝에 있어요.   It's on the other end of this coach.
17. 이 열차에 식당차 있어요?   Do we have a dining car on this train?
    네, 있어요.   Yes, we have one.
18. 식당차가 어디 있어요?   Where's the dining car?
    이 열차의 끝에 있어요.   It's on the tail end of this train.
19. 어떻게 가야 합니까?   How do I get there?
    다섯 칸 지나가셔야 합니다.   You have to pass through five coaches.
20. 다섯 칸이오, 여섯 칸이오?   Five coaches or six coaches?
    다섯 칸이오.   Five coaches.

B. What Do You Say?

Work with your instructor or classmate in the following series of role-playing.

1. Ask your friend whether the best way to go to Taegu is the plane or the train.
2. Say that the train is safer and more comfortable.
3. Ask your friend how long it takes to go to Taejŏn.
4. Ask your friend if you could buy the ticket at the station.
5. Ask a stranger at the station where you could buy a train ticket for Taegu.
6. Ask a stranger at the station which platform the train for Kwangju departs from.
7. Ask a passenger next to you on the train where you are now.
8. Ask that person if Kyŏngju is a long way to go.
9. Ask the conductor on the train where the lavatory/dining car is.
10. Respond properly to each of the questions list above, as needed.

C. Vocabulary Exercise

Follow the steps given below as you work on each exercise question.

Step 1. Cover the English portion on the right. Your instructor will read to you a key Korean word or phrase and then an exchange in Korean containing the same word or phrase.

Step 2. Try to understand what your instructor says. Uncover the English portion and see if your knowledge is correct.

Step 3. Now cover the Han-gŭl portion on the left, and say correctly the Korean equivalent of the English exchange listed under the cue.

Step 4. Uncover the Han-gŭl portion and see if your answer is correct.

1. You hear : 안전하다　　　　to be safe
   비행기 안전해요?　　　　Is the airplane safe?
   기차가 더 안전해요.　　　The train is safer.
   Cue : Is it safe here at night?
   　　　No, it is not.

2. You hear : 편하다　　　　to be comfortable
   버스가 편해요.　　　　The bus is comfortable.
   기차가 더 편해요.　　　The train is more comfortable.

Cue : This bed is expensive.
But it's very comfortable.

3. You hear : 걸리다   to take (as of time)
시간 많이 걸렸어요.   It took a lot of time.
열 시간 걸려요.   It takes 10 hours.
Cue : How long does it take to go to Taegu ?
It takes about 4 hours.

4. You hear : ㅡ야 하다   must; have to
지금 가야 해요.   I must go now.
내일 오셔야 해요.   You have to come tomorrow.
Cue : Do I have to read this now ?
Yes, you have to.

5. You hear : ㅡ행 열차   the train (bound) for
이것 부산행 열차입니까 ?   Is this the train for Pusan ?
아니오, 대구행 열차입니다.   No, it's for Taegu.
Cue : Is that the train for Mokp'o ?
No, that's for Taejŏn.

6. You hear : 출발하다   to depart
몇 시에 출발합니까 ?   What time do you depart ?
아직 몰라요.   We don't know yet.
Cue : What time does the train for Pusan depart ?
At seven thirty.

7. You hear : 멀었다   to be a long way
대전까지 멀었어요 ?   Is it a long way to Taejŏn ?
아직 멀었어요.   It's a long way yet.
Cue : Is it a long way to Kwangju ?
Yes, it is.

8. You hear : 칸   coach (of a train); compartment
화장실 어디 있어요 ?   Where's the lavatory ?
이 칸의 끝에 있어요.   It's at the end of this coach.
Cue : There are a lot of people in this coach.
There aren't many in that coach.

D. Grammar Exericse

1. Convert each of the following verb forms on the left into an obligation form.

Dictionary form   Obligation form

하다	"to do"	_____
있다	"to be"	_____
가다	"to go"	_____
사다	"to buy"	_____
끝나다	"to end"	_____
떠나다	"to depart"	_____
내다	"to pay"	_____
오다	"to come"	_____
보다	"to see"	_____
쓰다	"to write"	_____
배우다	"to learn"	_____
알다	"to know"	_____
먹다	"to eat"	_____
읽다	"to read"	_____
기다리다	"to wait"	_____

2. When the honorific suffix —시— is attached, the combination of 시 and 어 results in 셔. Convert each of the plain forms on the left into a honorific obligation form.

Plain form   Honorific form

해야 돼요	_____
있어야 돼요	_____
가야 돼요	_____
와야 돼요	_____
써야 됩니다	_____
알아야 됩니다	_____
먹어야 됩니다	_____
기다려야 됩니다	_____

3. Respond to the following questions affirmatively.

(a) 해야 돼요?   (c) 기다려야 돼요?

(b) 가야 돼요?   (d) 나가야 됩니까?

(e) 사야 됩니까?   (h) 시작하셔야 됩니까?

(f) 계셔야 됩니까?   (i) 찾으셔야 돼요?

(g) 일하셔야 돼요?   (j) 읽으셔야 됩니까?

4. The following questions are specifically directed to you as the subject, with the honorific form in each. Respond affirmatively, using the non-honorific form.

(a) 서울 가셔야 돼요?   (e) 물어보셔야 해요?

(b) 기차로 가셔야 합니까?   (f) 건너가셔야 돼요?

(c) 여기 계셔야 됩니까?   (g) 한국말 배우셔야 합니까?

(d) 그분 보셔야 돼요?   (h) 전화 받으셔야 됩니까?

5. Answer each of the following questions, using each of the cues.

> *Example* : Question : 뭐로 가세요?   What (means) are you taking ?
> Cue : train
> Answer : 기차로 갑니다. I am leaving by train.

(a) 뭐로 가세요?

    Cues : bus, airplane, train, taxi, express bus

(b) 이 길을 어떻게 건너가요?

    Cues : that intersection, overpass, underpass

(c) 어떻게 연락 드릴까요?

    Cues : telephone, letter, public telephone

(d) 뭐로 쓸까요?

    Cues : pencil, ball-point pen, pen

Reading and Writing

1. There are many Korean words that are borrowed from English. Such words are called loan words. Since there are many Enlgish sounds that are difficult to approximate in Korean, the shapes of such loan words are often radically modified. You should, however, be able to detect the English counterparts for most of them. Read the following loan words and write down their English sources, using your best judgment.

(a) 호텔 _____ (f) 카메라 _____

(b) 버스 _____ (g) 커피숍 _____

(c) 터미널 _____ (h) 택시 _____

(d) 터널 _____ (i) 카운터 _____

(e) 커피 _____ (j) 라디오 _____

2. Read and translate the following into English.

고 선생은 이번 주말에 부산에 가야 한다. 부산에 기차로 간다. 그 기차가 9시 반에 서울역에서 떠난다. 부산에 오후 3시에 도착한다. 부산역에 고 선생의 친구가 나온다. 고 선생은 다음 수요일에 돌아온다.

3. Answer in written Korean the following questions in line with the contents of the reading material provided above.

(a) 고 선생이 어디 갑니까?

(b) 언제 가요?

(c) 어디서 떠나요?

(d) 기차가 부산에 몇 시에 도착해요?

(e) 고 선생이 언제 돌아와요?

4. Complete the sentences by filling in the blanks. Each Korean sentence should express the idea contained in the English sentence.

(a) 고속버스_____ 가야 _____.

I must go by express bus.

(b) 내일_____ 회의를 _____합니다.
The conference will begin (starting) tomorrow.

(c) _____가 다시 연락 _____.
I will contact you again.

(d) _____에 _____돼요?
Do you have to go out to the station?

5. Translate the following sentences into English, using a Korean-English dictionary.
(a) 지하철로 수원에 가요.
_____

(b) 신발 벗어야 돼요?
_____

(c) 나는 여섯 시까지 역에 나가야 합니다.
_____

(d) 다섯 시까지 꼭 돌아오세요.
_____

(e) 안내양한테 다시 물어 보시지요.
_____

Summary of Verb Forms

—어야 되다 ("have to")

STATEMENT
Present

	LONG	SHORT
HON	되십니다	되세요
PLN	됩니다	돼요(되어요)

Past

	LONG	SHORT
HON	되셨습니다	되셨어요
PLN	됐습니다 (되었습니다)	됐어요 (되었어요)

QUESTION
Present

	LONG	SHORT
HON	되십니까?	되세요?
PLN	됩니까?	돼요?

Past

	LONG	SHORT
HON	되셨습니까?	되셨어요?
PLN	됐습니까?	됐어요?

REQUEST

(not applicable)

SUGGESTION

(not applicable)

PROPOSITION

(not applicable)

떠나다 ("to leave")

STATEMENT
Present

	LONG	SHORT
HON	떠나십니다	떠나세요
PLN	떠납니다	떠나요

Past

	LONG	SHORT
HON	떠나셨습니다	떠나셨어요
PLN	떠났습니다	떠났어요

QUESTION
Present

	LONG	SHORT
HON	떠나십니까?	떠나세요?
PLN	떠납니까?	떠나요?

Past

	LONG	SHORT
HON	떠나셨습니까?	떠나셨어요?
PLN	떠납니까?	떠났어요?

REQUEST

	LONG	SHORT
HON	떠나십시오	떠나세요
PLN	(not introduced)	

SUGGESTION

HON	떠나실까요?
PLN	떠날까요?

PROPOSITION

HON	떠나십시다
PLN	떠납시다

Words and Phrases

걸리다	to take (as of time)
그러면	then
기차	train
끝	end
더	more
도착하다	to arrive
떠나다	to leave
매표구/매표소	ticket window
매표원	ticket girl
맨앞에	at the very front of
멀다	to be a long way
비행기	airplane
빠르다	to be fast
승무원	railroad crew
식당차	dining car
안전하다	to be safe
—어야 되다/하다	must; have to; should
여객	passenger
여행사	travel agency
역	railroad station
열차	train
차표	(train) ticket
출발	departure
출발하다	to depart
칸	coach
편하다	to be comfortable
플랫폼	platform
한가운데	in the middle of
한참	quite
—행	(bound) for...

THE REFERENCE SECTION

HAN-GŬL : THE LETTERS
AND SOUNDS

There are two types of writing systems used today in Korea: one is a phonetic system called Han-gŭl,("the Korean script"), and the other is an ideographic system called *Hancha* ("the Chinese characters"). The former is the native Korean writing system, while the latter is the writing system borrowed from Chinese. The modern Korean writing is done either exclusively in Han-gŭl or occasionally in a mixed writing, with *Hancha* scattered here and there. But almost all public signs and billboards in Korea today use Han-gŭl exclusively. Therefore, you will only need to concern yourself with Han-gŭl in this course.

Han-gŭl is a phonetic—or phonemic if you will—writing system with relatively small number of letters: 24 altogether. It is traditionally held that there are 10 vowel symbols and 14 consonant symbols.

Roughly as the English letters are combined into words, the 24 letters in Korean are variously combined to form words—with some different rules of combination. We will discuss those rules shortly in Unit 1. For now, we will take a simplified overview of Han-gŭl.

1. Vowel Symbols: ㅏ, ㅓ, ㅗ, ㅜ, ㅡ, ㅣ, ㅐ, ㅔ

2. Consonant Symbols: ㄱ, ㄴ, ㄷ, ㄹ, ㅁ, ㅂ, ㅅ, ㅇ, ㅈ, ㅊ, ㅋ, ㅌ, ㅍ, ㅎ

Note : Traditional Korean grammar books list ㅏ, ㅑ, ㅓ, ㅕ, ㅗ, ㅛ, ㅜ, ㅠ, ㅡ, ㅣ as ten basic vowel symbols, while this text book classifies the vowel symbols in such a way that it will promote the understanding of the English-speaking student of Korean. For example, in this textbook the y- vowels ㅑ, ㅕ, ㅛ, ㅠ vowels like ㅐ, ㅔ are treated as basic vowels.

3. Direction of Lines (or Rows of Words): There are two ways: one is

traditional and the other modern, as shown next. Both ways are equally common, but the modern style is gaining popularity.

    a. Traditional : Words are written TOP-TO-BOTTOM and lines proceed RIGHT-TO-LEFT (as in Chinese).

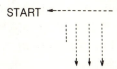

    b. Modern : Words are written LEFT-TO-RIGHT and lines proceed TOP-TO-BOTTOM (as in English).

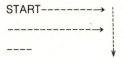

UNIT 1

How Korean syllables are formed: Although Han-gŭl is a phonetic script consisting of consonants and vowels like English, the way words are formed in Han-gŭl is somewhat different from the way of English. Korean symbols (letters) are first grouped into SYLLABLES rather than WORDS (unless they coincide). Then, syllables are put together to form words. In this unit, you will learn some basic rules of forming syllables.

1. Six Simple Vowels

Listen to the model pronunciation of the six vowels as you look at the written symbols below:

Vowel #1 : 아   Vowel #2 : 어   Vowel #3 : 오

Vowel #4 : 우   Vowel #5 : 으   Vowel #6 : 이

Each of the six vowels above consists of a circle and one or two lines. The little circle " ㅇ " represents a "zero" consonant, that is, the absence of a consonant. This is because <u>any</u> <u>written</u> <u>syllable</u> <u>in</u> <u>Han-gŭl</u> <u>must</u> <u>begin</u> <u>with</u> <u>a consonant</u> <u>symbol</u>. When you write a vowel alone (or when there is no initial consonant), you still have to begin with " ㅇ ."

Now, notice the relative positions of the consonant (a zero in this case) and the vowel in each syllable above. There are two kinds of arrangements. A vowel symbol (lines or sticks with a short twig attached) is placed either to the <u>right</u> of, or <u>below</u>, the consonant.

(1) LEFT-TO-RIGHT   (2) TOP-TO-BOTTOM

as in   아   (#1)   as in   오   (#3)

          어   (#2)   우   (#4)

          이   (#6)   으   (#5)

Pronunciation of the Vowels

The following notes are not to be taken as the precise descriptions of the Korean vowels. None of the Korean vowels are exactly like their English counterparts. Listen carefully to the model pronunciation.

		Approximate English sound	International phonetic symbol	ROK/MR*
#1	아	Like the a in father	[ɑ]	a
#2	어	Like the u in burn	[ə]	ŏ
#3	오	Like the o in own	[o]	o
#4	우	Like the oo in too	[u]	u
#5	으	Like the oo in book (without lip rounding)	[u]	ŭ
#6	이	Like the ee in feet	[iː]	i

> *ROK (The Republic of Korea) officially uses the McCune-Reischauer system in maps, public signs, etc. In this textbook this system will be used whenever romanization is called for.

How to write Han-gŭl (Stroke Orders): It is important to learn correct stroke orders from the beginning. If you know the proper stroke orders, it will be easier for you to recognize later sloppy hand-written letters.

Let us begin with two general rules of writing.

> Rule 1: Everything HORIZONTAL moves from LEFT-TO-RIGHT. This applies to the movement of a stroke, as well as to writing a sequence of symbols (e.g., the consonant first, then the vowel.)
>
> Rule 2 : Everything VERTICAL moves from TOP-TO-BOTTOM.

Following the stroke orders shown above, write each of the following syllables, stroke by stroke, in the spaces provided.

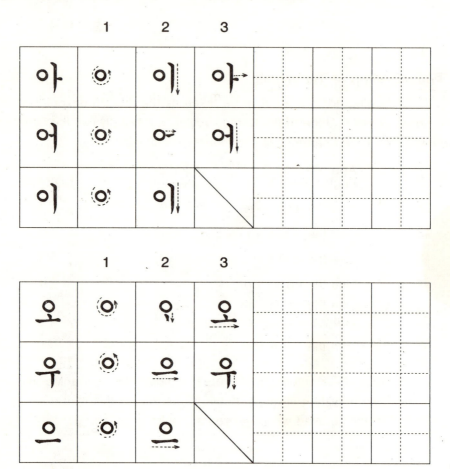

2. First Three Consonants

Now you will learn how to write consonants. You will proceed in the Korean alphabetical sequence, which is used for arranging vocabulary in dictionaries. In this unit you will learn the first three consonants and how they combine with vowels.

§. Consonant #1

The first consonant is pronounced like the k in kiss, or the c in call, but is not accompanied by a heavy puff of air (aspiration).

How to write it: It is done in one stroke as shown by dotted lines.

How to combine a consonant with a vowel: Remember the basic rule of Han-gŭl given in the beginning of this unit: any written syllable in Han-gŭl must begin with a consonant. This means that you will replace the zero consonant " ㅇ " with a consonant symbol before you write in the vowel. Do not add a new consonant on to the zero consonant.

For example, to write a syllable <u>ka,</u> you replace ㅇ with ㄱ to form 가, but not ㄱ아.

Now write the syllables <u>ka</u>, <u>kŏ</u>, and <u>ki</u> in the boxes below.

가					
거					
기					

Top-to-Bottom Arrangement

Now write the syllables: <u>ko</u>, <u>ku</u>, and <u>kŭ</u>.

고					
구					
그					

Reading Practice

Read aloud the following words. They are all real Korean words and English translations are given for your reference. Compare your pronunciation against the model pronunciation.

1. 이   tooth
2. 오이   cucumber
3. 고기   meat
4. 그이   that person
5. 아이   child
6. 거기   there
7. 기구   tool
8. 아기   baby

§. Consonant #2

The second consonant in Han-gŭl is pronounced like the <u>n</u> in <u>nature</u>.

How to write it: The movement is from top to bottom and then to the right.

Write the following syllables in the boxes provided.

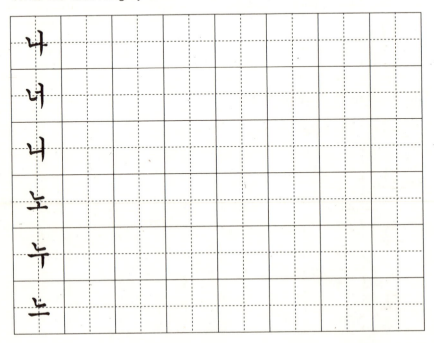

§. Consonant #3

The third consonant in Han-gŭl is pronounced like the t in tall, but it is not accompanied by a heavy puff of air, and the tip of the tongue will be touching the back of the upper teeth. Note that for an English t the tip of the tongue is farther back, touching the gum ridge.

How to write it : This symbol is written with two strokes.

Write the following syllables in the boxes provided.

Reading Practice

Syllables listed below are real Korean words. Read them aloud, and then compare your reading against the model pronunciation.

1. 다   all
2. 어느   which
3. 누구   who
4. 더   more
5. 이   tooth
6. 구두   shoes
7. 어디   where
8. 거기   there

Listening and Writing Practice

The model voice will say 8 words, each pronounced twice. As you hear each word, complete the Han-gŭl below. Check your answers against the key.

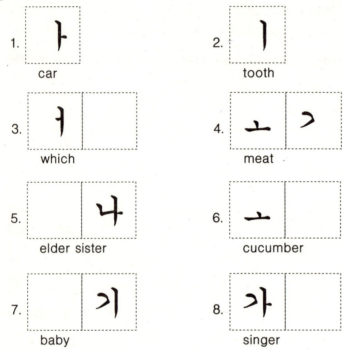

1. 아   car

2. 이   tooth

3. 어   which

4. 고 ᄀ   meat

5. 나   elder sister

6. 오   cucumber

7. 기   baby

8. 가   singer

Key : 1. 차   2. 이   3. 어느   4. 고기   5. 누나   6. 오이   7. 아기   8. 가수

UNIT 2

1. Two Additional Vowels

The two new vowels will complete the eight vowels of Korean. Listen and repeat after the vowel sounds of the model voice as you look at the letters below:

 Pronounced like <u>a</u> in <u>apple.</u>

 Pronounced like the <u>e</u> in <u>end.</u>

Each of these vowels was historically derived from the combination of two vowels:

$$ 아 \quad + \quad 이 \quad \longrightarrow \quad 애 $$
$$ 어 \quad + \quad 이 \quad \longrightarrow \quad 에 $$

Han-gŭl was devised in the 15th century, and the six basic vowels introduced above were the only simple vowels in the 15th century. Modern Korean ("Standard Korean" and most other dialects) has typically eight simple vowels.

How to write them: As usual, move from left to right. Each vowel symbol is written with three strokes.

Note the different lengths of the two downward strokes in each vowel symbol; the downward stroke on the left is slightly shorter.

Writing Practice

Following the stroke order shown above, write each vowel, stroke by stroke, in the spaces provided.

	1	2	3	4					
애	어	이	아	애					
에	어	어	어	에					

Reading Practice

The following are real Korean words. Read them aloud, and then compare your pronunciation against the model pronunciation.

1. 개   dog   2. 네   yes

3. 게   crab   4. 아내   wife

5. 아기   baby   6. 네 아이   four children

7. 내가   I (1st person subject)   8. 어디에   where (to)

Listening and Writing Practice

The model voice will say twice. As you hear each word, complete the Han-gŭl below. Check your answers against the key.

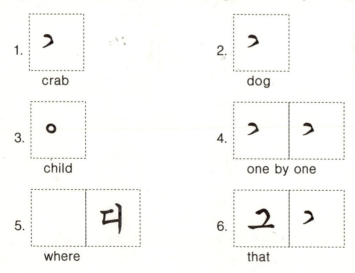

1. ㄱ   2. ㄱ

     crab   dog

3. ㅇ   4. ㄱ ㄱ

     child   one by one

5. 디   6. ㄱ ㄱ

     where   that

7. 개

four things

8. 내

wife

Key : 1. 게 2. 개 3. 애 4. 개개 5. 어디 6. 그게 7. 네개 8. 아내

2. Five More Consonants

§. Consonant #4

The fourth consonant is pronounced like the r in three. The tip of the tongue taps lightly against the gum ridge when you pronounce ㄹ. Note that the American r is normally produced with the tip of the tongue not touching the gum ridge, as in radio and red.

How to write it : This symbol is written with three strokes.

Write the following syllables in the boxes provided.

라						
래						
러						
레						
로						
루						

르						
리						

§. Consonant #5

The fifth consonant in Han-gŭl is pronounced like the <u>m</u> in <u>map</u>.

How to write it : This symbol is written with three strokes. Note that the little box formed is slightly narrower at the bottom.

Write the following syllables in the boxes provided.

마							
매							
머							
메							
모							
무							
므							
미							

§. Consonant #6

The sixth consonant in Han-gŭl is pronounced like the p in pen. Unlike the English p, however, the Korean ㅂ is not accompanied by a heavy puff of air.

How to write it : This symbol is written with four strokes.

Write the following syllables in the boxes provided.

바							
배							
버							
베							
보							
부							
브							
비							

§. Consonant #7

The seventh consonant in Han-gŭl is pronounced like the s in sky, but before i it is pronounced like the sh in she.

How to write it: This symbol is written with two strokes.

Write the following syllables in the boxes provided.

사							
새							
서							
세							
소							
수							
스							
시							

§. Consonant #9

ㅈ

The ninth consonant in Han-gŭl is pronounced like the <u>ch</u> in <u>child</u>. (The eighth is the ㅇ consonant.) Unlike the English <u>ch</u>, however, ㅈ is not accompanied by a puff of air.

How to write it: This symbol is written with three strokes.

Write the following syllables in the boxes provided.

자								
재								
저								
제								
조								
주								
즈								
지								

3. The Dictionary Sequence of Consonants

Now that you have learned eight consonants, let us put them in the traditional sequence used in dictionaries and word lists. Combine each consonant with the vowel ㅏ, and then pronounce the syllables in this order. Note that ㅇ is regarded as a consonant, and 아 is placed after 사 in the traditional sequence of Han-gŭl: 가, 나, 다, 라, 마, 바, 사, 아, 자.

While reading aloud the consonants in sequence, write them in the spaces provided.

가							
나							

다								
라								
마								
바								
사								
아								
자								

Reading Practice

Read the following Korean words aloud and compare your pronunciation against the model pronunciation.

1. 배	boat	2. 새	bird
3. 지도	map	4. 버스	bus
5. 나무	tree/wood	6. 도로	road
7. 바지	pants	8. 아버지	father
9. 다리	bridge	10. 어머니	mother
11. 라디오	radio	12. 미스 리	Miss Lee

Listening and Writing Practice

The model voice will say eight words, each pronounced twice. As you hear each word, complete the Han-gŭl below. Check your answers against the key.

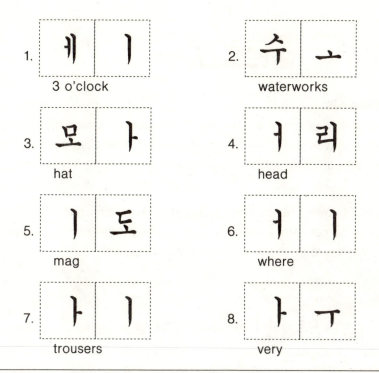

1. 케 ㅣ
3 o'clock

2. 수 ㅗ
waterworks

3. 모 ㅏ
hat

4. ㅓ 리
head

5. ㅣ 도
mag

6. ㅓ ㅣ
where

7. ㅏ ㅣ
trousers

8. ㅏ ㅜ
very

Key : 1. 세시 2. 수도 3. 모자 4. 머리 5. 지도 6. 어디 7. 바지 8. 아주

UNIT 3

1. The Y-Vowels

The sound of y in <u>year</u>, <u>you</u>, etc. are considered a consonant in English. In Korean, however, y is a vowel coloring rather than a consonant. The Korean vowels that are preceded by the sound of y may be called the y-vowels.

Six of the eight vowels (excluding 으 and 이) may be preceded by y. The vowels 으 and 이 do not form y-vowels. Listen to the model voicing on each pair of vowels as you look at the written symbols below:

1. 아 ⇨ 야   Pronounced like the <u>ya</u> in <u>yard</u>.

2. 어 ⇨ 여   Pronounced like the <u>yə</u> in <u>yearn</u>.

3. 오 ⇨ 요   Pronounced like the <u>yo</u> in <u>yo-ho</u>.

4. 우 ⇨ 유   Pronounced like the <u>yu</u> in <u>useful</u>.

5. 애 ⇨ 얘   Pronounced like the <u>yæ</u> in <u>yak</u>.

6. 에 ⇨ 예   Pronounced like the <u>ye</u> in <u>yet</u>.

As you see, the y sound is represented by an additional stroke in each of the six vowel symbols.

Reading Practice

Read aloud the following Korean words and compare your pronunciation against the model pronunciation.

1. 야 구   baseball
2. 여 자   woman
3. 요 리   cooking
4. 유 리   glass
5. 우 유   milk
6. 자 유   freedom
7. 셔 츠   shirts
8. 애 기   story/talk
9. 묘   grave
10. 교 사   teacher

Listening and Writing Practice

The model voice will say eight words, each pronounced twice. As you hear each word, complete the Han-gŭl below. Check your answers against the key.

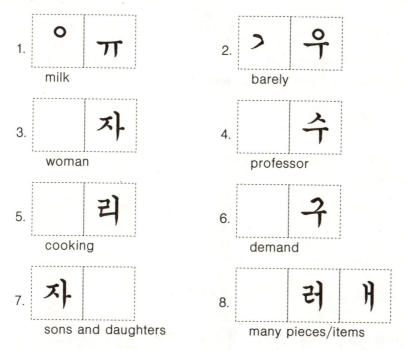

1. ㅇ ㅠ
   milk

2. ㄱ 우
   barely

3. 자
   woman

4. 수
   professor

5. 리
   cooking

6. 구
   demand

7. 자
   sons and daughters

8. 러 ㅐ
   many pieces/items

Key : 1. 우유 2. 겨우 3. 여자 4. 교수 5. 요리 6. 요구 7. 자녀 8. 여러개

2. The Dictionary Sequence of Vowels

Words in dictionaries and word lists are arranged according to the traditional sequence of Korean consonants and vowels.

The followings are the vowels included in the traditional sequence. Write the symbols for the vowels in the boxes provided.

아 야 어 여 오 요 우 유 으 이

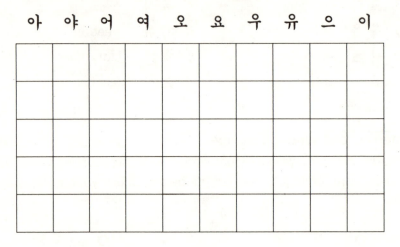

What about Y-Vowels 애, 얘, 에, and 예 ? : These symbols were made by adding 이 to 아, 야, 어, and 여.

아 + 이 → 애   야 + 이 → 얘
어 + 이 → 에   여 + 이 → 예

Therefore, they appear in the dictionary directly after 아, 야, 어, and 여, respectively.

아   야   어   여
↑   ↑   ↑   ↑
애   얘   에   예

Write the following syllables in the boxes provided.

가	걔	갸	걔	거	게	겨	계	고	교	구	규

나	내	냐	냬	너	네	녀	녜	노	뇨	누	뉴
다	대	댜	댸	더	데	뎌	뎨	도	됴	두	듀
라	래	랴	럐	러	레	려	례	로	료	루	류
마	매	먀	먜	머	메	며	몌	모	묘	무	뮤
바	배	뱌	뱨	버	베	벼	볘	보	뵤	부	뷰
사	새	샤	섀	서	세	셔	셰	소	쇼	수	슈
아	애	야	얘	어	에	여	예	오	요	우	유
자	재	쟈	쟤	저	제	져	졔	조	죠	주	쥬

Note that there is little difference in sound between the paired syllables (one with a simple vowel and one with the corresponding y vowel) that begin with ㅈ.

3. The Final Consonants

All the syllables you have learned so far end with a vowel (as in 가, 소, 비, etc.), but many Korean words (and syllables) also end with a conso-nant.

The final consonant (of a syllable) is placed directly below the preceding consonant and vowel, regardless of how they are arranged (i.e., whether horizontally or vertically).

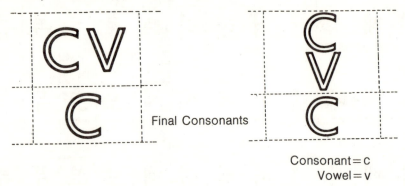

Final Consonants

Consonant = c
Vowel = v

A block forming a syllable with three symbols (C-V-C) will naturally be more conjested than a block with two symbols (C-V). However, each syllable (or block) should be approximately of the same size, regardless of the number of symbols contained in it. It is, therefore, necessary to make the size of symbols smaller when a syllable contains three or four symbols, as you see in the examples below.

| Reading Practice |

Read aloud the following Korean words and compare your pronuncia-tion against the model pronunciation.

1. 박   Park (surname)   2. 닭   chicken

3. 손   hand   4. 봄   spring (season)

5. 은   silver   6. 금   gold

7. 미국   U.S.A.   8. 서울   Seoul (city)

9. 부산   Pusan (city)   10. 언제   when

Pronunciation of the Final Consonants

Every consonant that you have learned so far can be used as the final consonant of a syllable. In other words, all of the following syllables are used in Han-gŭl. However, there are some changes in the phonetic values of these final consonants (as indicated by Roman letters below).

1. 악   2. 안   3. 앝   4. 알   5 암
   ak   an   at   al   am

6. 압   7. 앗   8. 앙   9. 앚
   ap   at   ang   at

You will note some irregularities in 3, 4, 7, 8, and 9. These are due to the following three general rules about Korean sounds.

Rule 1 : No final consonants are "released" in Korean. Releasing means opening your mouth to let the air escape at the end of a word.

   In English, the consonant p in tip may be either "released" or "not released". In Korean, the final consonant is not released. The consequences of this explains why (3) 앝, (7) 앗, and (9) 앚 in the above examples are all pronounced the same: at.

Rule 2 : The consonant ㄹ is pronounced like r in three when followed by a vowel, but is pronounced like l at the end of a word or syllable. The example (4) 알 is, therefore, pronounced like al.

Rule 3 : The zero symbol ㅇ, which indicates the absence of a consonant in the beginning of a syllable, is also used to indicate the sound of ng, as in sing, at the end of a syllable. In other words, ㅇ as a final consonant stands for ng.

Reading Practice

1. Now, keeping Rule 1 in mind, read aloud the following words, and compare your pronunciation against the model pronunciation.

(a) 옷 clothes   (b) 숟가락 spoon   (c) 믿다 to believe

(d) 붓 brush   (e) 벚나무 cherry   (f) 낮 daytime

2. The following words end with ㄹ. Read them aloud, and then compare your pronunciation against the model pronunciation.

(a) 말   words   (b) 물   water   (c) 불   fire

(d) 서울 Seoul   (e) 오늘 today   (f) 일본 Japan

3. The following words end with the symbol ㅇ. Read them aloud, and then compare your pronunciation against the model pronunciation.

(a) 강   river   (b) 궁   palace   (c) 상   table

(d) 중국 China   (e) 선생 teacher   (f) 명동 Myŏng-dong

4. The followings are some samples of Han-gŭl in different styles of print. They include some new words, but you should be able to pronounce most of them. Read them aloud, and then compare your pronunciation against the model pronunciation.

(a) 갈비   (b) 영 어

(c)

서 울 올림픽

(d) 오늘의 토픽

| Listening and Writing Practice |

As you hear the model voice, complete the following writings in Han-gŭl. Check your answers against the key.

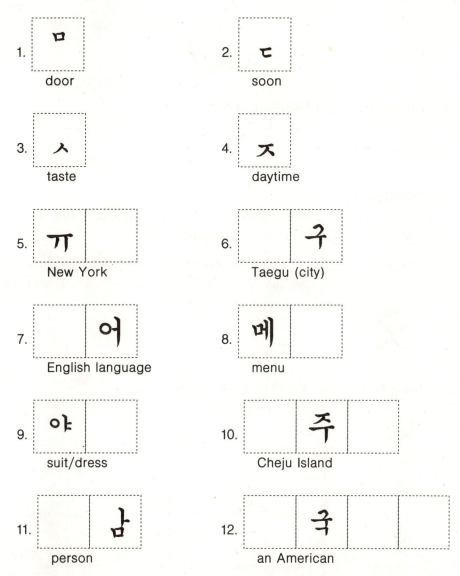

1. ㅁ
door

2. ㄷ
soon

3. ㅅ
taste

4. ㅈ
daytime

5. ㄲ
New York

6. 구
Taegu (city)

7. 어
English language

8. 메
menu

9. 야
suit/dress

10. 주
Cheju Island

11. ㅁ
person

12. 국
an American

Note : When the final consonants ㄷ, ㅅ, and ㅈ are all pronounced like t̲ (unreleased) as in items (2), (3), and (4) above, how is one to know how to spell correctly them by the sounds alone ? One simply can't, unless he/she already knows the meanings, and the spellings, of the words.

Key : 1. 문 2. 곧 3. 맛 4. 낮 5. 뉴욕 6. 대구 7. 영어 8. 메뉴
9. 양복 10. 제주도 11. 사람 12. 미국 사람

UNIT 4

1. Five Aspirated Consonants

The last five consonants in Han-gŭl are characterized by a heavy puff of air accompanied.

§. Consonant #10

The 10th Han-gŭl consonant is pronounced like the <u>ch</u> in <u>chin</u>, followed by a strong puff of air.

How to write it: The first stroke is a dot. With the remaining three strokes you write the ㅈ symbol, which you have already learned.

Write the following syllables in the boxes provided.

차					
초					
책					
춘					
칠					
처					

§. Consonant #11

The 11th Han-gŭl consonant is pronounced like the <u>k</u> in <u>kick</u>, with a heavy puff of air accompanying it.

How to write it: To the ㄱ symbol simply add a second stroke, slightly slanting up.

Write the following syllables in the boxes provided.

콰						
크						
코						
켜						
콩						
콸						
캥						

§. Consonant #12

The 12th Han-gŭl consonant, ㅌ, is fully aspirated and is pronounced like the <u>t</u> in <u>tin</u>.

How to write it: The first stroke is a horizontal bar, and beneath that bar comes the ㄷ symbol you have already learned.

Write the following syllables in the boxes provided.

타							
투							
티							
톤							
탈							
턱							
통							

§. Consonant #13

The 13th Han-gŭl consonant is pronounced like the <u>p</u> in <u>park</u>, and with a stronger puff of air.

How to write it: This symbol is written with four strokes.

Write the following syllables in the boxes provided.

파							
포							
필							
플							
팔							
파	리						
포	장						
풍	선						

§. Consonant #14

The 14th and last consonant in Han-gŭl is pronounced like the <u>h</u> in <u>have</u>. When ㅎ precedes ㄱ, ㄷ, ㅅ, ㅈ, it causes them to become aspirated.

How to write it: This symbol is written with three strokes. The first stroke is a dot, the second is a horizontal bar and the third is a zero.

Write the following syllables in the boxes provided.

하								
호								
형								
후								
힘								
핵								

Reading and Writing Practice

Read the following words aloud as you write them in the boxes provided. (The English meanings are given for your reference only.)

	천	당						
1.

heaven

	포	도						
2.

grape

	총	장						
3.

university president

4. 특권

privilege

5. 타자

typing

6. 크다

to be big

7. 한국

Korea

8. 허가

permission

Listening and Writing Practice

The model voice will say 15 words. As you hear each word, complete the Han-gŭl syllable(s). Check your answers against the key.

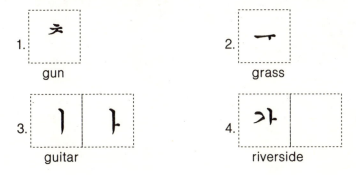

1. ㅊ

gun

2. ㅜ

grass

3. ㅣ ㅏ

guitar

4. 가

riverside

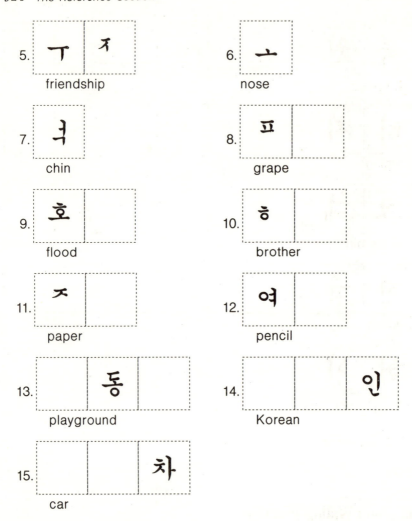

5. ㄱ ㅈ
friendship

6. ㅗ
nose

7. ㅓ
chin

8. ㅍ
grape

9. 호
flood

10. ㅎ
brother

11. ㅈ
paper

12. 여
pencil

13. 동
playground

14. 인
Korean

15. 차
car

Key : 1. 총 2. 풀 3. 기타 4. 강가 5. 우정 6. 코 7. 턱 8. 포도
9. 홍수 10. 형제 11. 종이 12. 연필 13. 운동장 14. 한국인
15. 자동차

UNIT 5

1. Four W-Vowels

You have already learned that six vowels may be preceded by a y-like sound. These y-vowels are 야, 얘, 여, 예, 요, and 유.

There are seven vowels that are preceded by a w-like sound. These w-vowels are 와, 워, 외, 위, 왜 and 웨 and 의. Each is formed by combining two vowel symbols.

As you see below, 와 and 워 are formed by combining two vowel symbols together as follows:

| 오 | + | 아 | ⇨ | 와 | Pronounced like the <u>wo</u> in <u>wobble</u>. |

| 우 | + | 어 | ⇨ | 워 | Pronounced like the <u>wa</u> in <u>was</u>. |

Write the following syllables in the boxes provided.

와							
과							
뇌							
봐							
쇄							

화							
워							
둬							
뭐							
줘							
퉈							
훠							

위 and 외 are also formed by combining two vowel symbols together, as follows:

우	+	이	⇒	위

Pronounced like the <u>wi</u> in w<u>ith</u>.

오	+	이	⇒	외

Pronounced like the <u>eu</u> in the French word j<u>eu</u>di.

Write the following syllables in the boxes provided.

위				외		
귀				되		

쉰			
휘			

빌			
퇴			

2. The Dictionary Sequence of the W-Vowels

The four w vowels are found in your dictionary directly following words that begin with the first half of the combinations.

오　　요　우　　　이
↑　　↑　　↑　　↑
와　　외　　워　위

Arrange each of the following groups of words in the dictionary sequence. All words in each group start with the same consonant, so they must be arranged according to the vowels. Check your answers against the key.

1. 좌석, 중, 죄명, 절　　2. 권, 겨울, 과자, 과

3. 우유, 외국, 완전, 원산　　4. 휘, 허리, 회, 향

Key : 1. 절, 좌석, 죄명, 중　　　2. 겨울, 과, 과자, 권

　　　3. 완전, 외국, 우유, 원산　　4. 향, 허리, 회, 휘

Reading and Writing Practice

Read the following words aloud as you write them in the boxes provided. (The English meanings are given for your reference only.)

되	다				

to become

권	위						

authority

전	화						

telephone

완	전						

perfection

최	고						

the best

조	화						

harmony

병	원						

hospital

위	성						

satellite

Listening and Writing Practice

The model voice will say 15 words. As you hear each word, complete the Han-gŭl syllable(s). Check your answers against the key.

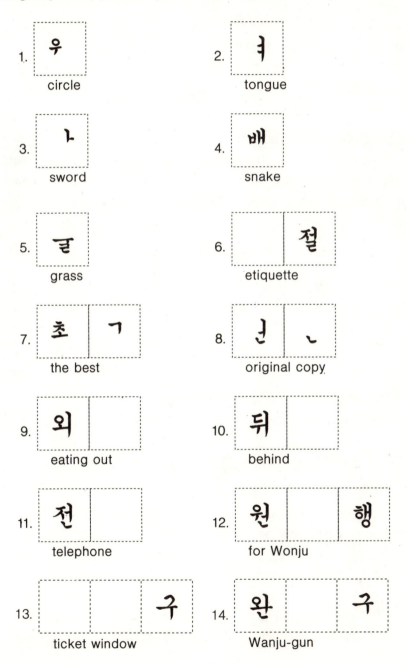

1. 우
   circle

2. ㅕ
   tongue

3. ㄴ
   sword

4. 배
   snake

5. 글
   grass

6. 절
   etiquette

7. 초 ㄱ
   the best

8. ㄹ ㄴ
   original copy

9. 외
   eating out

10. 뒤
    behind

11. 전
    telephone

12. 원 행
    for Wonju

13. 구
    ticket window

14. 완 구
    Wanju-gun

15.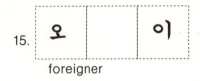

foreigner

Key : 1. 원 2. 혀 3. 칼 4. 뱀 5. 풀 6. 예절 7. 최고 8. 원본
       9. 외식 10. 뒤에 11. 전화 12. 원주행 13. 매표구 14. 완주군
       15. 외국인

Sound Discrimination Pracitce

The model voice will say 10 syllables. As you listen, circle the syllable that you think corresponds to what you have heard. Check your answers against the key.

1. 달	2. 전	3. 반	4. 걔	5. 잘
탈	천	판	깨	찰
6. 월	7. 괴	8. 와	9. 뉘	10. 돠
왈	귀	외	뇌	둬

Key : 1. 달 2. 천 3. 반 4. 걔 5. 잘 6. 왈 7. 괴 8. 와 9. 뇌 10. 둬

3. Position of Consonants in Spelling

The Korean word for "soldier" is pronounced <u>kunin</u> and spelled

The position of the consonant in the middle of the word, in this case ㄴ, is important in spelling. How do you know which syllable it belongs to ?

There are two basic principles of Han-gŭl spelling, or the grouping of symbols into syllables:

Rule 1: Words consisting of two or more syllables are grouped so that their meaningful components are in separate syllables.

For example, the word for 군인 is spelled 군 plus 인 because it has two meaningful components: 군 means "military" and 인 means "person."

> CAUTION: This does not mean, however, that the word is pronounced like 군 plus 인. It is still pronounced 구닌.

You may be under the impression that you have no way of knowing the proper grouping until you are told. Exactly! You have to learn the proper grouping when you are first introduced to a word. There is no other way.

> Rule 2: If a word has no smaller meaningful components, the sounds are "evenly grouped" into syllables.

"Evenly grouped" means that a consonant in the middle of a word is placed at the beginning of the second syllable (rather than at the end of the first). For example,

누구 is spelled 누 | 구 but not 늑 | 우

How about a noun and its suffix?   According to the first spelling rule introduced above, a suffix (-이 or -에) is a meaningful element distinct from the noun to which it is attached. Therefore, a suffix is written as a separate unit (as in 책이 and 미국에), even though a suffix is always pronounced as part of the noun. Compare the following pronunciations and spellings:

Pronounced	Spelled	
지베	집에	at home
미구기	미국이	America (as subject)
서우레	서울에	to/in Seoul .

The model voice will say 8 nouns with suffixes. Write them in the spaces provided. Check your answers against the key.

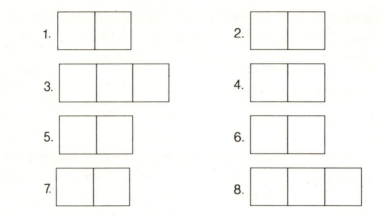

Key : 1. 문이   2. 손이   3. 수첩에   4. 불이   5. 벽에   6. 책이   7. 집에
8. 한국은

How about syllables ending in ㅇ ?   Any consonant may come in the middle of a word, and therefore the position of such a consonant may be either at the end of the first syllable or at the beginning of the second syllable. But there is one exception to the above: that is when ㅇ carries the -ng sound.

The symbol ㅇ can stand for the consonant sound ng only at the end of a syllable. Therefore, to spell the ng sound in the middle of a two-syllable word, ㅇ must be placed with the first syllable.

So far, you have learned only one word that contains ㅇ in the middle: 종이]. Practice writing the word in the spaces provided.

종 이

What to do with two consonants in the middle of a word ? Many Korean words have two consonants in the middle. Read the following words:

칠판, 전화, 학교, 의사, 남자, 학생, 선생, 양복

When you see them by the spellings alone, the two middle consonants in each word are split between two syllables—one consonant at the end of the first syllable and the other at the beginning of the second.

Occasionally, however, two consonants in the middle of a word are kept together in the same syllable, if they both belong to one part of the word. The existence verb 있습니다 and its negative 없습니다 are two such examples. Both ㅆ and ㅄ belong to the stem portions of the verbs:

Stem   +   Ending
있   +   습니다   There is
없   +   습니다   There isn't

Write these verbs in the spaces provided.

있습니다

없습니다

What about other verbs? Sometimes it is impossible to write the stem and the ending in separate syllables, although they are separate meaningful elements. We have already seen examples in 갑니다("go") and 옵니다 ("come"). Whenever a verb stem ends with a vowel, a part of the polite form ending ㅂ is placed below the stem. Practice writing these verbs in the spaces provided.

갑니다

옵니다

4. Punctuation and Spacing

In the past, Korean sentences were written like strings of beads, without any spaces between words. In fact, there were no spaces between sentences, either. This situation made reading extremely difficult, because one could hardly tell where a word, a clause, or a sentence started and ended.

Early in this century, Western-style punctuation was introduced into

Han-gŭl writing. So today periods, commas, question marks, exclamation marks and so forth are used, just as in English writing. Furthermore, Korean words are now separated by spaces.

It's all very easy, since the basic Korean rules for punctuation and spacing are more or less the same as the rules in English. Only two Korean rules for spacing need to be stated here:

Rule 1 : The suffix is attached to the noun, with no space between.

For example: 책이   but not 책 이

바다가 but not 바다 가

Rule 2 : There is no space between the verb stem and the verb ending.

For example: 있습니다 but not 있 습니다

갑니다   but not 가 ㅂ니다

UNIT 6

1. Verb Forms in the Dictionary

When you look up a verb in a Korean-English dictionary, you have to know the basic form of the verb. It is almost always the stem followed by an ending. The dictionary entry has –다 after the stem.

For example, 갑니다 is made up of the stem 가 plus the ending ㅂ니다. The dictionary entry is 가다 ("to go"). 먹습니다 is made up of the stem 먹 plus the ending 습니다. The dictionary entry is 먹다 ("to eat").

2. Three More W-Vowels

You learned that w- vowels 와, 워, 위, and 외 are the combinations of two vowels. The same is true of the other three w- vowels.

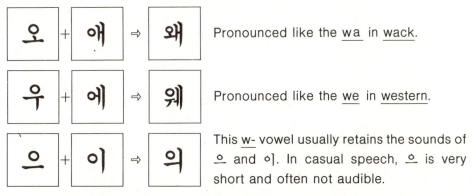

오 + 애 ⇒ 왜   Pronounced like the wa in wack.

우 + 에 ⇒ 웨   Pronounced like the we in western.

으 + 이 ⇒ 의   This w- vowel usually retains the sounds of 으 and 이. In casual speech, 으 is very short and often not audible.

Are two different Korean written syllables pronounced the same? Yes. Although most written syllables have one unique pronunciation, 외 and 웨 are pronounced practically the same.

How do you know which way to spell the sound? Speaking of the sound alone, there is no way for you to know which way to spell it: 외 or 웨. You have to learn which spelling is used for a particular word—in the same way that you learned the different spellings for "right" and "write."

Isn't there some kind of clue? No, but in nine out of ten cases, the sound is spelled 외 rather than 웨. Therefore, your chance of being correct is very good if you spell 외 when you hear the sound we, as in "western."

Reading and Writing Practice

Read the following words aloud as you write them in the boxes provided. (The English meanings are given for your reference only.)

왜			

why

궤			

box

외	국					

foreign nation

웨	이	터						

waiter

의	자					

chair

괭	이					

hoe

의	심					

doubt

정	의					

justice

Listening and Writing Practice

The model voice will say 12 words. As you hear each word, complete the

Han-gŭl syllable(s). Check your answers against the key.

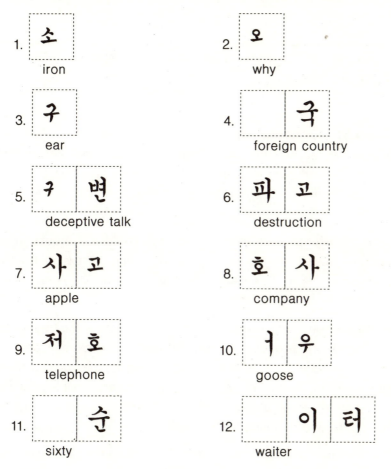

1. 소 — iron
2. 오 — why
3. 구 — ear
4. 국 — foreign country
5. ㅋ 변 — deceptive talk
6. 파 고 — destruction
7. 사 고 — apple
8. 호 사 — company
9. 저 호 — telephone
10. ㅓ 우 — goose
11. 순 — sixty
12. 이 터 — waiter

Key : 1. 쇠 2. 왜 3. 귀 4. 외국 5. 궤변 6. 파괴 7. 사과 8. 회사
9. 전화 10. 거위 11. 예순 12. 웨이터

Sound Discrimination Practice

The model voice will say 10 words. As you listen, circle the syllable that you think corresponds to what you have heard. Check your answers against the key.

1. 와   2. 궤   3. 의   4. 쇠   5. 죄
   왜   귀   위   쉬   줘

6. 바다	7. 소리	8. 창구	9. 광산	10. 외국
파다	서리	장구	강산	애국

Key : 1. 와 2. 궤 3. 위 4. 쇠 5. 쥐 6. 바다 7. 서리 8. 창구
9. 광산 10. 외국

3. The "Double" Consonants

You have so far learned the 14 Korean consonants included in the dictionary sequence. Five more consonants will be introduced here. These five "double" consonants are represented by double symbols: ㄲ, ㄸ, ㅃ, ㅆ, and ㅉ.

The "double" consonants are pronounced as you hold your mouth tense and then suddenly release the sound without aspiration (that is, without a puff of air accompanying it). Read aloud the following double consonants with the vowel ㅏ : 까, 따, 빠, 싸, 짜.

What are the closest English sounds? No consonants at the beginning of an English word are pronounced like Korean "double" consonants. However, when t, p and k come after s in English words, they do not have aspiration and therefore sound very much like the Korean "double" consonants ㄲ, ㄸ and ㅃ. Read aloud "sky," "style," and "spy", paying attention to k, t and p. Now pronounce the Korean consonants: 까, 따, 빠.

Aren't the "double" consonants somewhat like g, d, and b? Yes, they are often heard as g, d, and b by English speakers. Conversely, Korean speakers occasionally transcribe English words beginning in g, d, and b with the corresponding "double" consonants. For example, "gas" would be spelled 까쓰.

Sound Discrimination Practice

The model voice will say 10 pairs of syllables. As you listen, circle the syllable that you think corresponds to what you have heard. Check your answers against the key.

1. 가—까
2. 다—따
3. 바—빠
4. 사—싸

5. 자—짜　　　　　　6. 굼—꿈
7. 디—띠　　　　　　8. 번—뻔
9. 살—쌀　　　　　　10. 재—째

Key : 1. 까　2. 다　3. 바　4. 싸　5. 자　6. 꿈　7. 띠　8. 번　9. 살　10. 재

What exactly is the difference between ㅅ **and** ㅆ **?** The difference between ㅅ and ㅆ (and also between ㅈ and ㅉ) is a very fine one since they are both sounds made by air friction at a narrow gap behind the gum ridge. The puff of air doesn't play much of a role in differentiating them.

One way to learn how to pronounce the "double" consonants is by exaggerating the sounds.

Now you will hear 10 more pairs of syllables. Circle the written syllable that you think corresponds to each one you hear. Check your answers against the key.

1. 가—까　　　　　　2. 기—끼
3. 도—또　　　　　　4. 달—딸
5. 배—빼　　　　　　6. 분—뿐
7. 삽—쌉　　　　　　8. 소—쏘
9. 저—쩌　　　　　　10. 준—쭌

Key : 1. 가　2. 끼　3. 또　4. 딸　5. 빼　6. 분　7. 삽　8. 쏘　9. 쩌　10. 준

Listening and Writing Practice

The model voice will say 10 syllables. As you hear each syllable, complete each one in the box. Check your answers against the key.

1. 　2. 　3. 　4. 　5.

6. 　7. 　8. 　9. ㄹ　10. 굼

Key : 1. 까 2. 쏘 3. 다 4. 떠 5. 부 6. 쪼 7. 빠 8. 고 9. 쌀 10. 꿈

---

4. The Dictionary Sequence of the "Double" Consonants

The positions of "double" consonants vary from one dictionary to another. There are at least three different ways of arranging them. The method you will learn now is based on the *Standard Korean-English Dictionary for foreigners* published by Hollym Publishers in and the *Pocket Korean-English Dictionary* published by Minjungseorim in Seoul.

There, each "double" consonant is found after the words beginning with the corresponding single consonant. For example, 까 is found after the last word of the ㄱ-series, 깊이

가 나 다 라 마 바 사 아 자 차 카 타 파 하

↑   ↑   ↑   ↑   ↑

까   따   빠 싸   짜

Arrange each of the following group of words in the dictionary sequence. Check your answers against the key.

1. 시간, 술, 쉬다, 쇠
2. 안주, 안치, 안심, 안양
3. 왜관, 되다, 완수, 뒷문
4. 꿀, 게, 뱀, 끼다
5. 사이, 봄, 싸다, 술

Key : 1. 쇠, 술 쉬다, 시간   2. 안심, 안양, 안주, 안치
3. 되다, 뒷문, 완수, 왜관   4. 게, 꿀, 끼다, 뱀
5. 봄, 사이, 술, 싸다

UNIT 7
Romanization of Korean

1. The Korean Letters and Their Romanized Forms
§. Vowels
(a) Simple:

Korean letter			Romanization	English sound
ㅏ	ㅏ	아	a	as a̲h̲
ㅓ	ㅓ	어	ŏ	as hu̲t̲
ㅗ	ㅗ	오	o	as o̲h̲
ㅜ	ㅜ	우	u	as do̲
ㅡ	ㅡ	으	ŭ	as take̲n
ㅣ	ㅣ	이	i	as i̲nk
ㅐ	ㅐ	애	ae	as ha̲nd
ㅔ	ㅔ	에	e	as me̲t̲

(b) Compound:

Korean letter		Romanization	English sound
ㅑ	야	ya	as y̲a̲rd
ㅕ	여	yŏ	as y̲e̲arn
ㅛ	요	yo	as y̲o̲-ho
ㅠ	유	yu	as y̲o̲u̲
ㅒ	얘	yae	as y̲a̲m
ㅖ	예	ye	as y̲e̲s
ㅘ	와	wa	as wa̲n
ㅝ	워	wo	as wo̲n
ㅟ	위	wi	as wi̲eld
ㅚ	외	oe	as Kö̲ln
ㅙ	왜	wae	as wa̲g
ㅞ	웨	we	as we̲t̲
ㅢ	의	ŭi	as take̲n̲+we̲

§. Consonants

  (a) Simple:

Korean letter	Romanization	English sound
ㄱ	k (g)	as king or grocer (lightly aspirated)
ㄴ	n	as name
ㄷ	t (d)	as toy or depend (lightly aspirated)
ㄹ	r (l)	as rain or lily
ㅁ	m	as mother
ㅂ	p (b)	as pin or book (lightly aspirated)
ㅅ	s (sh)	as some or shift
ㅇ	ng	as king
ㅈ	ch (j)	as zoo or razor
ㅊ	ch'	as church
ㅋ	k'	as kite
ㅌ	t'	as tank
ㅍ	p'	as pump
ㅎ	h	as high

  (b) Double:

Korean letter	Romanization	English souna
ㄲ	kk	as sky
ㄸ	tt	as stay
ㅃ	pp	as spy
ㅆ	ss	as essence
ㅉ	tch	as joy

2. Guidelines for the Romanization of Korean

§. Summary of the Transcription System

  (a) Vowels are transcribed as follows:

Simple vowels	ㅏ	ㅓ	ㅗ	ㅜ	ㅡ	ㅣ	ㅐ	ㅔ	ㅚ
	a	ŏ	o	u	ŭ	i	ae	e	oe

Compound vowels ㅑ ㅕ ㅛ ㅠ ㅒ ㅖ ㅢ ㅘ ㅝ ㅙ ㅞ ㅟ

ya yŏ yo yu yae ye ŭi wa wo wae we wi

Note: Long vowels are not marked in transcription.

(b) Consonants are transcribed as follows:

plosives (stops)	ㄱ	ㄲ	ㅋ
	k, g	kk	k'
	ㄷ	ㄸ	ㅌ
	t, d	tt	t'
	ㅂ	ㅃ	ㅍ
	p, b	pp	p'
affricates	ㅈ	ㅉ	ㅊ
	ch, j	tch	ch'
fricatives	ㅅ	ㅆ	ㅎ
	s, sh	ss	h
nasals	ㅁ	ㄴ	ㅇ
	m	n	ng
liquids	ㄹ		
	r, l		

Note 1: ㄱ, ㄷ, ㅂ and ㅈ are transcribed respectively as g, d, b and j, between vowels, or between ㄴ, ㄹ, ㅁ, or ㅇ and a vowel; otherwise they are transcribed as k, t, p, and ch.

e.g. 가구 kagu 바둑 paduk 갈비 *kalbi*
제주 Cheju 담배 tambae 받침 patch'im

Note 2: ㅅ is transcribed as s except in the case of 시, when it is transcribed as sh.

e.g. 시루 shiru 신안 Shinan 신촌 Shinch'on
부산 Pusan 상표 sangp'yo 황소 hwangso

Note 3: ㄹ is transcribed as r before a vowel, and as l before a consonant or at the end of a word: ㄹ ㄹ is transcribed as ll.

e.g. 사랑 sarang 물건 mulgŏn 발 pal
진달래 chindallae 벌레 bŏlle

§. Special Provisions for Transcription

(a) When Korean sound values change as in the following cases, the results of those changes are transcribed as follows:

i.   The case of assimilation of adjacent consonants

e.g. 냇물   naenmul   부엌문   puŏngmun
      낡는다 nangnŭnda   닫는다   tannŭnda
      갚는다 kamnŭnda   진리   chilli
      심리   shimni   압력   amnyŏk
      독립   tongnip   꽃잎   kkonnip

ii. The case of the epenthetic ㄴ and ㄹ

e.g. 가랑잎 karangnip   낮일   nannil
      담요   tamnyo   홑이불   honnibul
      풀잎   p'ullip   물약   mullyak

iii. The case of palatalization

e.g. 굳이   kuji   해돋이   haedoji
      같이   kach'i   샅샅이   satsach'i

iv. The case when ㄱ, ㄷ, ㅂ and ㅈ are adjacent to ㅎ

e.g. 국화   kuk'wa   낳다   nat'a
      밟히다 palp'ida   맞히다   mach'ida

Note: The tense (or glottalized) sounds, which occur when morphemes are compounded as in the examples below, are transcribed by voiceless consonants.

e.g. 장기 (長技) changki   사건   sakŏn
      냇가   naetka   작두   chaktu
      신다   shinta   산불   sanpul

(b) When there is a possibility of confusion in pronunciation, or a need for segmentation, a hyphen '-' may be used.

e.g. 연구   yŏn-gu   잔기 (殘期) chan-gi
      물가에 mulka-e   종로에   Chongno-e

Note: In the transcription of personal names and names of administrative units, assimilated sound changes before or after a hyphen are not transcribed.

e.g. 김복남 Kim Pok-nam
      사북면 Sabuk-myŏn

(c) The first letter is capitalized in proper names.

    e.g. 인천 Inch'ŏn   대구   Taegu

        세종 Sejong   새마을호 Saemaŭl-ho

(d) Personal names are written by family name first, followed by a space and then the given name. A hyphen will separate given names, except that non-Sino-Korean given names may be joined without a hyphen.

    e.g. 김정호   Kim Chŏng-ho

        남궁 동자 Namgung Tong-cha

        손 미회자 Son Mi-hŭi-cha

        정 마리아 Chŏng Maria

(e) In spite of the **Note** to (b) above, administrative units such as 도, 시, 군, 구, 읍, 면, 리, 동 and 가 are transcribed respectively as do, shi, gun, gu, ŭp, myŏn, ri, dong, and ga and are preceded by a hyphen.

    e.g. 충청북도   Ch'ungch'ŏngbuk-do

        제 주 도   Cheju-do

        의정부시   Ŭijŏngbu-shi

        파 주 군   P'aju-gun

        도 봉 구   Tobong-gu

        신 창 읍   Shinch'ang-ŭp

        주 내 면   Chunae-myŏn

        인 왕 리   Inwang-ri

        당 산 동   Tangsan-dong

        봉천 2 동   Pongch'ŏn 2-dong

        종로 2 가   Chongno 2-ga

        퇴계로 5 가 T'oegyero 5-ga

   Note: Terms for administrative units such as 특별시, 직할시, 시, 군, 읍 and so on may be omitted.

       e.g. 부산직할시 Pusan   신창읍 Shinch'ang

(f) Names of geographic features, cultural properties, and man-made structures may be written without hyphens.

    e.g. 남산   Namsan

        속 리 산   Songnisan

금강	Kŭmgang
독도	Tokto
해 운 대	Haeundae
경 복 궁	Kyŏngbokkung
도산서원	Tosansŏwon
불 국 사	Pulguksa
현 충 사	Hyŏnch'ungsa
독 립 문	Tongnimmun

Note: Hyphens may be inserted in words on five syllables or more.

e.g. 금동 미륵보살 반가상 Kŭmdong-mirŭkposal-pan-gasang

(g) Some proper names, which cannot be abruptly changed in view of international practices and common longstanding transcriptions, may be written as follows:

e.g. 서울 Seoul   이순신 Yi Sun-shin

연세 Yonsei   이화   Ewha

이승만 Syngman Rhee

(h) When they are difficult to print or to typewrite, the breve ' ˘ ' in ŏ, ŭ, yŏ, and ŭi, and the apostrophe ' ' ' in k', t', p', and ch', may be omitted as long as there is no confusion in meaning.

Korean Alphabet I

	ㄱ k(g)	ㄲ kk	ㄴ n	ㄷ t(d)	ㄸ tt	ㄹ r(l)	ㅁ m	ㅂ p(b)	ㅃ pp
ㅏ a	가 k(g)a	까 kka	나 na	다 t(d)a	따 tta	라 r(l)a	마 ma	바 p(b)a	빠 ppa
ㅐ ae	개 k(g)ae	깨 kkae	내 nae	대 t(d)ae	때 ttae	래 r(l)ae	매 mae	배 p(b)ae	빼 ppae
ㅑ ya	갸 k(g)ya	꺄 kkya	냐 nya	댜 t(d)ya	땨 ttya	랴 r(l)ya	먀 mya	뱌 p(b)ya	뺘 ppya
ㅒ yae	걔 k(g)yae	꺠 kkyae	냬 nyae	댸 t(d)yae	떄 ttyae	럤 r(l)yae	먜 myae	뱨 p(b)yae	뺴 ppyae
ㅓ ŏ	거 k(g)ŏ	꺼 kkŏ	너 nŏ	더 t(d)ŏ	떠 ttŏ	러 r(l)ŏ	머 mŏ	버 p(b)ŏ	뻐 ppŏ
ㅔ e	게 k(g)e	께 kke	네 ne	데 t(d)e	떼 tte	레 r(l)e	메 me	베 p(b)e	뻬 ppe
ㅕ yŏ	겨 k(g)yŏ	껴 kkyŏ	녀 nyŏ	뎌 t(d)yŏ	뗘 ttyŏ	려 r(l)yŏ	며 myŏ	벼 p(b)yŏ	뼈 ppyŏ
ㅖ ye	계 k(g)ye	꼐 kkye	녜 nye	뎨 t(d)ye	뗴 ttye	례 r(l)ye	몌 mye	볘 p(b)ye	뼤 ppye
ㅗ o	고 k(g)o	꼬 kko	노 no	도 t(d)o	또 tto	로 r(l)o	모 mo	보 p(b)o	뽀 ppo
ㅘ wa	과 k(g)wa	꽈 kkwa	놔 nwa	돠 t(d)wa	똬 ttwa	롸 r(l)wa	뫄 mwa	봐 p(b)wa	뽜 ppwa
ㅙ wae	괘 k(g)wae	꽤 kkwae	놰 nwae	돼 t(d)wae	뙈 ttwae	뢔 r(l)wae	뫠 mwae	봬 p(b)wae	뾔 ppwae
ㅚ oe	괴 k(g)oe	꾀 kkoe	뇌 noe	되 t(d)oe	뙤 ttoe	뢰 r(l)oe	뫼 moe	뵈 p(b)oe	뾔 ppoe
ㅛ yo	교 k(g)yo	꾜 kkyo	뇨 nyo	됴 t(d)yo	뚀 ttyo	료 r(l)yo	묘 myo	뵤 p(b)yo	뾰 ppyo
ㅜ u	구 k(g)u	꾸 kku	누 nu	두 t(d)u	뚜 ttu	루 r(l)u	무 mu	부 p(b)u	뿌 ppu
ㅝ wo	궈 k(g)wo	꿔 kkwo	눠 nwo	둬 t(d)wo	뚸 ttwo	뤄 r(l)wo	뭐 mwo	붜 p(b)wo	뿨 ppwo
ㅞ we	궤 k(g)we	꿰 kkwe	눼 nwe	뒈 t(d)we	뛔 ttwe	뤠 r(l)we	뭬 mwe	붸 p(b)we	뿴 ppwe
ㅟ wi	귀 k(g)wi	뀌 kkwi	뉘 nwi	뒤 t(d)wi	뛰 ttwi	뤼 r(l)wi	뮈 mwi	뷔 p(b)wi	쀠 ppwi
ㅠ yu	규 k(g)yu	뀨 kkyu	뉴 nyu	듀 t(d)yu	뜌 ttyu	류 r(l)yu	뮤 myu	뷰 p(b)yu	쀼 ppyu
ㅡ ŭ	그 k(g)ŭ	끄 kkŭ	느 nŭ	드 t(d)ŭ	뜨 ttŭ	르 r(l)ŭ	므 mŭ	브 p(b)ŭ	쁘 ppŭ
ㅢ ŭi	긔 k(g)ŭi	끠 kkŭi	늬 nŭi	듸 t(d)ŭi	띄 ttŭi	릐 r(l)ŭi	믜 mŭi	븨 p(b)ŭi	쁴 ppŭi
ㅣ i	기 k(g)i	끼 kki	니 ni	디 t(d)i	띠 tti	리 r(l)i	미 mi	비 p(b)i	삐 ppi

Korean Alphabet Ⅱ

	ㅅ s	ㅆ ss	ㅇ ng	ㅈ ch(j)	ㅉ tch	ㅊ ch'	ㅋ k'	ㅌ t'	ㅍ p'	ㅎ h
ㅏ a	사 sa	싸 ssa	아 a	자 ch(j)a	짜 tcha	차 ch'a	카 k'a	타 t'a	파 p'a	하 ha
ㅐ ae	새 sae	쌔 ssae	애 ae	재 ch(j)ae	째 tchae	채 ch'ae	캐 k'ae	태 t'ae	패 p'ae	해 hae
ㅑ ya	샤 sya	쌰 ssya	야 ya	쟈 ch(j)ya	쨔 tchya	챠 ch'ya	캬 k'ya	탸 t'ya	퍄 p'ya	햐 hya
ㅒ yae	섀 syae	썌 ssyae	얘 yae	쟤 ch(j)yae	쨰 tchyae	챼 ch'yae	컈 k'yae	턔 t'yae	퍠 p'yae	햬 hyae
ㅓ ǒ	서 sǒ	써 ssǒ	어 ǒ	저 ch(j)ǒ	쩌 tchǒ	처 ch'ǒ	커 k'ǒ	터 t'ǒ	퍼 p'ǒ	허 hǒ
ㅔ e	세 se	쎄 sse	에 e	제 ch(j)e	쩨 tche	체 ch'e	케 k'e	테 t'e	페 p'e	헤 he
ㅕ yǒ	셔 syǒ	쎠 ssyǒ	여 yǒ	져 ch(j)yǒ	쪄 tchyǒ	쳐 ch'yǒ	켜 k'yǒ	텨 t'yǒ	펴 p'yǒ	혀 hyǒ
ㅖ ye	셰 ssye	쎼 ssye	예 ye	졔 ch(j)ye	쪠 tchye	쳬 ch'ye	켸 k'ye	톄 t'ye	폐 p'ye	혜 hye
ㅗ o	소 so	쏘 sso	오 o	조 ch(j)o	쪼 tcho	초 ch'o	코 k'o	토 t'o	포 p'o	호 ho
ㅘ wa	솨 swa	쏴 sswa	와 wa	좌 ch(j)wa	쫘 tchwa	촤 ch'wa	콰 k'wa	톼 t'wa	퐈 p'wa	화 hwa
ㅙ wae	쇄 swae	쐐 sswae	왜 wae	좨 ch(j)wae	쫴 tchwae	쵀 ch'wae	쾌 k'wae	퇘 t'wae	퐤 p'wae	홰 hwae
ㅚ oe	쇠 soe	쐬 ssoe	외 oe	죄 ch(j)oe	쬐 tchoe	최 ch'oe	쾨 k'oe	퇴 t'oe	푀 p'oe	회 hoe
ㅛ yo	쇼 syo	쑈 ssyo	요 yo	죠 ch(j)yo	쬬 tchyo	쵸 ch'yo	쿄 k'yo	툐 t'yo	표 p'yo	효 hyo
ㅜ u	수 su	쑤 ssu	우 u	주 ch(j)u	쭈 tchu	추 ch'u	쿠 k'u	투 t'u	푸 p'u	후 hu
ㅝ wo	쉬 swo	쒸 sswo	워 wo	줘 ch(j)wo	쭤 tchwo	춰 ch'wo	쿼 k'wo	퉈 t'wo	풔 p'wo	훠 hwo
ㅞ we	쉐 swe	쒜 sswe	웨 we	줴 ch(j)we	쮀 tchwe	췌 ch'we	퀘 k'we	퉤 t'we	풰 p'we	훼 hwe
ㅟ wi	쉬 swi	쒸 sswi	위 wi	쥐 ch(j)wi	쮜 tchwi	취 ch'wi	퀴 k'wi	튀 t'wi	퓌 p'wi	휘 hwi
ㅠ yu	슈 syu	쓔 ssyu	유 yu	쥬 ch(j)yu	쮸 tchyu	츄 ch'yu	큐 k'yu	튜 t'yu	퓨 p'yu	휴 hyu
ㅡ ǔ	스 sǔ	쓰 ssǔ	으 ǔ	즈 ch(j)ǔ	쯔 tchǔ	츠 ch'ǔ	크 k'ǔ	트 t'ǔ	프 p'ǔ	흐 hǔ
ㅢ ǔi	싀 sǔi	씌 ssǔi	의 ǔi	즤 ch(j)ǔi	쯰 tchǔi	츼 ch'ǔi	킈 k'ǔi	틔 t'ǔi	픠 p'ǔi	희 hǔi
ㅣ i	시 shi	씨 ssi	이 i	지 ch(j)i	찌 tchi	치 ch'i	키 k'i	티 t'i	피 p'i	히 hi

NUMBERS IN KOREAN

Technically speaking, there are three different number systems in Korean: native Korean numbers, Sino-Korean numbers, and Arabic numbers. In general, native Korean numbers are used in informal speech, and both Sino-Korean and Arabic numbers are used in formal speech.

Native Korean numbers are represented always by Korean words. For example,

하나	둘	셋
one	two	three

We see here that these Korean number words represent the sounds as well as the symbol. They work just as their English equivalents ("one," "two," and "three") do. On the other hand, Sino-Korean numbers are represented by Chinese letter symbols and Arabic numbers by Arabic numerical symbols. For example,

Chinese :	一	二	三
Arabic :	1	2	3

Interestingly enough, these first three numbers are not pronounced 하나, 둘, 셋 as in the native Korean number system. There is another pronunciation system that works both for Sino-Korean and Arabic numbers. For example,

一 and 1 are both pronounced <u>il</u>   (일)

二 and 2 are both pronounced <u>i</u>   (이)

三 and 3 are both pronounced <u>sam</u>   (삼)

Unlike the case of native Korean numbers, 일, 이, and 삼 are used not as symbols but merely as sounds.

In modern Korean formal writing, you may encounter both Chinese letter numbers and Arabic numbers, but the latter is more frequently used. This is partly because less and less Chineses letters are being used in contemporary Korean.

Nevertheless, we shall limit ourselves to using two terms : "Sino-Korean numbers" as against "native Korean numbers." The reason is a historical one. That unique, Koreanized pronunciation system (일, 이, 삼, etc.), now used for both Sino-Korean numbers and Arabic numbers, had been developed first for the Chinese letters, not for the Arabic numerals. The Chinese letters had been part of Korean culture over so many years, while the Arabic numbers were introduced into Korea much later.

In this textbook, therefore, Arabic numbers in Korean will come under the category of Sino-Korean numbers, even though, in practice, Arabic numbers may occur far more frequently than Sino-Korean numbers.

UNIT 1

Native Korean Numbers

1. Cardinal Numbers : One to Ten

하나	one	여섯	six
둘	two	일곱	seven
셋	three	여덟	eight
넷	four	아홉	nine
다섯	five	열	ten

2. Cardinal Numbers : Eleven to Nineteen

To form one of the number words from eleven to nineteen, just add one of the number words from one to nine to the number word 열.

열하나	eleven	열여섯	sixteen
열둘	twelve	열일곱	seventeen
열셋	thirteen	열여덟	eighteen
열넷	fourteen	열아홉	nineteen
열다섯	fifteen		

3. Cardinal Numbers : Twenty to Ninety-nine

The words for the first nine numbers remain the same, but multiples of ten have individual names.

스물	twenty	예순	sixty
서른	thirty	일흔	seventy
마흔	forty	여든	eighty
쉰	fifty	아흔	ninety

To form one of the number words from twenty-one to ninety-nine, just add one of the number words from one to nine to one of the number words listed above. To give random examples,

스물둘	twenty-two	마흔넷	forty-four
서른셋	thirty-three	쉰다섯	fifty-five

예순여섯	sixty-six	여든여덟	eighty-eight
일흔일곱	seventy-seven	아흔아홉	ninety-nine

4. Cardinal Numbers : Over One Hundred

There used to be the native Korean word for "one hundred", but it is no longer in use. Instead, the Sino-Korean word 백 is being used for all purposes, formal and informal. Thus, to get one of the number words from one hundred and one to one hundred and ninety-nine, there are two ways. One is the native Korean way, which works like this: just add one of the number words from one to ninety-nine to the number words 백. To give random examples,

백하나	one hundred and one
백열	one hundred and ten
백스물둘	one hundred and twenty-two
백예순여섯	one hundred and sixty-six
백아흔아홉	one hundred and ninety-nine

The other is the Sino-Korean way, which will be discussed shortly.

5. Ordinal Numbers : the First to the Tenth

To form one of the ordinal number words from the first to the tenth, basically just add 째, the word meaning "the position in an ordered group of thing" to one of the cardinal number words from one to ten. The exception here is 첫째 ("the first") instead of 하나째.

첫째	first	여섯째	sixth
둘째	second	일곱째	seventh
셋째	third	여덟째	eighth
넷째	fourth	아홉째	ninth
다섯째	fifth	열째	tenth

6. Ordinal Numbers : the Eleventh to the Nineteenth

To form one of the ordinal number words from the eleventh to the nineteenth, just add one of the ordinal number words from the first to the ninth to the number word 열. The exceptions here are 열한째 ("the eleventh") instead of 열첫째; 열두째 ("the twelfth") instead of 열둘째. Hence,

열한째	eleventh	열여섯째	sixteenth
열두째	twelfth	열일곱째	seventeenth
열셋째	thirteenth	열여덟째	eighteenth
열넷째	fourteenth	열아홉째	nineteenth
열다섯째	fifteenth		

7. Ordinal Numbers : Over the Twentieth

The word-groups for the first nine ordinal numbers remain the same, except 첫째 changing to 한째 and 둘째 changing to 두째. One of those word-groups may be preceded by one of the words indicating multiples of ten. To give random examples,

스물한째	twenty-first	마흔여섯째	forty-sixth
스물두째	twenty-second	쉰일곱째	fifty-seventh
스물셋째	twenty-third	예순여덟째	sixty-eighth
서른다섯째	thirty-fifth	일흔아홉째	seventy-ninth

UNIT 2

Sino-Korean Numbers

1. Cardinal Numbers : 1 to 10

일	1		육	6
이	2		칠	7
삼	3		팔	8
사	4		구	9
오	5		십	10

2. Cardinal Numbers : 11 to 19

To form one of the number words from 11 to 19, just add one of the number words from 1 to 9 to the word 십. Hence,

십일*	11		십육*	16
십이*	12		십칠	17
십삼	13		십팔	18
십사	14		십구	19
십오*	15			

Note : 십일 is pronounced like 시빌, 십이 like 시비, 십오 like 시보, 십육 like 심뉴.

3. Cardinal Numbers : 20 to 99

To form a multiple of ten, add the number word 십 to one of the cardinal numbers from two to nine.

이십	20		육십	60
삼십	30		칠십	70
사십	40		팔십	80
오십	50		구십	90

To form any other number between 20 and 99, just add one of the cardinal numbers from one to nine to one of the multiples of ten listed above.

To give random examples,

이십일	21		육십오	65
삼십이	32		칠십육	76
사십삼	43		팔십칠	87
오십사	54		구십팔	98

4. Cardinal Numbers : Over 100

To form one of the number words from 101 to 199, just add one of the number words from 1 to 99 to the number word 백. To give random examples,

백일	101		백오십오	155
백오	105		백육십육	166
백십	110		백칠십칠	177
백이십이	122		백팔십팔	188
백삼십삼	133		백구십구	199

To form the multiples of hundred, just add the number word 백 to one of the cardinal numbers from 2 to 9.

이백	200		육백	600
삼백	300		칠백	700
사백	400		팔백	800
오백	500		구백	900

5. Cardinal Numbers : Over 1,000

To form the multiples of thousand, just add the number word 천 to one of the cardinal numbers from 2 to 9.

이천	2,000		육천	6,000
삼천	3,000		칠천	7,000
사천	4,000		팔천	8,000
오천	5,000		구천	9,000

6. Cardinal Numbers : Over 10,000

To form the multiples of ten thousand, just add the number word 만 to one of the cardinal numbers from 2 to 9.

이만	20,000	육만	60,000
삼만	30,000	칠만	70,000
사만	40,000	팔만	80,000
오만	50,000	구만	90,000

7. Cardinal Numbers : Over 100,000

To form the multiples of hundred thousand, just add the number word 십만 to one of the cardinal numbers from 2 to 9.

이십만	200,000	육십만	600,000
삼십만	300,000	칠십만	700,000
사십만	400,000	팔십만	800,000
오십만	500,000	구십만	900,000

8. Cardinal Numbers : Over 1,000,000

To form the multiples of million, just add the number word 백만 to one of the cardinal numbers from 2 to 9.

이백만	2,000,000	육백만	6,000,000
삼백만	3,000,000	칠백만	7,000,000
사백만	4,000,000	팔백만	8,000,000
오백만	5,000,000	구백만	9,000,000

9. Ordinal Numbers : the 1st to the 10th

To form one of the ordinal number words from the 1st to the 10th, just put 제, the word meaning "the position in an ordered group of things," before one of the cardinal numbers from 1 to 10.

제일	1st	제육	6th
제이	2nd	제칠	7th
제삼	3rd	제팔	8th
제사	4th	제구	9th
제오	5th	제십	10th

UNIT 3
Counters Used with Numbers

There are a good number of counter words in Korean. Native counters are used exclusively with native Korean numbers, while Sino-Korean counters are used with either native Korean or Sino-Korean numbers. If a counter is not specifically needed in communication, a number word will serve the purpose.

You recall that the words for the first four numbers in the native Korean number system are 하나, 둘, 셋, 넷. Only these four words change in form when they are used with counters. For example,

하나 is changed to 한, as in 한 사람
둘   is changed to 두, as in 두 사람
셋   is changed to 세, as in 세 사람
넷   is changed to 네, as in 네 사람

How do Koreans say "a cup of coffee"? 한 잔의 커피? That is not the way Koreans usually say; they say, 커피 한 잔. The English word order may occur in a Korean sentence in a very special circumstance, but at least that is not the way Koreans commonly speak.

1. List of Native Korean Counters

(a) 가지 a kind; a sort; a variety   신문 다섯 가지
(five kinds of newspapers)

(b) 그릇 a container; a bowl   밥 두 그릇
(two bowls of cooked rice)

(c) 단   a bundle   무 세 단
(three bundles of radish)

(d) 마리 number of animals   새 한 마리 (a bird);
개 두 마리 (two dogs)

(e) 묶음 a bunch; a sheaf   꽃 한 묶음 (a bunch of flowes); 서류 두 묶음 (two sheaves of papers)

(f) 번   a time   한 번 (a time); 세 번 (three times)

(g) 벌   a set; a suit   찻잔 한 벌 (a set of tea things);

옷 한 벌 (a suit of clothes)

(h) 사람 a person   학생 네 사람 (four students)

(i) 송이 a cluster; a blossom   포도 한 송이 (a cluster of grapes);

꽃 한 송이 (a blossom of flowers)

(j) 자루 a piece; a bag   연필 한 자루 (a pencil);

쌀 한 자루 (a sack of rice)

(k).잔   a cup, a glass   차 한 잔 (a cup of tea);

우유 한 잔 (a glass of milk)

(l) 장   a leaf; a sheet   종이 다섯 장 (five sheets of paper)

(m) 채   a building   집 여섯 채 (six houses)

(n) 켤레 a pair   구두 세 켤레 (three pairs of shoes)

(o) 통   a pail; a barrel   물 한 통 (a pail of water); 휘발유

두 통 (two barrels of gasoline)

2. List of Sino-Korean Counters

(a) 개   a piece, an item   사과 십 개 (10 apples)

(b) 권   a volume   책 오 권 (5 books)

(c) 대   a car; a plane   자동차 사 대 (4 cars)

(d) 매   a leaf; a sheet   백지 삼 매 (3 sheets of white paper)

(e) 명   a person   한국인 이 명 (2 Koreans)

(f) 번* a number in a series   팔 번 (No. 8)

(g) 원* Korean monetary unit   십 원 (10 won)

(h) 층* a floor; a story   오 층 (the fifth floor)

The Sino-Korean counters listed above may be used with native Korean numbers as well, except for 번, 원, 층, where the counter refers to something in a series or to any monetary unit.

UNIT 4
Numbers Used for Telephone Communication

1. Korean Telephone Numbers

Telephone numbers in Seoul have prefixes of three digits followed by four-digit numbers. Each prefix stands for the station (국) serving the area. Regional cities have four-digit numbers with prefixes of two digits.

A typical Korean telephone number consists of two parts : The station number and the individual telephone number.

Station Number   Individual Number

774   –   **3584**

2. How to Read Korean Telephone Numbers

Unlike the English way of reading, Korean telephone numbers are often read with suffixes: 국의 ("station's") follows the station number and 번 ("number") follows the individual number.

Station Number   Individual Number

612 국의   **9023** 번

"station"   "_'s"   suffix for the serial number

Telephone numbers are always read in the Sino-Korean way. There are two ways of reading them: the regular reading (as introduced under "Numbers in Korean") and the digit-by-digit reading. For example,

Regular Reading   3584 as 삼천오백팔십사(번)
Digit-by-digit Reading   3584 as 삼오팔사

There are two more things that you need to know in the digit-by-digit reading.

(1)   0 (Zero) is read as 공.

(2)   The suffixes -국 and -번 are often omitted.

To sum up, there are four ways to read a Korean telephone number. For example, 774-3584 is read as :

	Station Number	Individual Number
(1)	칠백칠십사국의	삼천오백팔십사번
(2)	칠백칠십사국의	삼천오백팔십사
(3)	칠백칠십사국의	삼오팔사
(4)	칠칠사의	삼오팔사

TIME: HOURS, DAYS, MONTHS AND YEARS

In designating points in time, an important general rule in Korean is that things proceed from a "larger" concept to a "smaller" one. For instance, when an English-speaking traveler writes "11 : 30, October 29, 1989," his points in time may be rendered into Korean this way : 1989년 10월 29일 11시 30분 ("1989, October 29, 11 : 30").

However, the need for time expressions is always greater in "smaller" concepts in ordinary conversation. Thus we will begin with Korean ways of counting hours.

Hours

1. Counting Complete Hours

In ordinary conversation, only native Korean numbers are used to express complete hour, such as one o'clock, two o'clock, etc. To form the expression for the complete hour, add the counter 시 ("hour") to a particular number word.

한 시	두 시	세 시
one o'clock	two o'clock	three o'clock

Even though a day consists of 24 hours, hours from one to twelve are ordinarily used, with either 오전 ("in the morning") or 오후 ("in the afternoon") preceding a particular hour, whenever such a specified expression is deemed necessary in the context.

오전 아홉 시	오후 세 시
9 o'clock in the morning	3 o'clock in the afternoon

List of Complete Hours (from One to Twelve)

한 시	1 o'clock	일곱 시	7 o'clock
두 시	2 o'clock	여덟 시	8 o'clock
세 시	3 o'clock	아홉 시	9 o'clock
네 시	4 o'clock	열 시	10 o'clock
다섯 시	5 o'clock	열한 시	11 o'clock
여섯 시	6 o'clock	열두 시	12 o'clock

The information center at a Korean terminal (for planes, trains, buses) uses a slightly different system in its broadcast announcements. Under that system, Sino-Korean numbers are used to express complete hours, although native Korean numbers are sometimes used on a limited basis (e.g., from one o'clock to nine o'clock). To clearly differentiate A.M. hours from P.M. hours, the information center at the terminal uses 공일 시("01 : 00"), 공이 시("02 : 00"), etc. up to 09 : 00. The word 공 here means "zero," which is also rendered as 영 in Korean.

The typical hours counting usage at the Korean transportation terminal is as follows:

공일 시	01 : 00	십삼 시	13 : 00
공이 시	02 : 00	십사 시	14 : 00
공삼 시	03 : 00	십오 시	15 : 00
공사 시	04 : 00	십육 시	16 : 00
공오 시	05 : 00	십칠 시	17 : 00
공육 시	06 : 00	십팔 시	18 : 00
공칠 시	07 : 00	십구 시	19 : 00
공팔 시	08 : 00	이십 시	20 : 00
공구 시	09 : 00	이십일 시	21 : 00
십 시	10 : 00	이십이 시	22 : 00
십일 시	11 : 00	이십삼 시	23 : 00
십이 시	12 : 00	이십사 시	24 : 00*

*Note: 이십사 시 ("24 : 00") is also called 영 시 ("zero hour"). In this case, 영시 is preferred to 공시.

2. Counting Half Hours

In ordinary conversation there is much need of expressing "30 minutes after a particular hour." To form the expression for the half-hour, put the word 반 ("half") right after the word meaning the complete hour. For example,

한 시 반   일곱 시 반
half past one   half past seven

In formal speech, however, it is quite common to indicate the half-hour in terms of 분 ("minute"). Just replace the word 반 with 삼십 분 ("30 minutes"). For example,

한 시 삼십 분   일곱 시 삼십 분
30 minutes after one   30 minutes after seven

3. Counting Minutes and Seconds

Sino-Korean numbers are used to express minutes and seconds in Korean. To form the expression for a certain minute, add the word 분 ("minute") to the number word. To form the expression for a certain second, add the word 초 ("second") to the number word. For example,

이십오 분 오 초   사십 분 사십이 초
25 minutes and 5 seconds   40 minutes and 42 seconds

4. Telling the Time Counterclockwise

This counterclockwise method is commonly used when the minute hand is at any point between 45 and 59 minutes after a particular hour. Let us take 10 : 55 as an instance. To say "5 minutes to 11" is more common than to say "55 minutes after 10." So when it is 45 minutes or more past any particular hour, you can say, "—시 —분 전." (The word 전 means here "before.") For example,

다섯 시 오 분 전   5 minutes to five
여섯 시 십 분 전   10 minutes to six
열 시 십오 분 전   15 minutes to ten

UNIT 2

Days and Weeks

1. Naming/Counting the Days of the Month

There are two ways to name/count the days of the month in Korean: one is the native Korean way and the other is the Sino-Korean way

(a) The native Korean way : Words used in this way are closely related etymologically to native Korean numbers. For example,

Native Korean Numbers	Native Korean Counting of Days
하나	하루
셋	사흘
넷	나흘
다섯	닷새
열	열흘
열하나	열하루
스물	스무날
스물하나	스무하루

Native Korean Naming/Counting of Days

하루	one day	열하루	eleven days
이틀	two days	열이틀	twelve days
사흘	three days	⋮	
나흘	four days	스무날*	twenty days
닷새	five days	서른날	thirty days
엿새	six days	마흔날	forty days
이레	seven days	쉰날	fifty days
여드레	eight days	예순날	sixty days
아흐레	nine days	아흔날	ninety days
열흘	ten days	백날	one hundred days

*Note : 날 ("day") is a native Korean word.

In ordinary conversation today, many of these words are no longer used, although older people in Korea still use them. However, you may encounter in conversation such words as 하루, 이틀, 열흘.

(b) The Sino-Korean way: This method is much simpler. Words used in this way have to do with Sino-Korean numbers. To form the expression for naming/counting a day, add the word 일 ("day") to a particular Sino-Korean number word.

일 일	1st day/1 day		삼십 일	30th day/30 days
이 일	2nd day/2 days		사십 일	40th day/40 days
삼 일	3rd day/3 days		오십 일	50th day/50 days
사 일	4th day/d days		육십 일	60th day/60 days
오 일	5th day/5 days		칠십 일	70th day/70 days
⋮			팔십 일	80th day/80 days
십 일	10th day/10 days		구십 일	90th day/90 days
십일 일	11th day/11 days		백 일	100th day/100 days
십이 일	12th day/12 days		백일 일	101st day/101 days
			⋮	
이십 일	20th day/20 days			

*Note : 일 ("day") is a Sino-Korean word.

2. Naming the Days of the Week

The Korean names of the days of the week are made up of words for different elements of nature or heavenly bodies. Each of these words is followed by the word 요일, meaning "the day of the week."

The Days of the Week (요일)

월요일	(월 means "moon")	Monday
화요일	(화 means "fire")	Tuesday
수요일	(수 means "water")	Wednesday
목요일	(목 means "wood")	Thursday
금요일	(금 means "metal or gold")	Friday
토요일	(토 means "earth")	Saturday
일요일	(일 means "sun")	Sunday

It is useful to practice saying the first syllables of these days of the week, stringing them in the traditional sequence, with Sunday coming last.

월—화—수—목—금—토—일

3. Counting Weeks

There are two ways to count weeks in Korean : one is to do so by using native Korean numbers and the other by using Sino-Korean numbers. To form the expression for counting a week, add the word 주일 ("week") to a particular number word, either native Korean or Sino-Korean.

Native Korean way	Sino-Korean way
한 주일	일 주일
두 주일	이 주일
세 주일	삼 주일
네 주일	사 주일
다섯 주일	오 주일
⋮	⋮
열 주일	십 주일
열한 주일	십일 주일
⋮	⋮

The native Korean way is used in informal speech, and the Sino-Korean way is used in both kinds of speech, formal and informal.

Months

1. Naming the Months of the Year

The Korean names of the months are made up of Sino-Korean numbers. Each of these words is followed by the word 월, meaning "month."

*일월/1월	January
이월/2월	February
삼월/3월	March
사월/4월	April
오월/5월	May
*유월/6월	June
칠월/7월	July
팔월/8월	August
구월/9월	September
*시월/10월	October
십일월/11월	November
십이월/12월	December

*Note : 일월 is pronounced <u>irwol</u>. The <u>l</u> sound of 일 changes to <u>r</u>. Why ? Because when 일 and 월 combine to form one word, the <u>l</u> sound in of 일 undergoes change as it is carried over to the vowel-beginning word 월. The <u>k</u> in 육 is dropped when the vowel-beginning word 월 follows. However, this dropping of the <u>k</u> sound does not always happen in the speech of the younger generation. Thus, <u>yugwol</u> may be considered acceptable.

The <u>p</u> in 십 is dropped when the vowel-beginning word 월 follows. However, <u>shibwol</u> is also used among the younger speakers of Korean.

2. Naming the Day and the Month Together

When a day and a month are designated together, the month precedes the day in accordance with the general rule that a "larger" concept comes first. For example,

1월 1일   January 1

3월 3일	March 3
5월 5일	May 5
7월 7일	July 7
9월 9일	September 9
11월 11일	November 11

3. Counting Months

There are two ways to count months in Korean : one is to do so by using native Korean numbers and the other by using Sino-Korean numbers. To form the native Korean expression for counting a month, add the word 달 ("month") to a particular native Korean number word. To form the Sino-Korean expression for counting a month, add the words 개월 ("number of month") to a particular Sino-Korean number word. For example,

Native Korean way	Sino-Korean way
한 달	1개월
두 달	2개월
다섯 달	5개월
열 달	10개월
열 아홉 달	19개월

The native Korean way is used in informal speech, and the Sino-Korean way issued in both kinds of speech, formal and informal.

Years

1. Naming Years

To say the year in Korean, Sino-Korean numbers are used, with the word 년 ("year") following the number. For example,

Written	Pronounced
1776년	천칠백칠십육 년
1885년	천팔백팔십오 년
1900년	천구백 년
1945년	천구백사십오 년
1950년	천구백오십 년
1980년	천구백팔십 년
1989년	천구백팔십구 년

Note : Another way to pronounce the above-listed years is to add 일 ("one"), such as 일천칠백칠십육년. Years should never be read as two separate numbers, as in English. For example, 십구-칠십구 ("19-79") is incorrect.

2. Naming the Day, the Month and the Year Together

When a day and a month are designated together, the year precedes the month and the day in accordance with the general rule that a "larger" concept comes first. For example,

1945년 1월 1일	January 1, 1945
1972년 3월 31일	March 31, 1972
1984년 5월 23일	May 23, 1984
1988년 9월 19일	September 19, 1988
1989년 12월 25일	December 25, 1989

3. Counting Years

There are two ways to count years in Korean: one is to do so by using native Korean numbers and the other by using Sino-Korean numbers. To form the native Korean expression for counting a year, add the word 해 ("year") to a particular native Korean number word. To form the Sino-Korean expression for counting a year, add the word 년 ("year") to a particular Sino-Korean number word. For example,

Native Korean way	Sino-Korean way
한 해	1년
두 해	2년
다섯 해	5년
열 해	10년
스무 해	20년

The native Korean way is used in informal speech, and the Sino-Korean way is used in both kinds of speech, formal and informal.

Words and Phrases; A Cumulative List

〈From Lesson 11 (page 150) on, verb forms are introduced in stems only.〉

Grammar Points

Proper Nouns